THE ROAD TO DISILLUSION

THE ROAD TO DISILLUSION

From Critical Marxism to Postcommunism in Eastern Europe

JAMES P. SCANLAN / USSR

FERENC FEHÉR / HUNGARY

LESLIE HOLMES / GDR

RAYMOND TARAS / POLAND

JAMES SATTERWHITE / CZECHOSLOVAKIA

VLADIMIR TISMANEANU / ROMANIA

MARK BASKIN / BULGARIA

OSKAR GRUENWALD / YUGOSLAVIA

Edited by RAYMOND TARAS

M.E. Sharpe, Inc.   Armonk, New York
London, England

Copyright © 1992 by M. E. Sharpe, Inc.
80 Business Park Drive, Armonk, New York 10504

Available in the United Kingdom and Europe from M. E. Sharpe, Publishers,
3 Henrietta Street, London WC2E 8LU.

Library of Congress Cataloging-in-Publication Data

The Road to disillusion : from critical Marxism to postcommunism in Eastern Europe /
edited by Raymond Taras.
p. cm.
ISBN 0-87332-790-X (Cloth)
ISBN 0-87332-791-8 (Paper)
Includes bibliographical references and index.
1. Communism—Europe, Eastern—History—20th century.
2. Europe, Eastern—Politics and government—1945–1989.
3. Europe, Eastern—Politics and government—1989–
I. Taras, Ray, 1946–
HX240.7.A6R63   1991
335.43′0947—dc20
90-27828
CIP

Printed in the United States of America
The paper used in this publication meets the minimum requirements of
American National Standard for Information Sciences—
Permanence of Paper for Printed Library Materials,
ANSI Z 39.48-1984.

MV   10   9   8   7   6   5   4   3   2   1

Contents

Acknowledgments

I am grateful to the Hoover Institution at Stanford University for providing support critical to the completion of this volume. In particular, I wish to thank Tom Henricksen and Wendy Minkin, responsible for the National Fellows program, for going beyond the call of duty and marshalling the resources of the Institution on my behalf.

It was inspiring to have Robert Conquest and John Dunlop prowling the Hoover corridors, ready to discuss the fate of Communism with all comers and at the drop of a hat. At the same time, Richard F. Staar made sure that I did not forget that Eastern Europe was being transformed into Central Europe.

Across the way in Stanford University's political science department, I derived immense intellectual inspiration from talking with Gabriel Almond, truly a man who represents all that is best about the field of comparative politics.

When I was very young, growing up in Montréal, and even before I could skate, I had an occasional babysitter whose name was Zbigniew Brzezinski. Only a Freudian can tell what influence he has had on my subsequent development. I wish to express my belated gratitude to him for the time he spent with me then; more importantly, I appreciate his interest in and support for my scholarly undertakings.

In the early stages of this study of critical Marxism's influence in Soviet and East European politics, Michael Shafir played a key role in developing the analytical framework that helped jumpstart this project. In the later stages of this project, Patricia Kolb of M. E. Sharpe, Inc. ensured that it would quickly see the light of day. I have known Pat for some ten years, and in a business that is all too often ruthless, she is striking by her selfless, longstanding commitment to furthering Russian and East European studies. I could not have wished for a more supportive senior editor.

Raymond Taras
October 1991

Contributors

Mark Baskin received his Ph.D. from the University of Michigan in 1986 and has specialized in Balkan politics. He has conducted field work in Bulgaria and Yugoslavia, and his research has focused on problems of ethnicity, nationalism, and public policy. He is currently Assistant Professor of Political Science at Manhattanville College.

Ferenc Fehér is Senior Lecturer in Humanities at the New School for Social Research in New York. He has published widely in the areas of aesthetics, the history of ideas, modern European history, and the theory and history of communism. In the last area, his publications include *Political Legitimation in Communist States* (1982, with T.H. Rigby), *Dictatorship Over Needs* (1983, with Agnes Heller and György Márkus), *Hungary, 1956 Revisited* (1983, with Agnes Heller), *Khrushchev and the Communist World* (1984, with Robert F. Miller), *Eastern Left, Western Left* (1987, with Agnes Heller), *Gorbachev—the Debate* (1989, with Andrew Arato), and the forthcoming volumes *Crisis and Reform in Eastern Europe* (with Andrew Arato) and *From Yalta to Glasnost* (with Agnes Heller).

Oskar Gruenwald, educated at the University of California–Berkeley and the Claremont Graduate School, where he completed a Ph.D., is the cofounder and president of the Institute for Interdisciplinary Research, Santa Monica, California. He is the author of *The Yugoslav Search for Man* (1983) and coeditor, with Karen Rosenblum-Cale, of *Human Rights in Yugoslavia* (1986). Dr. Gruenwald also edits the new *Journal of Interdisciplinary Studies: An International Journal of Interdisciplinary and Interfaith Dialogue*.

Leslie Templeman Holmes was born in London and has received degrees in modern languages and political science at the universities of Hull, Essex, Berlin, and Leningrad. He has taught at the universities of Essex, Wales, and Kent and is currently Professor of Political Science at the University of Melbourne, Australia. His numerous publications include *The Policy Process in Communist States* (1981), *Politics in the Communist World* (1986), and *Crisis, Collapse and Corruption in the Communist World* (1991).

James Satterwhite is Associate Professor of History and Political Science at Blufton College in Ohio. From 1970 to 1973 he taught in Czechoslovakia and Poland, then returned to the United States to complete his M.A. and Ph.D. at the University of Washington. He has published in the area of the history of social thought in Eastern Europe and is currently editing a volume of Czech philosopher Karel Kosík's essays, to be published in English in 1992.

James P. Scanlan is Professor of Philosophy and fellow at the Center for Slavic and East European Studies at Ohio State University. He received his M.A. and Ph.D. degrees from the University of Chicago. He has visited the Soviet Union for extended periods over the past twenty years, working at Moscow State University and the Institute of Philosophy of the Soviet Academy of Sciences. Among his publications is *Marxism in the USSR: A Critical Survey of Current Soviet Thought* (1985).

Raymond Taras was born in Montréal, Québec, and studied in universities in Canada, England, and Poland. In the United States he has taught at the universities of Michigan and Kentucky and at Tulane University, where he is Associate Professor in Political Science. Most recently he has been National Fellow at the Hoover Institution, Stanford University. He has authored and edited a number of books in comparative politics, including *Ideology in a Socialist State* (1984), *Leadership Change in Communist States* (1989), *Political Culture and Foreign Policy in Latin America* (1991), and *Handbook of Political Science Research on the Soviet Union and Eastern Europe* (1992).

Vladimir Tismaneanu teaches Soviet and East European politics at the University of Maryland (College Park) and is a senior fellow of the Foreign Policy Research Institute in Philadelphia. His books include *The Crisis of Marxist Ideology in Eastern Europe: The Poverty of Utopia* (1988) and *In Search of Civil Society: Independent Peace Movements in the Soviet Bloc* (1990). He is currently completing a political history of Romanian communism.

THE ROAD TO DISILLUSION

1

The "Meltdown" of Marxism in the Soviet Bloc

An Introduction

Raymond Taras

For historians, *fin-de-siècle* Europe may in time become closely associated with *fin-de-communisme* in the former Soviet bloc. On the threshold of the 1990s, in the countries that used to comprise geopolitical Eastern Europe as well as in individual republics that made up the USSR, Marxist ideocracies abruptly collapsed under the weight of nationalist sentiment, free-market impulses, and liberal democratic values. State Marxism became discredited and even reformist and critical schools of Marxism no longer served as centers of philosophical controversy. To the extent that ideological discourse was perceptible in these states, it was characterized by a bandwagoning process of siding with victorious counter-Marxist ideals. A witness to *fin-de-sièclisme* in the region would do well to recall an aphorism of, appropriately enough, Winston Churchill: "Defeat is an orphan, but victory has a thousand fathers." Today in the old Soviet bloc, Marxism has indeed been orphaned.

Why undertake a study of East European Marxism now, in view of the historic political changes that occurred in the region in 1989? Put another way, what can we learn from the fate of Marxism in the shattered Soviet bloc? The objectives of this book are to describe how Marxism as critique helped undermine Marxism as ideology, and at the same time to show how oppositional Marxists dissected "real"—that is, "actually existing"—socialism to expose the failings of the system. This study is about the process of dismantling the ideocracies that were established when Marxism was adopted as a totalistic state ideology, and it is about the intellectual odysseys of one-time Marxists who were increasingly repulsed by the official ideology and sought alternative belief systems. In this respect the book chronicles the road certain Russian and East European thinkers traversed from Marxist faith to disillusionment.

It is now clear to Soviet and East European specialists that the socialist states they study were built with a doctrinal house of cards. Because Marxism—and the economic relations and political and legal superstructures it engendered—crumbled so quickly in societies as different and distant from one another as Central Europe and Central Asia, the Balkans and the Baltic states, East Germany and Azerbaijan, there had to have been much less life left in the ideology and its institutional appendages than was commonly believed. It becomes all the more important, therefore, to examine the philosophical and ideological thrusts that initially helped weaken Marxism once the Stalinist era ended. This volume undertakes a cross-national analysis of these thrusts in eight states of the former Soviet bloc, including the USSR itself.[1]

The central thesis that informs this study is, then, the existence of linkage, however tenuous and indirect, between recent political change and past Marxist dissent in the Soviet alliance system. In seeking to capture the contradictions inherent in Marxist ideocracies, we might want to argue that what undermined Marxism in the Soviet bloc was precisely the coexistence of the "two Marxisms" about which Alvin Gouldner wrote—the "scientific" Marxism adopted by socialist states and the "critical" Marxism appropriated by those opposed to monolithic Muscovite ideology.[2] Such an argument oversimplifies the range of Marxist thought in existence while also distorting the relationship between the two, which oftentimes could be complimentary as well as antagonistic. We use the term critical Marxism in a more specific way than Gouldner: it includes theorists who utilized the Marxian paradigm as the basis for a critique of the real socialism of the Soviet bloc and who remained political outsiders rather than members of the ruling elite. The pioneer of dissent against the Stalinist model of socialism in the postwar period was Josip Broz Tito. As a power holder himself, however, he defined Yugoslavia's state Marxism, which in turn engendered an idiosyncratic variant of critical Marxism in that country. In 1953, five years after he had triggered the schism with Stalinism, the Yugoslav leader's understanding of the socialist project was itself challenged by the Marxist dissident Milovan Djilas. Elsewhere in the Soviet bloc, Marxist revisionism remained until 1956 largely an "ivory tower" form of dissent, limited to debates and conflicts over arcane and obscure philosophical issues. Nonetheless, even such differing and nuanced interpretations of the Marxian world view, based on exegesis and couched in Aesopean language, represented the first cracks in the monolith of Marxism that had been constructed by Lenin and consolidated by Stalin.

After Khrushchev's 1956 de-Stalinization speech, revisionism—the Marxist-grounded critique of official state Marxism—began to spread to intellectual circles not subordinated to the party. Before successive eras of dissident activism, samizdat, underground organizations, then broader social movements, revisionism represented the most serious challenge to the ideological state apparatus of communist regimes. Its crowning success was the selection of Alexandr

Dubček to head a liberal Marxist administration in Czechoslovakia in January 1968. But Dubček's normative framework remained alien to the country's ideological apparatus: the latter remained impervious to critical Marxist penetration, and to that extent the Czechoslovak leader remained an outsider to official Marxism. Revisionism's grand failure came with the overthrow of Dubček's shaky coalition of liberal Marxists following the Warsaw Pact invasion of August 1968.

With hindsight we know that revisionist Marxism was neither as insurrectionary and "counterrevolutionary" as then-communist rulers made out, nor was it particularly successful in bringing about political change. To employ Robert Sharlet's terminology, its principal goal was to engage in "self-limiting dissent" that "demonstrated varying degrees of deference to the unwritten 'rules of the game.' "[3] To give the early revisionist Marxists their due, they began the process of corroding the state ideology with liberal and democratic ideas, as chapters in this volume describe. Many in their number were "creeping democratizers" whose chief objective was to expand democracy within the communist parties. Others, like the eminent Soviet physicist Andrei Sakharov in his early writings, were willing to entrust democratization of the political system to the Communist Party.[4] The manner in which their programs were veiled was Marxist, and they fully merited the epithet "loyal opposition." Over time, it is possible to see how they eroded official Marxism until it ceased to provide guidelines to action for the communist leaders themselves.[5]

There is a logical and persuasive explanation for the plethora of Marxist analysis conducted in the failing socialist systems of the 1960s and for the threat it posed to political rulers. Michael Shafir put it this way: "It is indeed hardly conceivable that criticism formulated in terms other than the Marxian jargon would have been considered seriously or would have provoked any response other than brutal and immediate suppression." But in addition to this defensive tactic adopted by Marxist revisionists, Shafir also underscored its longer-term, offensive thrust: "Criticism employing a Marxian 'frame of reference' is a necessary stage . . . in the effort to institute 'civil society.' "[6] For in a strange way, the amount and level of creativity of Marxist critiques under socialism served as a barometer of the strength and vitality of opposition to incumbent rulers. No less an authority on political dissent under socialism than Adam Michnik stressed the centrality of revisionism in carrying the struggle to the communist regimes.[7]

Critical Marxists: Posttotalitarians or Maggots?

Let us accept, then, that critical Marxists were crucial to the early struggle against the Leninist party-state. They were pioneers in the effort to create independent space for philosophical discourse, and in their critiques they were

among the first to reject totalitarian culture. In this capacity they helped (applying Jeffrey Goldfarb's thesis) to "deconstruct the distinctive totalitarian amal-
gamation of force and a purported absolute truth" and to "bring into being very
significant changes in the politics and language of officialdom and officially accepted critics." They therefore represented an embryonic form of the post-
totalitarian mind.[8] The emergence of critical Marxists into intellectual life
opened up an autonomous public sphere not only because they successively
proselytized about "humanist Marxism," thereby expanding the breadth of discourse and the number of its adherents; they also represented models of activism
rather than of apathy, of political engagement in contrast to the sense of political
inefficacy prevalent within society at that time. By the 1970s, they went beyond
self-limiting dissent to put forward "contrasystems" serving as alternative social, cultural, and even economic models.[9] Finally, as Stuart Hughes wrote, even
if for no other reason, "those who thought or think *otherwise* deserve respectful
attention."[10]

From this account the reader may conclude that early critical Marxists
were nothing short of romantic revolutionaries singlehandedly taking on the
power of the socialist state in the quest for liberal and democratic values. So
let us for a moment portray critical Marxists as unromantic revisionists. In
Miklós Haraszti's study of the cultural intelligentsia under socialism, a more
sanguine analysis of the role of the well-meaning dissident is presented. Progress in liberalizing the state's hold over the individual is reduced to the discovery that what the writer "can publish *today* would not have been published *yesterday*. . . . It is indeed very good to be alive and write things my father could
not have written." Were not the critical Marxists who are the subject of this
book just such unambitious and smug liberals, readily bought off by the smallest
of concessions? Worse, were revisionists not the social reformers of Haraszti's
metaphor?

> This "struggle" is like an argument between an old-fashioned prison warden and
> a humane social reformer with a well-developed aesthetic sense. The latter
> wishes to replace the rusty iron chains with designer shackles. The warden fails
> to understand. The reformer becomes so vexed that he declares that jailers should
> not meddle in the business of handcuff production, as clearly everyone prefers
> stainless steel: it is better and more pleasing to look at.[11]

Clearly there were critical Marxists involved in the reproduction of ideological purity who preferred the aesthetic look of Marxism cast in stainless steel
rather than corroding iron. From accounts given in the essays that follow, the
reader will observe different trajectories in their political careers. Sometimes
such argumentation caused them to be co-opted into the ideological state apparatus, as in the case of the Soviet Union during the heyday of perestroika. At other
times and in other places, the preference for "stainless-steel Marxism" led to
loss of party position and even to execution, as in the case of Romania after the
war. Most often, such preference eventually evoked a transition to "melancholy

Marxism'' in its adherents and then a move away from Marxism altogether, as witnessed in the generation of disillusioned Poles who experienced the communist regime's backlash following the March 1968 protests.

A question related to the fate of apologetic Marxists is the extent to which they may have bought time for the socialist regimes of the Soviet bloc. The answer must be not at all. On the contrary, even putting different window dressing on the doctrine was likely to produce cognitive dissonance among the initiated; and for the rest of society, the very act of revising part of a petrified ideology probably served to justify existing skepticism and, in this way, proved dysfunctional to the state-socialist colossus. The fact that apologists themselves converted in great numbers to other ideological pathways underscored the fragility of their original doctrine.

What status did oppositional Marxists enjoy when the systemic transition to postcommunism began in Eastern Europe? Even in the generally anticommunist climate of the region in the early 1990s, there was grudging recognition of the part played by reformist communists in attacking the socialist system. Let us take the case of Poland. In an article titled ''Tomb of the Unknown Reformer,'' an establishment journalist of the ancien régime, Daniel Passent, wrote, ''The tragedy of revisionists–liberals–reformers is that they desired improvements, they possessed good intentions, they perceived the crisis of the state and of the formation that engendered it.'' But what happened subsequently was that ''reformers became disillusioned and were discarded by both their own circles and those of the opposition.''[12] At the other end of the political spectrum, the noted editor of an underground journal, Marcin Król, in characterizing the transition to postcommunism, observed how ''the orphans in this process are reform-communists. I feel sorry for them. They started the process of change and now they are disappearing.''[13] Sympathy for the plight of Marxist reformers thus came from radically different political positions. Similar recognition of the contribution yet transience of Marxist reformers could be found in some of the other ex-bloc states.

As a possible clinching argument in defense of the approach taken by critical Marxists, we can refer to Timothy Garton Ash's observation that ''it is easy now to forget that until almost the day before yesterday, almost everyone in East Germany and Czechoslovakia was living a double life: systematically saying one thing in public and another in private.'' Marxist-based discourse was forced upon much of the population of Eastern Europe until communist governments were finally ousted. The reason was obvious: ''By demanding from the ordinary citizen seemingly innocuous semantic signs of outward conformity, the system managed somehow to implicate them in it.''[14] In a paradoxical way, then, critical Marxists were closer to ''living in truth'' when they took on the communist system's ossified and oppressive ideology than were those who resigned themselves to living a double life. It is nonetheless true that their version of Marxism may have been, in retrospect, a form of false consciousness, particularly when juxtaposed with others' few illusions about the reformability of the system.

It seems as incorrect, therefore, to belittle the intellectual contribution, courage, and, in most cases, even the good faith of critical Marxists as it would be to view as banal the small protest delivered by Václav Havel's greengrocer, who one day refused to put a sign in the shop window exhorting the workers of the world to unite.[15] Living in truth was difficult to do in Haraszti's *Velvet Prison*, and the consequences of such a lifestyle seemed trivial anyway, but it is Havel's approach that has been vindicated. Similarly, Michnik's rehabilitation of the "maggots" in Polish history who were trying to save what could be saved from reform thrusts gone blunt would be viewed as inconsequential by moralists, who saw the world differently from oppositionists or historians. "Moralism enables the individual to notice the ethical traps that lie in wait for anyone who takes on active responsibility, but it also favors an exaggerated cult of 'clean hands.'" In 1979, on the eve of the Solidarity movement, Michnik poured scorn on the moralizers: "The angel who demands heroism not only of himself but of others, who denies the value of compromise, who perceives the world with a Manichean simplicity and despises those who have a different concept of obligations toward others—this angel, loving heaven as he may, has already started on the path that leads to hell."[16] While it is debatable whether Solidarity was not indeed composed more of angels than of maggots in 1980, Michnik's adherence to a broad coalitional struggle against authority caused him, a full decade later, to hear still the echoes of his adversaries' call that he was a crypto-communist.

In sum, it seems advisable not to rush in with moral judgments about the motivations behind critical Marxist writing. Probably the majority started out as believers in reformist Marxism as the only road to nirvana, were convinced about its intrinsic goodness when they were writing, and became disillusioned with it subsequently. A minority of calculating thinkers may have been driven by an intention to implode Marxism: Marxist critiques were to serve as the thin edge of a wedge to be driven into the ossified ideocracy so as to destroy it. Of course, political opportunism may to varying degrees have underlain the critical Marxism of other writers. For our purposes such exploration into the realm of psychology seems both sterile and superfluous when dealing with political animals.[17] What is ultimately important is the impact that their writings had on the political system of socialism.

Marxist Critiques: The Diversity of Approaches

The essays in this book represent a search, then, for the intellectual roots of the Soviet bloc's collapse.[18] They include accounts of individuals who skillfully used Marx against Marxism. In this capacity, these intellectual renegades followed a dictum of Marx himself who at one time claimed he was no Marxist. The intellectual beginnings of Marxist meltdown in the region can be traced to the search for the humanist thought of the young Marx, which, the presumption ran, was very different from the state Marxism espoused by Leninist party-states.[19] By the 1970s, groups of "sophisticated rebels" had emerged who no longer sought to effect change from within the establishment, as the revisionists had done. Rather, "protest took on a variety of novel guises, working for the most part with quiet tenacity on the margin or periphery rather than at the center of established power." The new opposition was less loyal than its predecessors but no more confrontational, and less Marxist and more ambiguous. In this way it was also more sophisticated—"sophisticated in the sense of recognizing realistic limits and frequently defying conventional classification as right or left."[20]

What could be added to the understanding of these "sophisticated rebels" operating in the Soviet bloc is the "ambiguous Marxism" of their writings. For as will become clear from the following chapters devoted to individual countries, the focus is on writers who, in some measure, used Marx to defy Marxism and employed a Marxist-type paradigm if only to couch their dissent in terms understandable to the ruling elite. The survey includes economists, historians, philosophers, playwrights, and political activists who confronted the authorities with Marxist-oriented critiques and then left Marxism behind altogether, in some cases to preside over postcommunist governments formed after 1989. Some lost interest in Marxism when they concluded it was outdated, irrelevant, oppressive, or plain useless. The chapters examine some critics who could never accept that Marxism was dying or dead. Other writers discussed here were interested in finding a social philosophy that would mitigate the problems of late twentieth-century capitalism. They used Marxism to criticize the culture of commerce and consumerism permeating advanced Western industrial societies while employing Western liberal-democratic values to attack real socialism. What such writers shared in the various countries was, in theoretical categories, a meta-Marxist quest and, in real-life terms, marginalization in their societies and even imprisonment and exile at the hands of the communist authorities. In these respects it was difficult to categorize them in traditional left–right terms.

The flourishing of Marxist critiques took place at different times and in different degrees in the countries of "real socialism." Moreover, the extent to which political and economic reforms implemented in the region from 1989 onwards were inspired by critical Marxist programs outlined by dissidents in the 1970s and 1980s varies considerably. Some political observers might argue, for example, that the concerns expressed in Djilas's early dissident tract about the emergence of a new class under socialism[21] remained relevant in the 1990s as the "national nomenklatura" of the former socialist states moved into the market economy. By contrast, Marxist critiques distinguishing between public and state ownership were superfluous in countries that opted for capitalism. Then there were Marxist (as well as non-Marxist) analyses of relations between the state and society under socialism that appeared to constitute the first issue to be addressed in the transition to postcommunism. Finally, while some dissidents outlined the class antagonisms that existed under socialism, they may well have felt that a new postcommunist social formation represented the introduction of new types of class antagonisms.

In short, the programmatic and axiological analyses of former Marxist-oriented critics (for example, the *Praxis* group in Yugoslavia, Bahro in East Germany, Kuroń in Poland, or Kosík in Czechoslovakia) were influential in shaping postcommunist systems to differing degrees. In the case of the Soviet Union, as James P. Scanlan argues in his chapter, it was precisely reformist Marxists like Aganbegian, Zaslavskaia, and Medvedev who set the agenda for and the direction of perestroika. They were anything but disillusioned with the possibilities of restructuring the system in the heady early years of Gorbachev's administration. Scanlan, then, offers a more sophisticated answer to the question raised by Estonian philosopher Eero Loone: "Has perestroika started as a result of Marxist analysis? No. . . . One feels that one is hungry, whether one is a human, a dog, an elephant or a rabbit."[22] To be sure, by 1990 many reformers no longer felt the need or the desire to invoke Marx as an authority for their blueprints for change, and Scanlan suggests that reformist Marxists increasingly felt trapped by their own paradigms. This belatedly followed the trend set elsewhere in the bloc, where change was quicker and more profound and the philosophical distance between new regime norms and *any* type of Marxism was greater.

There is another distinction among Marxist critiques that originates in the nature of dissidents' analyses. It can be reduced to the profound but impossible question of which set of views represents the core of Marxian thought. For many of the critics whose writings are examined in this volume, a system's commitment to transforming the economic base of a society, as envisaged in Marx's model of a socialist formation, was the most crucial litmus test of Marxism. Thus, some critics held that Marxism had gone awry in real socialism because the system emphasized state ownership of the means of production rather than public control over them. Others pointed to another component in the economic base—the relations of production—and argued that socialism had not eliminated exploitation.

The point of departure for other Marxist critiques of East European socialist societies was oftentimes the nature of the political and legal superstructure, and of ideology and social consciousness, under real socialism. Such critics would inquire whether these accurately reflected Marx's superstructural analysis, such as the need for a developed social consciousness and a socialist culture, the independence of organizations from party tutelage (but not from economic relations), and the establishment of a transitional dictatorship of the proletariat (rather than a permanent dictatorship over it).

Probably the single most all-encompassing and simultaneously devastating Marxist critique of the socialist project was carried out by the Budapest school.

Ferenc Fehér's chapter reflects upon the reasons both for the thorough indictment of Hungary's economic base and political and ideological superstructure and for the extraordinary theoretical sophistication that characterized this critique. Carried out primarily by the pupils of György Lukács, the "collective voice" of oppositional Marxists represented for many years the only audible expression of discontent with the Kádárist regime, making them pariahs in the system. Fehér, himself a distinguished product of the Budapest school, argues that their critical Marxism rested on the philosophical postulate that the Marxist ideal project had to be contrasted to its pathetic operationalization in socialist systems, and that this ideal project contained, in itself, all the necessary tools for undertaking such a critique. Eventually, shedding Marxist tenets proved to be both philosophical and personal emancipation for these writers. The comparative analysis provided by this volume strongly suggests that the apogee of critical Marxism in the Soviet bloc was reached in the works of the Budapest school.

The critique of socialist-constructed bureaucracy and of the functioning of other institutions under socialism were common themes running through many Marxist critiques. In Leslie Holmes's chapter on East Germany, we learn how such dissident writers as Rudolf Bahro, Wolfgang Harich, and Robert Havemann focused on the deleterious policy outputs of socialist institutions. Holmes credits East German critical Marxists with closely mirroring concerns expressed by social critics in Western Europe (for example, concerning environmental issues), and perhaps for this reason he concludes that their influence in macropolitical questions such as bringing down the Wall in November 1989 or fostering German unification in October 1990 was negligible.

Vladimir Tismaneanu's essay on Romania points to the essential irrelevance of Marxist critiques in the overthrow of the Ceauşescu dictatorship and the shaping of the new political system. In contrast to the case of East Germany, however, it was the anemia of Romanian Marxist resistance to totalitarianism rather than its narrowly focused agenda setting that produced its irrelevance. Tismaneanu uses the special case of the postwar communist leader Lucreţiu Pătrăşcanu to underscore the tameness of Romanian dissent, but he also assesses the later, calibrated critiques of Silviu Brucan and Pavel Campeanu to illustrate the limitations placed on even Marxist-grounded thought in the country's personal dictatorship.

By contrast, the chapter on Poland describes the major role played by critical Marxists in launching a nationwide dissident movement that culminated in the Solidarity experiment in 1980-81. There was, to be sure, a wide spectrum of critical Marxist writing in the country, from the Polish October of 1956 to latter-day party revisionists of the late 1980s. But the "dramatis personae" in the antiregime struggle overlapped across three decades, and central critical themes recurred in first Marxist, then post-Marxist guise. For example, the notions of a civil society and a civic culture figured prominently in the writings of an initially critical but subsequently disillusioned Marxist like Michnik, jailed in three separate decades, then serving as member of parliament in the fourth.

James Satterwhite's chapter on Czechoslovakia also points to the centrality of Marxist critiques in ushering in political change, seen most dramatically in the philosophical preparation that preceded the reforms enacted during the Prague Spring. Satterwhite focuses on the general questions of consciousness and culture in Czechoslovak society, and he highlights the contributions made to a critique of socialist culture by philosophers Karel Kosík and Ivan Sviták and other writers, concluding with Václav Havel. Whether oppositional Marxists or simply dissidents, all helped expose the deformed nature of this superstructural component. As a result, the intellectual heritage of the country, Satterwhite contends, cannot be understood without reference to the revisionist Marxist views that paved the way for the 1968 experiment of socialism with a human face, and they remain as a guide map to further reform today.

In the case of Bulgaria, Mark Baskin presents further evidence pointing to the marginality of critical Marxist thought in dismantling the country's state socialism. The author explains why critique of the system was limited and ineffective and turns to the part played by nationalism in diverting the attention of skeptical intellectuals away from attacks on the system. Baskin then shows how a belated interest in critical Marxist values on the part of reformist communist leaders helped the restructured party perform respectably in Bulgaria's 1990 elections.

Finally, Oskar Gruenwald's chapter on Yugoslavia describes the evolution of critical Marxist thought from the well-known *Praxis* group that began the return to Marxist humanism in the 1960s through the camp literature that, though less known in the West, produced alternative dissident critiques of Yugoslavia under Tito. Gruenwald concludes that the liberal tradition established by critical Marxists had a central place in challenging Tito's revisionist authoritarianism, but that in the post-Tito period dissenting groups including *Praxis* have broken down along nationalist lines.

From our comparative research it becomes clear, therefore, that the significance, sophistication, utility, and impact of critical Marxism varied from one country to another. Yet perhaps it is enough of an achievement that in at least some cases over past decades such thought helped bring about the transition from totalitarianism.

The End of Critical Marxism?

The historic political, philosophical, and geopolitical changes that occurred in the former Soviet bloc at the end of the 1980s had, of course, many sources. Not least of the causes for the fall of socialism were the sheer economic inefficiency of socialism and the pervasive contempt that society had for its rulers. Yet part of the etiology of the malaise of real socialism could already be found in the writings of Marxists themselves, as this volume documents. And while we certainly would not propose to explain what has happened solely by reference to the critical Marxists, we can evaluate their theoretical and practical contributions to the collapse of the Marxist monolith, which range from great in the USSR and Poland to minimal in East Germany and Romania. The contributors to this book are far from wishing to advance the view that the ongoing vitality and creativity of Marxism are best seen in the works of oppositional Marxists; but we do share the perspective that over several decades critical Marxists operating within these states were the first line of attack on real socialism. In some countries the emergent new polities owe a modest intellectual debt to them today.

On the other hand, it is possible that along with other types of Marxism, critical Marxism, too, may have outlived its usefulness. In a book published in 1988, the Yugoslav philosopher Svetozar Stojanović captured the self-negating dynamic of this school of thought: "Critics of existing communism who rely on Marx's communism are threatened with a new, now deadly danger: that of becoming conservative." As dogmatists lost influence throughout the region in the aftermath of Gorbachev's perestroika program, their critics on the Left were positioned to succeed them. Their task would undoubtedly have been to carry out salvaging work for the Marxist project. Instead, an unexpected development occurred: if perestroika represented the traditional Russian revolution from above, in Eastern Europe the so-called "velvet revolution" was a revolution from below. Although largely peaceful (Romania being a tragic exception), the velvet revolution did nothing less than leave "communism with its teeth kicked in," as Michnik graphically put it. Critical Marxists became part of the discredited ancien régime. As Stojanović presciently observed, "Symptomatically, the force of the Marxist critique of ruling communism has increasingly waned as real prospects have opened up for its liberalization."[23]

In order to convey the length of the road traveled by critical Marxists in the Soviet bloc, to the point that they have made themselves superfluous, let me now juxtapose their development with that of their counterparts in China. A number of studies have richly documented the ideological zigzags that the Chinese Communist Party has pursued since Mao's death.[24] Often these entailed a switchback to revisionist views (Deng's aphorism dealing with the color of the cat), then to dogmatist ones (the campaign against spiritual pollution). Writing in 1989, Bill Brugger and David Kelly concluded, as had so many observers before them at different times and in different contexts, that in recent Chinese politics "Marxist categories and arguments may be used ideologically to rationalize any situation one pleases." Referring to the four modernizations, they speculated whether revisionist theorists could produce an additional dimension—the modernization of Marxism. But this purported modernization might then produce, paradoxically, a "Marxism without Marx." The authors reported that the consensus in revisionist philosophical circles for bracketing out Marx was quite broad: "It is undoubtedly the hidden or unconscious agenda of many individuals inside and outside the establishment but is not openly admissible by more than a few marginal intellectuals like Fang Lizhi.''[25] Is this not how the unraveling of Marxism began in Eastern Europe in the years following Stalin's death?

Implicitly recognizing that contemporary China was not in the near future likely to make the ideological transition from critical Marxism to postcommunism, Arif Dirlik introduced the notion of ''postsocialism'' as a type of intermediary stage between real socialism and its *telos*. Postsocialism described a historical situation in which ''socialism has lost its coherence as a metatheory of politics.'' The diluting of socialism was the result of a number of phenomena. First, it had been conditioned by the structure of real socialism, which had made its compromises with the capitalist world order while engaging in a distorted application of Marxism. It was therefore important ''to recognize that these systems are historical products of the pursuit of socialism and that they point to fundamental problems within the concept of socialism as a political concept.'' Second, its ''vernacularization'' into different national contexts was the product of compromises with overriding cultural factors in many countries. Such ''localization'' of socialism ''has undermined its claims as a unitary discourse that derives its plausibility from its promise of a universal end to human history.'' Third, its bifurcation into reality and utopia, present and future, system and process, meant that ''the present has ceased to derive its inspiration from a conviction in the immanent relevance of the socialist vision.''[26]

At the same time, according to Dirlik, postsocialism was also postcapitalist. It sought to save and sustain itself by looking beyond itself toward the experience of capitalism and simultaneously to supersede the deficiencies of modern capitalist systems. Like postmodernism, it was dominated by incredulity: ''The characteristic of socialism at present is a loss of faith in it as a social and political metatheory with a coherent present and a certain future.''[27] What little remained socialist in postsocialism was that ''it strives to keep alive a vague vision of future socialism as the common goal of humankind while denying to it any immanent role in the determination of present social policy.''[28]

The objective of critical Marxists in the former Soviet bloc may at one time have been to create a system of postsocialism. Following upheavals in the region in the late 1980s, however, this agenda was in large part appropriated from critical Marxists by ousted Communist Party leaders to be presented as what they would prefer to term the program of European social democracy. Ironically, postsocialism is a concept now most enthusiastically supported by the transformed communist parties. For this reason we should return instead to the idea of postcommunism as the *Endziel* of East European societies. But what exactly is this postcommunism that the writers surveyed here helped bring about?

For Zbigniew Brzezinski, whose scholarship over the decades was grounded in the conviction that communist totalitarianism would prove to be a grand failure, the retreat from communism could lead either to postcommunist pluralism or to authoritarianism, depending on the competing strengths of liberal democratic or nationalist impulses present in a society. In either case, "post-Communism, very simply, will be a system in which self-declared 'Communists' just do not treat communist doctrine seriously as the guide to social policy."[29]

The defining characteristic of postcommunism appears, therefore, to be negative: what it is not. Retaining a Marxian conceptualization, it is possible to capture the essence of postcommunism as "the negation of the negation," or as the nullification of a nullity, which was real socialism. To a large extent it is shaped by anticommunism and anti-Sovietism. As such, it is a phase that must be transitional: once the harmful effects of the communist order have been undone, postcommunist societies will take on positive features, for example, the embourgeoisement that Iván Szelényi considers imperative.[30] Any one of a number of alternative futures then becomes possible. Generalizing about political development, individual countries can return to the tradition of the 1920s when parliamentary democracy existed, or to the pattern of the 1930s when nationalist, royal, and military dictatorships dominated. Or indeed, some mystical "third way," as Szelényi advocates, may become viable.

In a similar way, Goldfarb describes posttotalitarian politics in essentially a negative way. It is defined by the second coming of the end of ideology (the first was reported in the early 1960s by Daniel Bell).[31] More specifically, Goldfarb suggests that Marxism should largely be stripped of its political significance, that it should cease to serve as the basis for praxis: "Ultimately I maintain . . . that Marxism belongs in the academy, in the realm of intellectual inquiry, discourse, and dispute, informing the politics of some, perhaps, but not as a substitute for politics, as in the case when Marxism becomes the organizing theory of a society."[32] Posttotalitarian politics is characterized, accordingly, by the purging of Marxist influence.

A more illuminating analysis that speaks to the theme of postcommunism in affirmative terms was offered by Martin Jay. In a study that antedated the fall of communism in Eastern Europe, Jay described "*fin-de-siècle* socialism" as an affirmation of the achievements of enlightenment emancipation, as the unequivocal recognition of the values of democratic politics, and as the abandonment of the yearning for totality and grand narrative.[33] Such philosophical discourse shares attributes with the postsocialism discussed above and, like it, might not be directly connected with the political aspirations of the states of the former Soviet bloc today. It is noteworthy, however, that features of *fin-de-siècle* socialism could be discovered in the writings of the critical Marxists examined in this book.

In conclusion it seems clear that, at the least, the process of not taking Marxist dogma seriously, which according to Brzezinski ushered in postcommunism, began with critical Marxists. They were best placed to expose the contradictions and inadequacies of the socialist state's ideology at an early stage. If, however inadvertently, many of them accelerated the intellectual decline of the doctrine through their own personal disillusionment, then some of these writers face the opportunity today to help formulate a postcommunist, postideological social philosophy for the states of the former Soviet bloc. It remains unclear what the nature of the new social philosophy will be, but we can be relatively certain that it will vary more from country to country than critical Marxism—itself a diverse and deviant form of Marxism—ever did.

Notes

1. Of the old East European communist states, only Albania has not been considered here. Its state Marxism was eclectic, its critical Marxism negligible, and Western expertise on either scant.
2. See Alvin Gouldner, *The Two Marxisms: Contradictions and Anomalies in the Development of Theory* (New York: Seabury Press, 1980).
3. Robert Sharlet, "Varieties of Dissent and Regularities of Repression in the European Communist States: An Overview," in *Dissent in Eastern Europe*, ed. Jane Leftwich Curry (New York: Praeger, 1983), 5.
4. Andrei Sakharov, "Progress, Coexistence, and Intellectual Freedom," in *Sakharov Speaks* (New York: Alfred Knopf, 1974), 117.
5. For a history of revisionism that includes second-generation Marxists, see Leopold Labedz, *Revisionism: Essays on the History of Marxist Ideas* (Plainview, NY: Books for Libraries Press, 1962).
6. Michael Shafir, "Political Stagnation and Marxist Critique," *British Journal of Political Science* 14, no. 4 (October 1984): 440.
7. See Adam Michnik, "A New Evolutionism," in *Letters From Prison and Other Essays* (Berkeley: University of California Press, 1985), 135-48.
8. Jeffrey Goldfarb, *Beyond Glasnost: The Post-Totalitarian Mind* (Chicago: University of Chicago Press, 1989), xxi.
9. Sharlet, "Varieties of Dissent," 8-10.
10. H. Stuart Hughes, *Sophisticated Rebels: The Political Culture of European Dissent* (Cambridge, MA: Harvard University Press, 1988), 4.
11. Miklos Haraszti, *The Velvet Prison: Artists under State Socialism* (New York: Basic Books, 1987), 75-77.
12. Daniel Passent, "Grób nieznanego reformatora," *Polityka*, no. 7 (17 February 1990): 16. Passent was considered a liberal journalist until martial law was declared. Because he then neither resigned his post nor was purged from it, he became identified as an apologist for the Jaruzelski regime.
13. "Post-Communist Eastern Europe: A Survey of Opinion," *East European Politics and Societies* 4, no. 2 (Spring 1990): 159. As editor of *Res Publica*, Król supported conservative policies similar to those of Western European Christian Democratic parties.
14. Timothy Garton Ash, *The Magic Lantern* (New York: Random House, 1990), 137.
15. From Václav Havel et al., *The Power of the Powerless: Citizens against the State in Central-Eastern Europe* (Armonk, NY: M.E. Sharpe, 1985).
16. Adam Michnik, "Maggots and Angels," in *Letters from Prison and Other Essays* (Berkeley: University of California Press, 1985), 176, 196.
17. If the reader wished to conduct a pilot study of the psychological bases of reformism, a starting point might be to analyze the statements of fourteen Soviet public

figures interviewed in Stephen F. Cohen and Katrina vanden Heuvel, *Voices of Glasnost: Interviews with Gorbachev's Reformers* (New York: W.W. Norton, 1989).

18. To learn more, see Andrew Nagorski, "The Intellectual Roots of Eastern Europe's Upheavals," *SAIS Review* 10, no. 2 (Summer-Fall 1990): 89-100; and see Timothy Garton Ash, *The Uses of Adversity: Essays on the Fate of Central Europe* (New York: Vintage Books, 1990).

19. For a comprehensive analysis of the search for the authentic Marx, see Leszek Kołakowski, *Main Currents of Marxism*, 3 vols. (Oxford: Oxford University Press, 1978). Kołakowski himself was a participant in the quest for a humanist Marxism supposedly to be found in Marx's early writings. For the eclectic view that "sterile Marxist dogmatism could be exploded by using the views of the later Marx," see Julius I. Loewenstein, *Marx Against Marxism* (London: Routledge and Kegan Paul, 1980), xi. For a cross-national study of the search for Marxism, see *A Critique of Marxist and Non-Marxist Thought*, ed. Ajit Jain and Alexander Matejko (New York: Praeger, 1986).

20. Hughes, *Sophisticated Rebels*, 13.

21. Milovan Djilas, *The New Class: An Analysis of the Communist System* (London: Thames and Hudson, 1957).

22. Eero Loone, "Marxism and Perestroika," *Soviet Studies* 42, no. 4 (October 1990): 791.

23. Svetozar Stojanović, *Perestroika: From Marxism and Bolshevism to Gorbachev* (Buffalo, NY: Prometheus Books, 1988), 156.

24. Bill Brugger, ed., *Chinese Marxism in Flux* (Armonk, NY: M.E. Sharpe, 1985); Bill Brugger and David Kelly, eds., *Chinese Marxism in the Post-Mao Era* (Stanford, CA: Stanford University Press, 1990); Stuart Schram, *Ideology and Policy in China Since the Third Plenum* (London: University of London, School of Oriental and African Studies, 1984).

25. Brugger and Kelly, *Chinese Marxism*, 171-75.

26. Arif Dirlik, "Postsocialism? Reflections on 'Socialism with Chinese Characteristics,'" in *Marxism and the Chinese Experience*, ed. Arif Dirlik and Maurice Meisner (Armonk, NY: M.E. Sharpe, 1989), 363-64, 375-76.

27. Ibid., 374.

28. Ibid., 364.

29. Zbigniew Brzezinski, *The Grand Failure: The Birth and Death of Communism in the Twentieth Century* (New York: Charles Scribner's Sons, 1989), 252.

30. Iván Szelényi, "Alternative Futures for Eastern Europe: The Case of Hungary," *East European Politics and Societies* 4, no. 2 (Spring 1990): 234.

31. Daniel Bell, *The End of Ideology: On the Exhaustion of Political Ideas in the Fifties* (Cambridge, MA: Harvard University Press, 1988).

32. Jeffrey C. Goldfarb, "Post-Totalitarian Politics: Ideology Ends Again," *Social Research* 57, no. 3 (Fall 1990): 548.

33. Martin Jay, *Fin-de-Siècle Socialism and Other Essays* (New York: Routledge, 1988), 11-13.

2

From Samizdat to Perestroika
The Soviet Marxist Critique of Soviet Society

James P. Scanlan

Although Soviet leaders from Stalin to Chernenko described their tightly con-trolled society as Marxism incarnate, over the years many independently think-ing Soviet Marxists have had their doubts about that society's fidelity to the principles of their master. Indeed, internal criticism of the USSR from a Marxist perspective has been a continuing fact of Soviet life for decades. While Stalin held sway, this criticism was limited to clandestine and fugitive expressions, cir-culated orally or in samizdat. Beginning with the "thaw" after Stalin's death in 1953, limited public manifestations of discontent became possible; Marxist dis-sidents such as Roy Medvedev and Andrei Sakharov gained an audience both at home and abroad. Finally, in the era of glasnost', the Soviet leadership itself loudly proclaimed Marxist principles in defense of the broad social critique that lay behind perestroika.

Many observers outside the USSR regarded perestroika as either the triumph of an *anti*-Marxist ideology or else the abandonment of ideology altogether in favor of pragmatism. But Mikhail Gorbachev and other advocates of perestroika purported to advance a *Marxist* critique of Soviet society as the basis of their reform program. We may of course wonder how genuine their devotion to Marxism really was, or is. But whether sincerely or hypocritically, many of perestroika's champions framed its rationale in Marxist terms, and in those terms their critique of Soviet reality takes its place as the culmination of a long line of attempts to turn the authority of Marx against what was claimed to be the most perfect social embodiment of his ideas.

In this essay we shall first look at some of the earlier Soviet Marxist attacks on Soviet society, then examine at greater length the Marxist "new thinking" that provided the justification for perestroika, and finally explore the issue of whether that "new thinking" was truly Marxist in character.

Early Marxist Criticisms of Stalinism

A common thread linking earlier Soviet Marxist criticisms of Soviet society with those of the present day is the thesis that Stalinism was a perversion of socialism and of the Marxist principles on which the socialist order should be built. Roy Medvedev dedicated his ground-breaking study *Let History Judge* to this thesis, taking as his task "to restore the idea of socialism by undoing the results of the cult of personality."[1] Medvedev argued that neither the idea of socialism in general nor the specific ideas of Marx can be blamed for the crimes and blunders of the Stalin era: these ideas retain their validity despite being tarnished by Stalin, whose actions tragically impeded rather than fostered the development of socialism in the USSR. Unfortunately, Stalin's socialist pretensions played into the hands of anti-Marxists, Medvedev contended: "By identifying the Stalinist regime with socialism in general," he writes, hostile propagandists "have long tried (and not without success) to represent socialism as a system in which there is no respect for law, where the rights and freedom of the individual are violated and suppressed."[2] In fact such evils are incompatible with Marxism, according to Medvedev; they are "deviations from the correct Marxist-Leninist revolutionary line."[3]

Throughout the period from Stalin until the death of Brezhnev, the Marxist voices such as Medvedev's that were raised against the existing order in the Soviet Union spoke above all of the betrayal of humanitarian values in the authoritarian Soviet state. Marxist criticism was addressed not so much to the economic system of the USSR as to its political, social, and cultural setting—its denial of freedom, self-expression, and individual growth.

The philosophical basis of such criticism was generally drawn from the early writings of Marx, above all the *Economic and Philosophic Manuscripts of 1844*, in which the young German philosopher championed the untrammeled development of human capacities and faulted capitalism for enslaving and alienating the worker. Orthodox Marxist-Leninists (i.e., Stalinists) in the Soviet Union generally dismissed these early writings as romantic, juvenile works excessively influenced by Hegel. But for many in the USSR, they provided an authentic Marxist yardstick with which to measure the ills of the society around them.

One outspoken critic in the 1960s and 1970s was the philosopher P.M. Egides, whose denunciation of what he considered pernicious, un-Marxian elements in Soviet Marxist-Leninist ideology (and correspondingly in Soviet society) eventually led to his arrest and forced emigration.[4] Egides's quarrels with a social system based on Marxism-Leninism were evident even in his views on abstract questions of philosophy. In opposition to the official Soviet conception of knowledge as consisting simply of the "reflection" of reality in the human mind—a view at odds with Marx's emphasis on the active, productive character of human thinking—Egides blames this "reflection" theory for promoting human alienation and even totalitarianism. The concept, he writes, fosters "recognition only of the blind, contemplative reflection of being by an alienated, unfree, timid, dutiful reason, fettered by all sorts of blinders, standards, patterns, and clichés; recognition . . . only of a state of affairs in which reason trudges along behind being, passively photographing it."[5]

In another essay, Egides attacks the Soviet dogmatists who mouth the official view that Soviet socialist society is free of alienation. Although they claim to be against alienation and against a life lived "according to algorithms," Egides writes, they are in fact "afraid to come forward, afraid to open their mouths against the specific perpetrators of the algorithmization of man and against specific algorithms."[6]

For Egides and other unorthodox Soviet Marxists who spoke out in the sixties and seventies—G.D. Bandzeladze, V.S. Shtein, O.G. Drobnitskii, and many others—humanism was the true content of their Marxism and the touchstone of their social criticism. They agreed with Marx that, as he phrased it in the 1844 manuscripts, "communism is humanism mediated with itself through the annulment of private property," and that the goal of historical development is not communism as such but "positively self-deriving humanism, *positive humanism.*"[7] On that ground they defended the socialist principle of public ownership of the means of production but judged Soviet reality to be defective in comparison with an authentic communist world in which human needs would truly be met, individual capacities would have full scope to develop, and alienation would be conquered. In the late sixties their heroes were the reformist Marxists of the "Prague Spring." Like those East European thinkers, Soviet Marxist dissidents rejected Stalinism in favor of what Egides called "the deepest and broadest democracy in all spheres of our life."[8]

The humanistic ideals of the young Marx continue to provide a conceptual framework for dissatisfaction with Soviet society in the present day, when indeed glasnost' has made possible the increasingly explicit and detailed expression of those ideals. For example, the late Rem Naumovich Blium, writing in one of the two principal Soviet journals of philosophy in 1988, points to the prevalence of alienation in Soviet life, despite all the official protestations to the contrary:

> How can we explain that to this day workers in industry, agriculture, and the cultural sphere have not yet in *real terms* realized their *proprietary* functions, and hence do not feel themselves the owners or proprietors of their own production? Is not the utilization of socialist property to extract unearned income a manifestation of alienation? Is not the cancer of bureaucracy that is eroding our society a direct and virtually an appropriate expression of political alienation? Are not phenomena so dangerous to socialism as consumerism, political apathy, indifference to public affairs, intellectual deadness, and the like—are they not testimony to the prevalence of alienated forms of consciousness?[9]

Such phenomena must be overcome, Blium argues, in order to create "the conditions for the realization of the Marxist ideal of a whole and rich human being acting in a free world rich in interrelations."[10]

Gorbachev's "New Thinking" as Marxist Critique

But if for many decades the humanitarian vision of the young Marx provided a ground for the condemnation of Soviet society by individual intellectuals who had little or no political influence, in recent years the economic and historical theories of the mature Marx have been marshaled against the Stalinist order by those at the pinnacle of Soviet power. Key elements of Marx's "historical materialism" are now invoked on the highest public authority to justify perestroika, the broad effort to replace Stalinist socialism with a superior variety.

The earlier Marxist critiques of the USSR deserve credit for nurturing a climate conducive to reform, but they offered little in the way of specific guidelines for change. Furthermore they contained no suggestion of particular urgency: humanization and the overcoming of alienation are timeless ideals no more appropriate now than they were fifty years ago.

What caused the shift in the Marxist critical stance in the USSR in the mid 1980s was a sense of impending economic crisis. Early in the decade it became evident that the socialist state built under Stalin was not only inhumane but economically unviable: the Soviet Union, its growth rates falling and shortages multiplying, was facing economic disaster. The new Marxist critique that has developed in this situation is one that directly addresses the economic ills of the society and provides indications of the practical direction of reforms—the measures needed to separate true socialism from its Stalinist perversion. Thus the new critique is a substantive elaboration of Medvedev's view that genuine Marxist socialism must be rescued from Stalinism.

The earlier affirmation of humanistic values is not abandoned in this new policy-oriented critique, but it takes a back seat to more concrete analysis of the socioeconomic situation. In this respect the development of the Marxist critique of Soviet society in recent decades has paralleled the intellectual career of Marx himself: it has moved from humanistic philosophical principles to concrete socioeconomic analysis—without, however, renouncing its philosophical starting points.

For an appreciation of the Marxist content of this new critique, which is part of what Gorbachev calls the "new thinking" in the USSR, it may be helpful to contrast it with the "old thinking" it is designed to replace.[11]

The preperestroika version of Soviet Marxist ideology was brought to a finished state during what is now ritually called "the period of stagnation"—roughly the years under Brezhnev, Andropov, and Chernenko. According to this doctrine the Soviet Union had become a "developed" socialist society by the late 1960s, meaning that the country was by then no longer in danger of being swept from the world scene by hostile forces and that it had a properly socialist economic system. In Marxist terms, the Soviet Union's "relations of production"—that is, the economic relationships among people which structure the society's activities of production, exchange, and distribution—were thoroughly and appropriately socialist, being based on public ownership of the means of production, central planning and control of the economy, and the principle of reward according to labor contribution ("From each according to his ability, to each according to his work").

But it would take many decades of further growth, Soviet ideologists said, for "developed socialism" to reach its full potential and become capable of making the transition from socialism to communism. Only under communism would there be complete freedom from class differences and from state coercion, full material abundance, and a citizenry so dedicated to socially useful labor that rewards need no longer be tied to labor contribution but would be proportional to need ("From each according to his ability, to each according to his need"). This view signified, it will be noted, the indefinite postponement of communism. But at the same time the existing socialist order in the USSR was trumpeted as a great achievement: the country was said to be economically and politically sound, moving forward on the road to ever greater socialist triumphs.

Anticipation of the smooth and consistent advance of the Soviet socialist economy was based on the premise, supposedly grounded in the writings of Marx and Lenin, that socialism is crisis-proof. *Socialist* relations of production, the ideologists of "developed socialism" assumed, cannot possibly come into "contradiction" with the material forces of production (i.e., with the labor power, tools, and technology available in the society) in the Marxist sense of "fettering" or impeding the use and further development of those forces.

According to Marx, it is just such a "contradiction," a lack of correspondence between productive forces and relations of production, that renders *capitalism* ultimately incapable of functioning to best advantage: by their nature, production relations based on private ownership and free enterprise inevitably create the swings of the business cycle, chronic unemployment, the wastes of competition, and other obstacles to maximum utilization of the productive forces. On the other hand, according to the doctrine of "developed socialism," once socialist relations of production based on public ownership and central planning are established, contradictions are eliminated because the new relationships "outstrip" the development of the productive forces. Like an oversized coat for a child, socialist relations of production are capacious enough to allow for further growth. They give full scope to the productive forces to develop without impediment—presumably for an unlimited time, especially taking into consideration the relatively low level of development of the productive forces in Russia at the time of the revolution. The result, under socialism, is ever-increasing productivity without further threat of disruption or need for radical change. Indeed, any contradictions that might arise within socialism were guaranteed by Lenin himself to be "nonantagonistic" and hence resolvable through the routine operations of the steadily advancing socialist system.

This was the dogma stubbornly affirmed by generations of Soviet leaders, who looked forward confidently to overtaking the capitalist world in the eventual future—usually in the face of a dismal performance by the Soviet economy.

The first cracks in this dogmatic edifice appeared well before Gorbachev assumed office, during the final years of the Brezhnev era. The slowing of economic growth in the USSR and the increasing evidence of the country's economic inefficiencies convinced some Soviet social scientists that all was not well with the world's first postcapitalist society. It was difficult to continue believing in the stimulating effect of socialist as opposed to capitalist relations of production when studies showed that for the production of one unit of industrial output, the USSR expends 80 percent more than the United States in fixed assets, 60 percent more in materials, 110 percent more in energy, and 100 percent more in shipping.[12] Further, events in Poland demonstrated that "crises" could occur in a socialist system. Scholarly response to these developments took the form in 1980-1982 of a debate on the nature of "contradictions" under socialism, in which P.N. Fedoseev, A.P. Butenko, and other Soviet scholars defended the unorthodox thesis that socialist contradictions could be serious and require radical treatment—that nonantagonistic contradictions, given "mistakes of a subjective character" (i.e., mistakes attributable not to the nature of socialism but to perversions of it by willful individuals), could, as they gingerly put it, "acquire the features of antagonistic contradictions."[13]

Still more important from the point of view of Marxist theory, some of these social scientists explicitly raised the possibility of a *fundamental* contradiction between relations of production and productive forces under socialism. The idea that socialist relations of production always outstrip the development of the productive forces, Butenko wrote in 1982, is "groundless." While it is true, he granted, that the juridical institution of public ownership of the means of production provides a capacious framework for the development of productive forces throughout the socialist period, the "real production relations" that arise in the society as a result of the manner in which the legal form is implemented may fail to correspond to the growth of the productive forces and hence may retard that growth. Without directly identifying such a situation in the Soviet Union, Butenko made clear that its possibility entailed a consequence unanticipated in the prevailing ideology but seemingly in keeping with Marxist analysis—namely, the need to deliberately change *socialist* production relations in order to insure their continued adequacy, not merely in times of crisis but regularly and continually: "Every important step in the development of the productive forces of socialism," Butenko wrote, "requires the correction and improvement of this whole real system of socialist production relations, for without adequate changes in this sphere the retardation of the development of the productive forces and the progressive fall in the tempos of economic growth are inevitable."[14]

Many Western observers first became aware of the depth of this new Marxist

challenge to the established conception of socialism in the USSR with the leak-
ing and publication in 1983 of a confidential report, now called the
"Novosibirsk Report," which had been presented by the sociologist Tat'iana
Zaslavskaia to a closed seminar sponsored by the Novosibirsk Institute of the
Economics and Organization of Industrial Production (a unit of the Siberian
Division of the USSR Academy of Sciences) in April of that year. The seminar
was attended by high-ranking officials of the Soviet economics establishment,
including representatives of Gosplan and the Central Committee.[15] In retrospect,
Zaslavskaia's paper, for which she received a party reprimand at the time, provides a remarkable anticipation of the reform agenda subsequently advanced by
the Gorbachev administration.

After a frank assessment of the declining growth rates of the Soviet
economy—from 7.5 percent during the Eighth Five-Year Plan (1966-70) to 2.5
percent during the first two years of the eleventh (1981-82)—Zaslavskaia argues
that the cause of this deteriorating economic performance is not incidental but is
structural or systemic, that it is a matter of "the inability of this system to ensure
complete and efficient enough utilization of the working and intellectual potential of society." And she identifies the structural problem in impeccably Marxist
terms: it consists, she writes, in the fact that "the existing system of production
relations has fallen considerably behind the level of development of the productive forces. Instead of promoting their accelerated development, it is turning all
the more into a brake on their forward movement."

In such a situation, Zaslavskaia argues, the piecemeal and gradual replacement of obsolete elements cannot succeed, for a given set of production relations
constitutes an integrated system that "rejects" individual elements, even more
efficient ones, drawn from other systems of production relations. Only a
"profound restructuring [*perestroika*]" can succeed, a restructuring that sub-
stitutes for the retarding set of relations a "new economic mechanism," Zaslavskaia asserts. In other words, what is needed is a new integrated system of
production relations capable of promoting accelerated economic growth—a system that will, nonetheless, remain socialist in character.[16]

According to Zaslavskaia's analysis in the "Novosibirsk Report," the economy of the USSR is too complex to be managed "administratively"—i.e., purely
by commands issued from a central planning authority. She argues that directive
or command-administrative methods of running the economy were appropriate
in the 1930s, when the Soviet economy was less complex and when a far less
sophisticated work force required strict management; in Marxist language, the
methods then in use corresponded to the level of development of the productive
forces at hand. But identification of these command-administrative production
relations with socialist production relations per se leads to retaining them even
after they cease to be appropriate to more advanced productive forces.[17]

These pre-Gorbachev conceptual developments were not confined to the
world of scholarship. Iurii Andropov, whose short tenure as general secretary

lasted from November 1982 until February 1984, incorporated some of them in an address devoted, appropriately enough, to the one-hundredth anniversary of the death of Karl Marx. Without employing the Marxist technical term "relations of production" and without admitting the possibility of "antagonistic" contradictions under socialism, Andropov nonetheless acknowledged that a socialist economy could fail to provide adequate scope for its own productive capacity, and he went beyond Butenko in explicitly if gently applying that analysis to the USSR: "Our work directed at the improvement and restructuring [*perestroika*] of the economic mechanism, of forms and methods of management," Andropov wrote, "has lagged behind the demands posed by the achieved level of material-technical, social, and intellectual development of Soviet society." Furthermore, Andropov called explicitly for change in the "forms of the organization of economic life"—that is, in relations of production—in order to "accelerate the progress of the productive forces" in Soviet society.[18] Although these theses were still argued using the terminology of "developed socialism," Andropov's clear espousal of change, including the introduction of "socialist people's self-management" and even of democratization within the Communist Party, suggests that if he had lived he would have been the architect of perestroika, no doubt with the enthusiastic support of his disciple, M.S. Gorbachev.

When Gorbachev referred later to the "theoretical quest" that had prompted the ideas of perestroika, it was presumably the above developments that he had in mind.[19] As early as December 1984, a few months before assuming the general secretaryship, Gorbachev called for "profound transformation in the economy and in the entire system of social relations," transformation that would "raise socialist society to a new and higher level."[20] In the same speech he adopted the term perestroika used by Zaslavskaia and Andropov before him, and he repeated almost word for word his mentor's call for "the restructuring of the forms and methods of economic management," in order, he went on, to "create an economic mechanism that meets the requirements of developed socialism."[21]

After Gorbachev's accession to power, this emphasis on the need for substantial change was expressed in the new Program of the Communist Party, prepared under his direction and adopted at the Twenty-seventh Party Congress in 1986. Far from suggesting (as the previous program had) satisfaction with the advanced level of socialism supposedly achieved in the USSR, the new program spoke of the need for profound change—not change from socialism to communism, but change *within* socialism. Referring to the "mistakes of the seventies and early eighties" (the heyday of "developed socialism"), the program called for accelerated growth and explicitly tied such growth to the alteration of relations of production. "The constant improvement of production relations, the maintenance of a stable correspondence between them and dynamically developing productive forces, and the prompt identification and resolution of nonantagonistic contradictions that arise between them," the program reads, "are necessary preconditions for the acceleration of the social and economic progress of society." And if the wording of this statement suggests gradualism, the expected improvement was itself described in more dramatic terms: it was to constitute "a qualitatively new state of Soviet society."[22] In Marxist terminology, a *qualitative* transformation is a radical change, not simply a modification but a transition from one *level* of change to another—the kind of transformation associated with revolution.

That Gorbachev had something like a Marxist economic revolution in mind was made evident in his Twenty-seventh Party Congress address. In that speech he presented the outlines of a revolutionary diagnosis of the Soviet Union's ills—a diagnosis that drew freely on the ideas expressed earlier by Andropov and Soviet social scientists and that is noteworthy for its blunt use of Marxist principles to diagnose the ills of Soviet socialist society. Specifically, he applied to the USSR the fundamental Marxist analysis of an economic order ripe for revolution—that is, an order in which the established system of relations of production no longer "corresponds" to the growth of the forces of production and must be transformed.

In the first place, he admitted the possibility that under socialism, too, relations of production can come into contradiction with productive forces in such a way as to hinder rather than foster the latter's use. He admitted, in other words, something that no Soviet leader before Andropov had even hinted at—namely, that there is no guarantee in the nature of socialism itself that it will promote economic growth more successfully than, say, capitalism does. "Practice has shown," Gorbachev stated, "the bankruptcy of notions according to which, in socialist conditions, *the conformity of production relations to the nature of productive forces* is ensured automatically, as it were. In life, everything is more complicated." Socialist production relations, he argued, must change so as to keep pace with the growth of productive forces and function as an effective framework for the further growth of these forces. But since the production relations do not change "automatically," they must be altered by deliberate political action or they will no longer promote economic advance.

Indeed, Gorbachev went on, just such a situation has come about in the Soviet Union. Existing production relations, perhaps effective earlier, "have gradually grown obsolete, have begun to lose their incentive role, and in some respects have become an impediment."[23] Hence the need for perestroika, to create new and better socialist production relations so as to "open up new scope for the development of productive forces."[24] It was this Marxist diagnosis of productive forces hobbled by outmoded economic structures that opened the way to the call for a new revolution in the USSR—a revolution *within* socialism.

This need for revolution was further stressed by Gorbachev at the January 1987 plenary session of the Central Committee,[25] at which he recited a long litany of the Soviet economic failures in the seventies and early eighties—surely the most damning portrait of the Soviet economy ever drawn publicly by one of its leaders. Using the same Marxist conceptual apparatus of productive forces and relations of production, Gorbachev spoke of "mounting crisis phenomena" in the Soviet economy, which urgently require "a change of direction and measures of a revolutionary nature."[26] Referring to contemporary Soviet socialism not as "developed" but as "developing," he affirmed that "the dialectics of its motive forces and contradictions" had been misunderstood. Existing socialist relations of production, he said, had been "absolutized" and erroneously regarded as essential elements of socialism. "The model of socialist production relations became set in stone, and the dialectical interaction between these relations and productive forces was underestimated."[27] Far from being required for socialism's progress, Gorbachev went on, the existing relations of production had become a "braking mechanism" weighing down the productive forces instead of stimulating their development.[28] Perestroika, he stated, means "scrapping the braking mechanism, and creating a reliable and effective mechanism of accelerating the social and economic development of Soviet society."[29]

In the years after 1987, the main outlines of the new revolutionary economic mechanism envisaged by Gorbachev and his supporters became evident, as incorporated in such Soviet legislation as the Law on the State Enterprise, the Law on Individual Enterprise, the Law on Cooperatives, and the Law on the Land. Briefly, these major pieces of legislation sought to move Soviet socialism in the direction of decentralization and marketization; they provided in various ways for a shift away from state ownership of all means of production and strict central control of the economy. State-owned enterprises were to be allowed to set their own five-year plans and retain a portion of their profits for distribution among the workers; concurrently, they were required to be self-financing, to acquire their raw materials on the wholesale market, and to satisfy market demands on pain of bankruptcy. Individuals and groups of individuals (the latter in the form of collectives or cooperatives) were permitted to go into certain lines of business for themselves, owning means of production and retaining after-tax profits. Lease holding and other forms of ownership compatible with retention of legal title by the state were introduced: for example, individuals and groups were permitted to take long-term, bequeathable leases on farm land.

A succinct but comprehensive description of the new Soviet model of a socialist economy was provided by Nikolai Ryzhkov, then chairman of the Council of Ministers of the USSR, in a speech in May 1988:

> first, the existence and close interaction of various forms of property—state, cooperative, personal, and the property of public organizations;
>
> second, qualitatively new areas in the use of state and cooperative property based on the broad development of rental relations, under which economic accountability achieves its greatest embodiment. At the same time, the state, while retaining its right of ownership of the means of production, including natural resources, will, on the rental principle, transfer some of them—primarily medium-sized and small means of production—to labor collectives of state and cooperative enterprises for their use;

third, state and cooperative enterprises, as socialist commodity producers, will have full economic autonomy and will bear direct material responsibility for the results of their activity. They form their property and develop production using their own income. Their relations with the state are regulated by economic instruments: normatives, taxes, rent payments and lease charges;

fourth and last, in conditions of a diversity of economic forms of management, commodity-money relations [i.e., market relations], which fuse organically with the new methods of centralized management of the national economy as a single whole, are the basic link between producers and consumers.[30]

After Ryzhkov spoke, still further steps were taken in the direction of marketization and the extension of ownership rights. In all these ways the architects of perestroika sought to accomplish what Marx said must be done when existing economic institutions impede the productive use and further growth of the material forces of production at a society's disposal—namely, break up the existing economic structure and replace it with a new complex of institutions (relations of production) that correspond to the productive forces at hand. In their view this was not a matter of replacing socialism with a nonsocialist economic system but of replacing the Stalinist perversion of socialism with a healthy Marxist socialism.

How Marxist Is the "New Thinking"?

The fact that Gorbachev and his supporters cited Marxist doctrines to justify the need for perestroika was not enough, however, to convince everyone that the "new thinking" was genuinely Marxist, particularly when the positive program derived from it took the form we have just seen. Communist parties from Cuba to Japan charged that there was more Marxist rhetoric there than Marxist principle, and that the social theory behind perestroika in fact contradicted established Marxist notions in a number of significant respects.

Without question there are aspects of the "new thinking" that appeared to fly in the face of accepted Marxist truths. By way of assessing its Marxist credentials, we shall concentrate here on just three points, of varying degrees of importance, at which the new outlook appeared to depart from traditional Marxist doctrine.

The first and perhaps least serious is that it envisaged, as Marx did not, the need for a *second* revolution to establish socialism on a firm foundation.

Second, the social critique behind perestroika was not couched in *class* terms. Whereas Marx argued that revolutions are needed in order to overthrow an exploiting class that benefits from an existing complex of production relations, there was no explicit identification of class antagonisms or of an exploiting class in the ideology advanced by the champions of perestroika.

Finally, the proposed program of economic reform, with its movement toward market relations and abandonment of the state monopoly on ownership, appeared to contradict the very core of Marx's teachings: it clashed with Marx's intense and persistent opposition to an economic system based on commodity production for profit and to private ownership as the essence of capitalism and the principal source of human alienation.

Can these divergences from orthodoxy be accommodated within Marxism? Let us consider the three points in turn.

(1) The second revolution, taking place *within* socialism, was not aimed at changing the broadly socialist character of Soviet society. This is paradoxical, for as a revolution perestroika was held to effect a qualitative leap in the development of society, and according to the Marxist laws of dialectics it would seem that for a socialist society to make a qualitative leap, its socialist base would have to be replaced by a base of a different order—by a fully communist or (retrogressively) a capitalist base. But Soviet theorists contended that the qualitative change in this case was from one *socialist* base to another, superior one.

To do this they had to make two assumptions new to Soviet Marxism-Leninism but not clearly inconsistent with Marxism. First, they had to assume that socialism is compatible with a range of different production relations, some better than others. Second, they had to assume that deliberate policy choices must be made as to which socialist relations to establish and how to modify them once established; proper relations are not generated or maintained spontaneously by the socialist situation. On this view even a long-established socialist economy can be wrongly established or can become counterproductive—can exhibit ''phenomena of stagnation'' and develop a ''braking mechanism.'' The elimination of such a mechanism, then, is simply a kind of re-creation of socialism, of starting over again from the beginning.

Defenders of the ''new thinking'' argued that Marx himself would be sympathetic to the need for a fresh start. As evidence they cited a passage in ''The Eighteenth Brumaire of Louis Napoleon,'' in which the founder of Marxism wrote that in proletarian revolutions it is necessary to ''return to what would seem to have been accomplished already, in order to begin it over again.''[31] Whether Marx would indeed have applied this statement to a situation that arose some seventy years after the Bolshevik revolution in Russia is of course an open question. But in any event it does not appear that a second socialist revolution is obviously ruled out by anything Marx wrote or said.

(2) A second respect in which the ''new thinking'' departed from Marxist orthodoxy was in its seeming rejection of a class-based analysis of the ''revolutionary'' situation confronting the USSR. In traditional Marxist terms, a revolution occurs when opposing classes are divided by antagonistic interests that cannot be reconciled within the existing socioeconomic order. But Gorbachev's revolution, ostensibly at least, was not a *class* revolution—i.e., it was not a revolution in which an oppressed class rises up and takes power from its oppressors. Indeed, there was no open identification of an oppressor class in the ''official'' literature of perestroika. Gorbachev on numerous occasions explicitly denied that there were *class* conflicts or ''antagonisms'' in present-day Soviet

society.[32] How can there be a *Marxist* revolution that is not analyzable in class terms?

In this case, the absence of class terminology may be a misleading indication of the actual content of the "new thinking." Although the pronouncements of the leadership generally avoided the language of classes and their antagonisms, the ideology of perestroika was not thereby necessarily abandoning the Marxist notion of a dominant exploiting class from which power must be seized. For the proponents of perestroika unanimously agreed that one social group was the principal opponent of the new order, and that group was the *bureaucracy*. Despite the fact that the bureaucracy is ordinarily not called a *class*, in the statements of the reformers it clearly played the Marxist role equivalent to that of an exploiting class.

The principal clash of interests that now exists in Soviet society, the reformers argued, is that between the interests of the bureaucracy and those of the general public. The Ukrainian philosopher Iurii Priliuk speaks of the former interests as "departmental" and "local"; formed in "the invisible school of training of the bureaucrat," they are the interests of "bureaucratic self-serving and despotism."[33] What others call the "braking mechanism" in Soviet society, Aleksandr Iakovlev calls the "mechanism of *bureaucratic* retardation"; bureaucracy can exist, Iakovlev writes, "only at the cost of strangling the interests of society."[34] Enemies of society, through the system of "bureaucratic centralism," have usurped control of the means of production which rightfully belong to the people, and they use these means to the detriment of the people's interests.

Gorbachev himself, despite his insistence that there were no antagonistic classes in the USSR, spoke in the same vein about the bureaucracy. He referred in one breath to "the forces of conservatism" and the need to break the power of the bureaucracy, to reduce it drastically in size and function (he once called for a 50 percent cut in all industrial ministries by 1990).[35] He railed against officials who turned the areas under their jurisdiction into "patrimonies" and urged that they be "dragged out into God's light."[36] Calling them "self-seeking opponents of restructuring" (as opposed to principled opponents, whose interests are not affected and who simply need to be reeducated), he cited as among them officials or managers who "run an enterprise, a district, a city or a laboratory as if it were their private domain" and people who use their positions for the embezzlement of state property and "private gain."[37]

These, clearly, are individuals for whom the system makes possible an abuse of power, and no doubt it was they whom Gorbachev had in mind when he spoke in 1987 of the resistance to perestroika as coming from "bureaucratic encrusted layers"—his first actual reference to social strata opposed to restructuring.[38] Soon thereafter the bureaucracy with its powers and privileges became the favorite focus of official Soviet attacks on the opponents of perestroika. Gorbachev henceforth spoke freely of "really existing contradictions of interest" among different groups of the Soviet population and opposed the interests of the people to those of "the bureaucratic style of activity." A revolution, he stated, echoing the words of Zaslavskaia's "Novosibirsk Report," "does not take place without conflicts."[39]

Why, then, did Gorbachev and his supporters resist calling the second revolution a *class* revolution? One possible answer is that since the second revolution was to be a revolution *within* socialism, the working class must be assumed to hold power before it as well as after it; the proletariat has no need to overthrow another class but only to use its power for socioeconomic reconstruction.

But another possibility is that the reform thinking was more authentically Marxist than met the eye—that the reformers' hidden agenda was precisely the overthrow of a dominant, exploiting class. On this interpretation, the bureaucracy would be openly identified as an oppressor class, were it not thought advisable to avoid the inflammatory rhetoric of the class struggle.

As well-read Marxists, the ideologists of perestroika could hardly fail to draw the appropriate inferences from their own judgment of the need to rid their society of "bureaucratic centralism." If their analysis is correct, it must require breaking the power of the bureaucracy, who have become the de facto owners of the means of production, and thus the dominant class, through their ability to control and dispose of those means. Transferring that control and disposition to collectives, cooperatives, enterprises, and even to some extent to individual workers is then a genuine *class* revolution. It means a fundamental transformation of property relations in Soviet society, and it entails a fundamental change in the livelihood, the social identity, and the social function of economically powerful groups that have dominated the society and exploited other groups. As the Soviet economist Abel Aganbegian expressed it, "Power must be taken from those used to giving orders."[40]

At the same time, as practical political leaders, Gorbachev and his supporters could not single-mindedly condemn the bureaucracy. For they were dependent on that very bureaucracy to implement the desired revolutionary changes in an energetic and orderly fashion. Theirs was a revolution in which a bureaucracy was asked to participate enthusiastically in its own destruction, and it no doubt seemed gratuitous to make that bureaucracy regard itself as a class enemy into the bargain. Not only gratuitous but counterproductive, for it would only further antagonize an already apprehensive group, and it could produce a kind of unmanageable antibureaucratic fervor in the society at large. The Soviet leaders were surely not unmindful of the excesses permitted in Mao Zedong's "cultural revolution" in the name of combating bureaucracy—not to mention the Stalinist terror, which was justified at the time as part of "the exacerbation of the class struggle" as socialism advances. Hence the avoidance of class terminology by the champions of perestroika may have been motivated more by concern for the orderly and controlled self-dissolution of a postcapitalist exploiting class—the bureaucracy—than by a genuine departure from a broadly Marxist theory of revolution, however novel the particular application of that theory may be in the present case.

(3) Ultimately the question of the Marxist character of the thinking behind perestroika must surely hinge, however, on the relation between Marx's vision of a noncapitalist, dealienated social order and the actual changes in Soviet society that were being recommended by the reformers. And here some Soviet opponents of perestroika had grave doubts about its claims to Marxist credentials.

A particularly distressing aspect of the new economic thinking, in the eyes of ideological purists in the USSR, was its call for broader use of "commodity-money relations"—an expression that is the preferred euphemism for market relations and dependence on the law of supply and demand. To ideological hardliners, other aspects of the reforms may have been tolerable, though fraught with dangers. But to rely on market forces in the operation of an economy—to accept "the authority of the ruble," as the reformers were fond of saying, and permit exchange and distribution to be determined by market conditions of supply and demand—this could be seen as striking at the heart of the Marxist idea. To purists, the expression "socialist market," found even in such authoritative texts as pronouncements by Politburo members, smacks of oxymoron.[41]

In fact even the euphemism "commodity-money relations" is enough to raise the hackles of some conservative Soviet economists—dubbed "anticommodityites" (antitovarniki) in debates during the sixties and seventies—who identify the production of goods as "commodities" with capitalism and who view socialist production on the Marxist model as the expenditure of what is called "socially necessary labor" (labor that produces goods not as commodities to be bought and sold for a profit but as objects that satisfy social needs). For the anticommodityites, any talk of the exchange of "commodities" for money as the central nexus of a supposedly socialist economy is an indication that the very essence of socialism is being subverted.[42]

The liberal economists who championed the reforms were "commodityites" (tovarniki), who argued that commodity production, though highly developed under capitalism, is not peculiar to that economic order but existed for thousands of years before it and is a legitimate feature of a socialist economy as well. Commodity-money relations have the same general characteristics under socialism that they have in any economic system in which they are present, according to the economist A. Malafeev: products of labor are made for sale, they are exchanged for money on an equivalent basis, and the laws of supply and demand and of money circulation operate. Both sound economic theory and the experience of other socialist countries have established the commodity character of socialist production and its compatibility with planning, according to the liberal economists. In their view the antipode to a planned economy was not a commodity-money economy but an economy that operates "spontaneously," or in other words anarchically; the opposite of a commodity-money economy, on the other hand, is a natural economy—that is, one in which there is direct distribution of goods and services to consumers without a monetary link, as under full communism.[43]

One source of the prejudice against commodity-money relations among some Soviet theorists, Malafeev contended, was that the latter failed to perceive the difference between the planned *character* and the commodity *form* of socialist production. He quoted Leonid Abalkin, Gorbachev's chief architect of economic reconstruction, as pinpointing the proper distinction: "Planning characterizes the system of production relations from the side of the *method* of conducting the economy. As for commodity-money relations, they characterize the *form* of economic relations." Under both capitalism and socialism, then, economic relations may have the same form. What distinguishes commodity production "on a socialist basis" from its capitalist counterpart is that in the former, the form has an entirely different *content*, stemming from the fact that the basis of commodity-money relations under socialism is not private ownership but social ownership of the means of production.

This difference in content is specifiable in a number of contrasts between the two economies: First, under socialism the *labor power* that produces commodities is not itself a commodity; it is not something to be sold and bought (offered for hire and hired) under market conditions, as it is in a capitalist economy. Second, the aim of commodity production under socialism is not private profit but the satisfaction of social needs. And third, what Malafeev called a "basic mass" of products is produced by socialist enterprises in accordance with a plan designed to assure the satisfaction of those needs.[44] Recognition of these differences, the reform theorists argued, should dispel the fear that market relations per se are incompatible with socialism or unacceptable to Karl Marx. On this view, then, properly regulated market relationships may be an appropriate mechanism to achieve the Marxist goal of an economic system which satisfies social needs while avoiding exploitation.

Equally critical in establishing the Marxist credentials of the reforms was a defense of the socialist character of innovations with regard to ownership of the means of production. For Marx, socialist relations of production are grounded in social ownership of the means of production. Consequently, once a society *is* socialist—i.e., is marked, as the USSR supposedly already is, by the dominance of socialist relations of production—how can ownership be "radically changed" in that society without destroying its socialist character and reverting to individual appropriation and exploitation?

The supporters of perestroika replied that the question presupposes a highly oversimplified view of social ownership. They deplored the widespread idea that once property is legally established in the hands of the state, it belongs to all the people—is thoroughly "socialized"—and that hence no further questions about ownership need be asked. "Socialist means public and public means state—that's the basic pattern," the economist Otto Latsis laments. "If property is 100 percent public (state ownership is desirable, collective farm ownership less so), then everything is in order where socialization is concerned, and every-thing in our country is completely socialist."[45] There is no justification in Marxism or the theory of socialism, A.N. Iakovlev and others have argued, for this "absolutization" of *state* ownership (a dogmatism promoted, Iakovlev contends, by the special interests of the bureaucracy).[46] The *ideal* of social ownership of the means of production, of course, is public ownership by the whole people, to be achieved eventually under full communism. Short of that, under socialism, social ownership should not be identified with or limited to state ownership, which is simply one mode of implementing the former—others being ownership by collectives of various sorts and even by individuals—provided no exploitation is involved, as we saw above. Marx, the reformers noted, described socialism, or the transitional stage preceding communism, only in the most general terms.

Latsis and others increasingly acknowledge that since ownership, from the point of view of its socioeconomic significance, means not legal title but effective control, where state ownership is absolutized the bureaucrats who actually wield state powers, not the citizens at large, are in effect the owners of the resources. Latsis asks whether "public" property misused by a state official (or other citizen) for personal gain should really be called "socialist." "The point is," he states, "that property can be nominally public and not be so in fact," and for that reason, he affirms, the real level of socialization of property in the USSR is not as great as has been claimed.[47] Zaslavskaia succinctly conveyed both the importance and the realities of the matter in the "Novosibirsk Report" in more abstract, theoretical terms:

> The central link in the system of production relations is the prevailing form of ownership of the means of production, *which is made concrete in relations of control, distribution, and use.* The system of these relations shapes the special features and different status of social groups, their interests and behavior. The concrete system of management of the national economy, reflecting one or another modification of production relations, conditions the corresponding distribution of influence among social groups.[48]

Such reflections, according to these Soviet scholars, dispel the notion that "state" ownership means ownership by all the people—since the group within the state that has the powers of "control, distribution, and use" dominates in any case—and at the same time these reflections entail that decentralization can be genuine only by actually transferring the powers to other groups. In this light, the provisions of the Law on the State Enterprise that gave to enterprises the right to "establish, set, and confirm" their production plans and that prevent the state from appropriating the profits of the enterprise are highly significant: they mean that the enterprise, not the state, is the effective "owner" of the resources. In principle this is a major shift in ownership relations, a relocation of proprietorship from the center (more precisely, from bureaucratic groups at the center) to outlying groups.

Rental arrangements, the leasing of land, and contractual work agreements are also viewed as altering the effective control of resources and thus as signifying "a profound transformation of state property" in which workers are no longer alienated from it but see it as their means of existence.[49] Thus the shift from a fixation on state ownership to encouraging a variety of forms of ownership in no way endangers the socialist character of the relations of production as Marx would view them, in the opinion of the ideologists of perestroika. Their position was well summarized by Academician Vladimir Kudriavtsev, director of the USSR's Institute of the State and Law:

> Production relations of the socialist type can be formed successfully not only within the framework of the state enterprise but on the basis of social (cooperative, collective) ownership and also in connection with individual activity that excludes exploitation and is likewise a socially useful variety of the division of labor. All these diverse forms of production relations in no way contradict socialism and its basic principle of distribution according to labor; on the contrary, they transform this principle into a genuinely operating instrument of social and economic development.[50]

The reform thinkers placed considerable emphasis on the last point in defending the Marxist character of their critique. Soviet society before perestroika, they said, was not in fact based on Marx's principle that rewards should be distributed according to labor during the "first phase" (socialism) of communist society; wage leveling and the lack of a proprietary interest in state-owned property prevented the principle from having its intended stimulating effect on labor. Marketization and the changes in property relations included in perestroika, on the other hand, were expected to ensure that the material incentives assumed by Marx's principle would operate.

In all these respects, then, the Marxist defenders of perestroika insisted that there was no conflict between Marxist doctrines and a conception of socialism that accommodates market relations ("commodity-money relations") and a diversity of forms of ownership.

In the end, of course, we must ask whether such arguments on the part of these Soviet critics of Stalinist socialism issued from sincere Marxist conviction or were simply lip service to a traditional authority—for many decades the *only* authority (along with Engels and Lenin, his supposed philosophical clones) who could be cited in Soviet ideological discourse. Marx's ideas were being employed against a system that was earlier raised in his name, but perhaps that was due not so much to belief in the ideas as to their monopoly position on the Soviet intellectual scene.

At present it is still difficult to distinguish between sincere belief, the force of custom, and expedient hypocrisy. But before long we may be able to discern the extent to which Marxism is still a serious intellectual force in the USSR.

For the fact is that the monopoly position of Marxism has been yielding to the forces of change in the Soviet Union. As early as 1988 some Soviet scholars began openly to trace the roots of Stalinism to Marx himself, thereby calling into question the infallibility with which the German philosopher had previously been invested. "The former conviction that everything written by Marx is truth of the highest order is hardly useful today," wrote the philosopher Aleksandr Tsipko in a provocative article in the mass-circulation magazine *Science and Life*.[51] Stalin, Tsipko argues, was formed in a Marxist milieu and drew his thinking and his policies from Marx's ideas. The problem is not that Stalin distorted these ideas; rather, the ideas themselves were of mixed value and limited application. And we should be all the more skeptical of them today: "We have a right—more than that, we have an obligation—to ask which things in Marx's theory have proven out, and what we intend to follow. What part of his teachings were true only for that era, the nineteenth century? And in what things were Marx and Engels mistaken?"[52] In Tsipko's view, the "fundamental truths" (his quotation marks) of Marxism have to do with its methodology and its value system and not with "notions of the future that are outdated and have not been vindicated in practice."[53]

In the Soviet scholarly literature, opposition to the uncritical acceptance of Marxist doctrines has grown steadily, though in large part it is justified simply on the ground that Marx's views were historically conditioned and hence are not automatically applicable to today's problems.

At a conference in Moscow in December 1989, sponsored by no less Marxist an authority than the Central Committee of the Communist Party, several speakers expressed misgivings about Marxism. In the present day, according to I. Pantin, editor-in-chief of the journal *The Working Class and the Contemporary World*, "we can clearly see the historical limitations of Marxism as a teaching, understand the evolution of this theory and decide which of its elements have outlived their usefulness and which are still essential."[54] It was the attempt to implement "Marx's dogma," according to another speaker, that led the Bolsheviks to create a dictatorial system.[55] Still another blamed Marxism for absolutizing the class struggle, rejecting "bourgeois democracy," and neglecting the psychological, moral, and political aspects of social development.[56]

Among the conference participants, it was again Tsipko who went furthest in iconoclasm. Original Marxism was only one among many valuable socialist teachings, Tsipko asserted, and he went on to argue that Marx, to his great discredit, ultimately abandoned socialism in favor of communism, thereby rejecting the humanistic orientation of his own earlier theory and espousing violence and dictatorial rule. Although Marx claims to defend freedom, Tsipko argued, in his later writings "he says nothing about concrete economic and political mechanisms for the protection of the freedom and dignity of the personality in the future society." Under the influence of the Hegelian conception of totality, Marx took a step back in his conception of social life—"a step back even in comparison with the Gospel."[57]

No other Soviet philosopher has dismissed Marx as decisively as Tsipko has, but there is no doubt that in general the German philosopher's authority is on the wane. Soviet writers today feel no need to cite the name of Marx in defense of their own ideas, which may have little in common with Marx's. Thus, it should eventually be possible to judge the extent to which Marxism retains a genuine hold on people's minds in the Soviet Union, as opposed to commanding only lip service. At that time we may find that what was presented by most Soviet theorists of perestroika as a *Marxist* critique of the old order in the USSR is in fact a more fundamental critique masquerading as Marxism.

Notes

1. Roy A. Medvedev, *Let History Judge: The Origins and Consequences of Stalinism*, trans. Colleen Taylor, ed. David Joravsky and Georges Haupt (New York: Alfred A Knopf, 1971), xxx.
2. Ibid., xxix.
3. Ibid., xxxiv.
4. James P. Scanlan, *Marxism in the USSR: A Critical Survey of Current Soviet Thought* (Ithaca: Cornell University Press, 1985), 283.
5. P.M. Egides, "K probleme tozhdestva bytiia i myshleniia," *Filosofskie nauki*, 1968, no. 4:179.
6. G.D. Bandzeladze, ed., *Aktual'nye problemy marksistskoi etiki (sbornik statei)* (Tbilisi: Izdatel'stvo Tbilisskogo gosudarstvennogo universiteta, 1967), 106-107.
7. Karl Marx, *Economic and Philosophic Manuscripts of 1844* (Moscow: Foreign Languages Publishing House, 1961), 164.
8. Bandzeladze, *Aktual'nye problemy*, 105.
9. R.N. Blium, "Alienation and Socialism," *Soviet Studies in Philosophy* 27, no. 2 (Fall 1988): 70.
10. Ibid., 72.
11. For a fuller exposition see Scanlan, *Marxism in the USSR*, 224-60.
12. These figures are taken from a Soviet study quoted by Academician E. Primakov; see "New Gains Seen for Soviet Foreign Policy," *The Current Digest of the Soviet Press* 40, no. 1 (3 February 1988): 1.
13. A.P. Butenko, "Protivorechiia razvitiia sotsializma kak obshchestvennogo stroia," *Voprosy filosofii*, 1982, no. 10:19.
14. Ibid., 21-22.
15. For the complete English text with a commentary by Igor Birman, see Tat'iana Zaslavskaia, "Paper to a Moscow Seminar," *Russia*, 1985, no. 9:27-50.
16. Ibid., 27, 30, 33, 36.
17. Ibid., 28-29.
18. Iurii Andropov, "Uchenie Karla Marksa i nekotorye voprosy sotsialisticheskogo stroitel'stva v SSSR," *Kommunist*, 1983, no. 3:13.
19. Mikhail Gorbachev, *Perestroika: New Thinking for Our Country and the World* (New York: Harper and Row, 1987), 25.
20. Ibid., 2, 27.
21. Ibid., 4.

22. *Current Soviet Policies IX. The Documentary Record of the 27th Congress of the Communist Party of the Soviet Union* (Columbus: The Current Digest of the Soviet Press, 1986), 140, 142.

23. Ibid., 23-24.

24. Ibid., 24.

25. "Gorbachev Addresses Party on Change—III," *The Current Digest of the Soviet Press* 39, no. 6 (11 March 1987): 14.

26. "Gorbachev Addresses Party on Change—I," *The Current Digest of the Soviet Press* 39, no. 4 (25 February 1987): 3, 6.

27. Ibid., 3.

28. Ibid., 3-4.

29. Ibid. 6. *The Current Digest*'s translation of *mekhanizm tormozheniia* as "mechanism of retardation" has been changed here for consistency with the above usage.

30. "The Supreme Soviet Session—I," *The Current Digest of the Soviet Press* 40, no. 21 (22 June 1988): 14-15.

31. Quoted by G. Smirnov in "Grounding Gorbachev's 'Renewal' in Theory," *The Current Digest of the Soviet Press* 39, no. 11 (15 April 1987): 24.

32. M.S. Gorbachev, "O zadachakh partii po korennoi perestroike upravleniia ekonomikoi. Doklad General'nogo sekretaria TsK KPSS M.S. Gorbacheva na Plenume TsK KPSS 25 iunia 1987 goda," *Pravda*, 26 June 1987, p. 1.

33. "Glavnoe—eto chelovek. 'Kruglyi stol' zhurnalov Kommunist, Kommunist Ukrainy, i Filosofs'ka dumka v Kieve," *Kommunist*, 1987, no. 5:100; cf. A.P. Butenko, "Teoreticheskie problemy sovershenstvovaniia novogo stroia: sotsial'no-ekonomicheskoi prirode sotsializma," *Voprosy filosofii*, 1987, no. 2:26-27.

34. "Perestroika i nravstvennost'. Vystuplenie chlena Politbiuro TsK KPSS, sekretaria TsK KPSS A.N. Iakovleva na vstreche s aktivom Kaluzhskoi oblastnoi partiinoi organizatsii," *Znamia* (Organ Kaluzhskogo obkoma KPSS i oblastnogo soveta narodnykh deputatov), 17 July 1987, p. 1 (emphasis added); "Yakovlev Assails Dogmatic Thinking," *The Current Digest of the Soviet Press* 39, no. 15 (13 May 1987): 12; cf. T. Zaslavskaia, "Social Justice and the Human Factor in Economic Development," *Problems of Economics* 30, no. 1 (May 1987): 12-15.

35. "Oktiabr' i perestroika: revoliutsiia prodolzhaetsia. Doklad General'nogo sekretaria TsK KPSS M.S. Gorbacheva na sovmestnom torzhestvennom zasedanii Tsentral'nogo Komiteta KPSS, Verkhovnogo Soveta SSSR i Verkhovnogo Soveta RSFSR, posviashchennom 70-letiiu Velikoi Oktiabr'skoi sotsialisticheskoi revoliutsii," *Izvestiia*, 3 November 1987, p. 4; "Soviet Industrial Ministries Will Lay off 60,000," *The Japan Times*, 12 November 1987, p. 9.

36. "Prakticheskimi delami uglubliat' perestroiku," *Kommunist*, 1987, no. 12:9.

37. "Gorbachev Speeches Push Restructuring," *The Current Digest of the Soviet Press* 39, no. 8 (25 March 1987): 8.

38. "Mikhail Gorbachev's Answers to Questions Put by 'L'Unita,'" *Moscow News*, 1987, Supplement to issue no. 22 (3270):5.

39. Gorbachev, "O zadachakh partii," 1; "Kak obnovliaetsia obshchestvo. Mikhail Gorbachev v dialoge s chitateliami 'Moskovskikh novostei,'" *Moskovskie novosti*, 1 November 1987, p. 9.

40. "Rebuilding Russia" (interview with Abel Aganbegian), *Newsweek*, 27 July 1987, p. 48.

41. N. Sliunkov, "Perestroika i partiinoe rukovodstvo ekonomikoi," *Kommunist*, 1988, no. 1:14.

42. The views of the anti-commodityites are sketched (unsympathetically) in Nikolai Petrakov's article "Zolotoi chervonets vchera i zavtra" in *Novyi mir*, 1987, no. 8 (August): 215ff.

43. A. Malafeev, "Tovarno-denezhnye otnosheniia i perestroika khoziaistvennogo mekhanizma," *Kommunist*, 1986, no. 18:79-80; see also V. Kulikov, "Tovarno-denezhnye otnosheniia v kontseptsii uskoreniia," *Kommunist*, 1986, no. 12:11-22. Even if commodity production is expected to cease under *communism*, when the categories of "commodity" and "money" would seem to have no application, according to Kulikov this does not mean that it must be eliminated or relentlessly diminished in significance during the *socialist* period (p. 16).

44. Malafeev, "Tovarno-denezhnye otnosheniia," 79-80.

45. "Myths of Stalinist 'Golden Age' Debunked," *The Current Digest of the Soviet Press* 40, no. 16 (18 May 1988): 3.

46. "Yakovlev Assails Dogmatic Thinking," 4; A.M. Cherepakhin, "O nekotorykh sotial'no-filosofskikh predposylkakh sovremennogo ekonomicheskogo myshleniia i putiakh ego perestroiki," *Voprosy filosofii*, 1987, no. 12:3-9.

47. "Myths of Stalinist 'Golden Age' Debunked," 3.

48. Zaslavskaia, "Paper to a Moscow Seminar," 34 (emphasis added).

49. "Reforming the Economy—A Scholar's Opinion: Take the Plant on a Rental Basis. What New Forms of Management Can Yield," *The Current Digest of the Soviet Press* 40, no. 20 (15 June 1988): 25-26.

50. V. Kudriavtsev, "Sovetskoe gosudarstvo: preemstvennost' i obnovlenie," *Kommunist*, 1987, no. 16:47.

51. "In Search of Stalinism's Deeper Causes," *Current Digest of the Soviet Press* 41, no. 10 (5 April 1989): 5.

52. Ibid.

53. Ibid., 1.

54. A. Volkov and V. Mironov, eds., *The Phenomenon of Socialism: Essence, Regularities, Perspectives* (Moscow: Global Research Institute, 1990), 183. These conference proceedings were privately distributed in an edition of 200 copies.

55. Ibid., 90.

56. Ibid., 159.

57. Ibid., 43-44.

3

The Language of Resistance
"Critical Marxism" versus "Marxism-Leninism" in Hungary

Ferenc Fehér

Introduction

The analysis starts at "Zero Hour." In today's Hungary, after the revolutionary change of 1989, there are neither Marxists nor Marxism, with the exception of a few true believers and the members of the "Karl Marx Society," founded by former party inquisitors and operating under the aegis of the fringe group of unreconstructed old and neo-Stalinists, the MSzMP.[1] This empty space, strewn with the debris of once proud *Weltanschauungen*, is all the more surprising since, together with Poland and Yugoslavia, Hungary was once the home of the largest and internationally best known contingent of "critical Marxism."[2] György Lukács, the only philosophical genius Marxism has produced after Karl Marx, an enigmatic heretic inside his Church, lived and worked for twenty-five years in Hungary after World War II. Lukács, after many failed attempts to found a philosophical school outside the official orthodoxy but inside the doctrine, finally succeeded in fathering a circle which he termed "the Budapest school" of critical Marxism.[3] Furthermore, the leading critical economists of Hungary, the best single group of devastating analysts of the ultimate irrationality of the Soviet-type command economy, were initially uniformly Marxist, and several of them retained elements of a Marxist criticism of the "Marxist regime" until the late 1980s.[4] Lukács's influence over the critical sociology of Hungary (resurrected in the 1960s after the long, conservative communist suppression of the critical social sciences, which once boasted such names as those of Karl Mannheim and Karl Polányi) was perceivable in the works of András Hegedűs, György Konrád, Iván Szelényi, Mária Márkus, and several others—not all of them Marxists, critical or otherwise.[5] Finally, a Marxist opposition completely unrelated to Lukács—one primarily political, not theoretical, in nature—was formed by the members of the opposition around Imre Nagy between 1953 and 1956. This group had a short political, theoretical (and, for several of its members, in the atmosphere of the post-1956 persecution, also a short physical) existence. They left behind no significant writings. Those who survived, either in emigration or in "internal emigration" after many years in prison, became liberals or "liberal conservatives," and they now have no sentimental memories of their Marxist youth. But the story of "critical Marxism" in Hungary cannot be written without mentioning them.[6]

Historically, critical Marxism appeared in Eastern Europe after Stalin. It is worth mentioning that it stood in no relation to the actual beginning, namely Trotskyism in Soviet Russia in the twenties and later in exile, despite the fact that a numerically weak, but intellectually not entirely insignificant, group of Hungarian Trotskyists was formed in the late thirties and during the war, in Paris and Budapest.[7] Only Stalin's death made a minimum of deviant self-expression physically possible, and even then quite often only in an Aesopean language. As long as the tyrant lived, maintaining silence instead of indulging in ritual self-criticism was the risky maximum only heroes or eccentrics could afford.[8]

Generally speaking, the fate of oppositional Marxism, even as a trend in philosophy and sociology, was closely connected to the historic junctures of politics. Despite the devastating defeat of the revolution in 1956, the spirit of resistance to the ruling Marxist-Leninist orthodoxy within the framework of Marxism was not broken; paradoxically, it was instead strengthened by a number of factors. Thanks to Imre Nagy's heroic resistance and the short but crucial emergence of the workers' councils during the revolution and its immediate aftermath, the great event lent itself to being interpreted as a corroboration, instead of a refutation, of reformed socialism and "nondogmatic Marxism." The emergence of a school of neo-Marxism in Poland, so unambiguously and articulately critical of "real socialism," together with similar trends in Yugoslavia, gave further encouragement. Furthermore, "Khrushchevism," despite its thoroughly reactionary role in the suppression of the Hungarian Revolution, did not then seem to have completely exhausted its reserves of reform and renewal. And if we read the "Khrushchev phenomenon" backwards, from the perspective of the "Gorbachev phenomenon," the utopian hope for a burgeoning trend toward the self-dismantling of the regime from the top appears to be more than a pipe dream; rather, it transpires as the first act of a historical drama.

The 1960s saw the peak period as well as the beginning of the decline of Hungarian critical Marxism. International and domestic factors combined in its enhanced cultural self-confidence. The growth of the Western New Left was not only an indication of the international, not merely domestic, relevance of its quest for renewal. It was also a model for critical Marxism's possible new identity as a radical-socialist, but noncommunist, and increasingly anticommunist, contingent. And the critical Marxists who did most for the new self-identity, primarily Agnes Heller, understood the New Left precisely from this aspect. Domestically, Kádárism's major effort of reconciliation with the nation whose revolution it had suppressed, beginning with its unexpected general amnesty of 1963 and reaching its peak in experiments (later miscarried) with a thorough economic reform, and its general self-advertisement as the only Khrushchevite country even after Khrushchev's fall,[9] further bolstered the critical Marxists' hope of a possible renewal of their ideas and movement.

The ebb of the New Left in Europe after the May 1968 events in Paris, together with the invasion of Czechoslovakia in August of the same year, spelled the historic end of Hungarian critical Marxism, although the actors continued their efforts in the same direction for another decade—some of them for an even longer period of time. In the wake of the fall of the Prague Spring, domestic reaction to the superficial loosening of the regime predictably set in. In an hour of internal crisis, Kádár, following Khrushchev's failed recipe, tried to appease his enemies by eliminating the rebellious intellectuals. A 1973 resolution of the Political Bureau of the Hungarian Communist Party proscribed the Budapest school as a group of dangerous subversive elements. It banned them from publication and, in general, from participation in any form of the cultural life of Hungary. Similar repressive measures were undertaken against several critical—but never Marxist—sociologists, most conspicuously against Szelényi and Konrád (while Hegedűs and Márkus were included in the case against the "Budapest school").[10] Some of the intellectuals affected left Hungary for exile in Europe, the United States, and Australia; others remained to become leading lights of the opposition to the regime and gradually bid adieu to their "reformed" or "neo"-Marxism.

Dimensions of Critical Marxism

A working definition of critical Marxism in the countries of "real socialism" can be given, first, by citing its philosophical postulate that the "ideal project" of Marxist socialism has to be contrasted to its appalling implementation in the Soviet-type societies; second, by pointing out its axiom that the "ideal project" contains all the necessary elements of an uncompromising critique of that "reality" as well as adequate criteria for such a criticism; finally, by emphasizing its conviction that no other world-view is suitable for this task. Hence critical Marxism's appeal for a return to Marx, launched by Lukács in the historic year of 1956;[11] hence the pathos of this appeal as well as its internal limitations.

The delicate balance of the critical theory—challenging reality in the name of the assumed ideals of that same reality—rested on the following philosophical theses. The Marxian grand narrative of the progression of the human species, with the predicted terminus of both precapitalist and capitalist "modes of production'' in a universal ''end of alienation,'' was not only maintained but even passionately affirmed. Emphasis on de-alienation, instead of on economic growth, was precisely the hallmark of the ethical and aesthetic ''humanism'' of the critical theory. However weak its political proposals, which are going to be mentioned below, the rejection of the appalling present was, nevertheless, vocal and unambiguous in critical Marxism. The political implications of the uncompromising statement that ''real socialism'' was yet another ''alienated'' society were correctly understood by the philosophically not particularly astute Kádárist secret police.

Widely diverging appraisals of ''alienated reality'' followed from the philosophical premise. Lukács himself, the paradigmatic figure of ''the unhappy consciousness'' of the Bolshevik era, who could never overcome the self-fragmentation and internal contradictions of his philosophy and politics, remained loyal to his maxim of faith, ''my party, right or wrong,'' from which the other, similar, maxim followed: ''The worst socialism is still better than the best capitalism.'' The verdict of others was curt, negative not just in content but also in form. For them, this society did not represent socialism of any kind (which of course suggested the retained presence of the Marxian grand narrative in this position). From the mid- and late 1970s onwards, the appellations proliferated: the regime was termed ''the class power of the intellectuals'' by Konrád and Szelényi, the implication being that it is only potentially, not actually, the intellectuals' power, hence its inadequacy; ''a new class society,'' in the original book by Bence and Kis; and ''the dictatorship over needs'' by Fehér, Heller, and György Márkus.[12]

The deconstruction of the official Marxist sociology—another overwhelmingly negative operation—was the second pillar of the critical Marxist position. The major target of deconstruction was the backbone (and the main mystery) of Marx's sociology: class theory, challenged from all directions. First, its pragmatic forecasting value turned out to be virtually nil. As the decades passed by, it became more and more evident that the nineteenth century, rather that the twentieth, was the era of proletarian revolutions. Second, and more embarrassing, insofar as the workers showed revolutionary zeal in any social arena, it was on the barricades, erected in Berlin, Poznań, and Budapest, against ''their own class power.'' A third, and major, dilemma for class theory was provided by ''real socialism,'' an allegedly classless society itself and one from which, in terms of the official theory, the ''antagonistic classes'' had already disappeared. This self-characterization yielded one of two options, neither of which made its partisans acceptable for ''Marxism-Leninism'': either the new society was indeed classless, and yet it produced a much more unbearable type of hierarchic domination than a so-called class society; or the new order was, as Djilas, for example, assumed, yet another scenario of class rule, class exploitation, and class domination.

The Hungarian debate on class theory was conducted, primarily in the works of Hegedűs and Mária Márkus, in an indirect fashion.[13] No frontal attack on Marx's theory was made. However, the term "class," particularly in the form it had been used in the official theory, was proven worthless for describing the genuine social problems Hungarian society confronted and was replaced by a "stratification model," making a realistic discussion of genuine problems feasible and having many followers (the best known of them being Zsuzsa Ferge).

An increasing disillusionment and a deconstruction of the major tenets (similar to what was happening in sociology) unfolded in the area of Marxist economics and completed its task by the late seventies. Two generations of critical, less and less Marxist, economists dissected the official doctrine with such incisiveness that neither the regime's claim to a superior rationality nor its other claim to a sustained and unparalleled economic growth could be upheld by any other means but an administrative fiat.[14] However, the critical economists refrained from a direct refutation of Marx's own economic system, in part perhaps because they wanted to avoid a head-on collision with the ruling orthodoxy (a position somewhat similar to that of the critical sociologists). But there was another reason for refraining from the task as well. Marx's critique of political economy represented a social philosophy, rather than a positive economic doctrine, and "the critique of the critique" would have needed a philosophical position, not merely economic expertise.

This important task was taken up by a book of strange fate, *Is Critical Economy Possible?*, written by the team of Bence, Kis, and György Márkus between 1970 and 1972. The book, which has never been published and probably never will be, fell victim to the parting ways of the dissident authors to the same extent as to the censorship of the nomenklatura. And yet it played a certain role in the clarification of oppositional ideas in its underground existence. In some sense, its philosophical critique, the conclusions of which were only partly drawn by the authors, relieved the conscience of the left-wing opposition in abandoning Marxist purity and turning toward the market. For the ultimate argument of the authors against Marx was his Enlightenment overestimation of the Promethean-Faustian element, his abundantly optimistic view of Man the Creator who can overcome scarcity of all kinds. Linking the subject of a dynamic system of needs to a world of ineradicable scarcity (ineradicable, if in no other terms but in those of disposable time for work), identifying *scarcity as the human condition*, served as more consolation for the oppositional Marxist actor than any Friedmanite enthusiasm *avant la lettre* for the free market,[15] the more so since the book retained the paraphernalia of a relevant cultural and social critique of modern market society.

Perhaps the most conspicuous constituent of critical Marxism was its *ethical dimension*, and its most important expression, not merely in Hungary but in the whole of the world of "real socialism," can be found in the work of Agnes Heller.[16] Ethical criticism had a simple, and seemingly merely academic, premise: the conspicuous absence of ethics from Marx and Marxism, excused, even hailed, by cynical references to Marx's journalistic dictum that the proletariat is not intent on realizing moral ideals of any kind. The emphasis on the necessity of writing a Marxist ethics, or at least one that can sustain harmonious relations with an author so clearly contemptuous of moral philosophy, had an obvious political edge even before Khrushchev's first revelations about Stalin and much more so afterwards. However Aesopean its language, every sentence of this "purely academic" critique was the moral condemnation of communism's crimes as well as a plea for a post-Machiavellian type of politics. The major theoretical stumbling block in this respect was the methodological postulate of every version of Marxism demanding the grounding of ethics in a "class position." This was in blatant contradiction to both the universalist "humanism" of the Hungarian Marxist opposition and its increasing doubts about class theory. Campaigning for ethical humanism resulted, first, in a moralistic and critical rereading of the history of Bolshevism (and ultimately in the complete rejection of this tradition) and, second, in undermining the Manichean dichotomy of "socialism" and "capitalism." Moral criticism had thus prepared the ground for a complete rethinking of the philosophy of history.

Political theory was decidedly not the strong suit of critical Marxists. For decades, typical pseudoproblems of how best to square the circle were discussed in their circles. The key term, indicating to what extent their groping in the dark was a far cry from a genuine political theory, was "democratization." "Democratization" was the favorite term of the Khrushchevite faction of the nomenklatura, magnanimous enough to agree to change everything theoretically, provided that everything remained unaltered practically. The maxim of "democratization" was spelled out to this author by Kádár's most insightful adviser, the secretary of the Central Committee, György Aczél, who, in a mixture of frustration and rage at the end of a conversation (unexpectedly not leading to the ideological capitulation of the "Budapest school"), coined the following interpretation, of unintended historic value, of what the term actually meant: "We are going to decide when, what, and to what degree we will democratize." And nothing proves more the captivity of the political mind of Lukács, who had been the founder and the leading spirit of oppositional Marxism in Hungary, than the fact that his political testament, an ad hoc pamphlet in reaction to the invasion of Czechoslovakia, had the title *Demokratisierung*. It contained a totally empty and self-contradictory political proposal.[17]

The tradition that saved Hungarian critical Marxism from complete political sterility and made it possible for some of its members to become political leaders of the opposition in the eighties as well as key political figures of postrevolutionary Hungary was the redeemed memory of the revolution of 1956. For strangers to the story it is difficult to conceive how deeply buried this tradition had remained under Kádárist brainwashing; the resurrection of the memory of the greatest historic event in Hungary after World War II would have been an emancipatory gesture in itself. But the works—written in exile and at home—by writers once belonging to the critical Marxist tradition,[18] books which for the first time hailed not only the darling of the cold war, but a great social and national revolution, were also documents of the self-education of the critical Marxists. In studying their own history, the critical Marxists have learned the premise of political theory, the perhaps not original but crucial idea that democracy is neither "bourgeois" nor "socialist" but the general technique of the freedom of the moderns.

Critical Marxist Theory and Other Opposition Forces

Two obvious questions can be posed at this point. The first is whether the critical Marxists had a privileged position in articulating Hungary's suffering among similar-minded oppositional voices. The second is whether they could express these grievances *by virtue of* or *in spite of* their inherited theoretical framework, which they gradually dismantled and abandoned, if to a varying degree and with varying retrospective emotional coloring.

The critical Marxism of Hungary did have a distinguished role within the suppressed, yet omnipresent, array of dissatisfied voices. It is their remaining glory, these days often forgotten with the usual ingratitude of democracies, that for a long period of time the collective voice of the critical Marxists was the only audible expression of dissatisfaction in Kádárist Hungary. It is equally (and equally unjustly) forgotten that they not only took great personal risks and bore heavy sacrifices but also faced a uniquely disinterested Western public opinion which for a long time had been positively infatuated with Kádárism, this "liberalizing miracle" of the communist world. Without doubt, critical Marxism, in Hungary and several other (but not all) countries of "real socialism," did have a certain advantage when compared to other voices of opposition: at least on the surface, their vocabulary seemed to be identical with the official language of the regime. Moreover, several members of the Marxist opposition sustained the self-delusion for so long a time that their conflict with the regime was a mere *querelle de famille*. The fate of Imre Nagy was, of course, a useful memento. After his execution as a traitor, almost to the day forty years after he had joined communism as a prisoner of war in Russia, the mirage of a troubled family atmosphere could no longer be upheld. But the ties of a common language still remained, and this at least made it possible for the critical Marxists to make attempts at public self-articulation. It also belongs to the story of self-delusion that whenever the Khrushchevite faction of the apparatus embarked on one of its regular (and regularly failed) exercises in nonconsequential reforms, for which they needed the authority of the critical Marxists outside the party, they always "discovered" the Marxist language of those whom they had normally treated as enemies, and they believed, or pretended, to see in this linguistic sign a certain warranty of their critics' trustworthiness—within strictly drawn limits. When at a significant political juncture—namely, at the time of the

Warsaw-Pact invasion of Czechoslovakia—György Márkus proposed pluralism within Marxism,[19] the sense of a "semantic confraternity" quickly evaporated from the apparatus.

It is to the credit of the critical Marxists that they had the resolve to translate what was a mere semantic potentiality of their vocabulary into the language of an actual politics of dissent. And in this resolve they had no competition for decades. In Hungary, for particular historic reasons, all parallel voices of opposition, characteristic of the scene in other countries, were almost completely missing. Hungary, unlike Poland, had no powerful Catholic contingent of dissent under communist rule. Not even the half-hearted pacifist disobedience of the East German Evangelical Church, which served as a weak shield against official oppression, could be perceived in the country. A Western-type liberalism, so familiar for Czechs, was a sporadic trend without roots and traditions in Hungary. The country once had a strong and influential social-democratic movement. But its almost traceless disappearance after the revolutionary change, its humiliatingly poor showing in the first free elections, explains in retrospect the fact, although not the causes, of its total absence from the oppositional panorama. What is usually called an *ouvrierist* opposition (a polemical expression of the workers' hostility to the regime, ruling in their name but against their best interests, the greatest example of which was Solidarity as a movement) appeared only in a perverted form in Hungary. Disaffected Stalinists of Kádár's team occasionally played upon the workers' always perceptible anger, and they hatched plots on behalf of policies that would have crippled the workers much more than those of the Kádárist nomenklatura. No serious theory or ideology of opposition could develop out of such a more-than-ambiguous position.

The populist intelligentsia alone can be described as the potential, but never actual, second stream of opposition. It is not at all accidental that two major political forces have emerged in postrevolutionary Hungary: the social liberals rallying around the Alliance of the Free Democrats (whose leaders and political cadres once belonged to the group of critical Marxists or were at least influenced by them), and the populist nationalists who, having joined the Christian conservatives, now dominate the party in government, the Hungarian Democratic Forum. The roots of this division can be traced back to the decades of opposition to communism, in which, as mentioned, the populists always represented a potential, never an actual, force. Their alienation from communism was genuine. Their intellectual leaders—writers, artists, and academics—always regarded communism as an enemy of the nation and of the peasant, as an urban and antirural, and often as a "Jewish," trend. The populists built up a widespread and very efficient personal network of reciprocal support under the vigilant eyes of communist surveillance. With flexible diplomacy, but also due to genuine convictions, they always kept open their lines of communication to traditional Hungarian conservatism and emigré groups as well as to major European conservative parties and institutions. They had excellent relationships, to the degree it was possible, with the Hungarians living in the "successor countries" (Romania, Yugoslavia, and Czechoslovakia). In addition, they had some of the great literary names in their ranks in a country where literature still dominates the cultural scene. Potentially, they seemed to be more dangerous to the communists than the critical Marxists, and, according to the testimony of confidential conversations with leading apparatchiks, the nomenklatura seemed to be more apprehensive of the populists than of the critical Marxists whose influence over the crowd they deemed insignificant. But in reality an old and dubious piece of Hungarian political wisdom prevailed among the populists, in terms of which one need not look for trouble unless necessary: one should rather wait for the moment of demise of the enemy, then join in the kill. As a result of heeding this maxim, the populists lived comfortably under the combined condition of official recognition and surveillance (while the critical Marxists were outcast pariahs). The populists undeniably kept emitting signals of their ultimate alienness to the regime, but they worked out no coherent ideology of opposition comparable to that of the critical Marxists.

Critical Marxism found rich possibilities of articulating certain grievances and social contradictions in its own vocabulary. At the same time it ran into difficulties at a certain point beyond which its mother tongue, characteristic vision, and traditions became an insurmountable obstacle to the proper and politically influential expression of major social issues. At this point its self-dissolution inevitably began.

Opposition to the Stalinist terror, much as it was the politically most sensitive and pragmatically most dangerous topic, lent itself easily to theoretical expression by the critical Marxists. They had been brought up in a "heroic" tradition whose maxims always demanded, even if its adherents did not always practice, a life based on principles and on nothing else, come what may. Therefore those who took the legacy seriously and not self-servingly could not remain silent once they were convinced that the terror served no "historically progressive cause" (in the terms of their initial vocabulary), merely the interests of an oppressive poser. From here it was a relatively smooth transition, at least theoretically, to draw decisive conclusions concerning a rule of terror in general and Bolshevism in particular.

Their vocabulary similarly supported the critical Marxists in developing a thorough criticism of not just the pragmatic malfunctions but of the *systemic irrationality* of a command economy. Although the critical philosophers learned extensively from the critical economists, they went further in their analysis. The creation of a superior type of rationality, embodied in the new society, was a *conditio sine qua non* of their philosophy of history; this was precisely the "mission" of the new society. Failure on this crucial point could not remain hidden from the eyes of the philosophers, nor could it be treated by them as a minor blemish on the escutcheon. Sensitivity to this crucial agenda made them at least suspicious of, if not completely negative to, the merely technocratic versions of economic reform. And the philosophically motivated suspicion paid off politically. The critical Marxist philosophers observed, sooner than anyone else and certainly sooner than the majority of economic experts would have been ready to admit, the failure of economic reform, reduced by the regime from the level of systemic changes and a quest for genuine rationality to that of a mere technical adjustment.

It was not specifically its Marxist tradition (one which has been, despite popular legends, always critical of the "petty-bourgeois" idea of equality) but rather the socialist tradition in general that made the critical Marxists and those influenced by them highly sensitive to the drastic inequalities created by the regime so proudly calling itself "socialist." An East European classic of descriptive sociology, the investigation of systematic inequalities in housing allotments, written by two non-Marxist writers, who were, however, influenced by the socialist–New Left opposition, Konrád and Szelényi,[20] best exemplifies that moderate egalitarianism which smoothly and naturally emerged from the socialist ethos of Hungarian critical Marxism. At the same time, the presence of this philosophical tradition, its superior criticism of absolute egalitarianism, made Hungarian Maoism a mere episode.[21]

The "New Left identity" of the oppositional Marxism of Hungary helped build a special dimension of its "deconstructive function": cultural criticism, and proposals of a "revolution of forms of life."[22] As far as the actual content of the latter is concerned, this is not the place to discuss in detail the relevance of its utopian elements; pointing out its social function will suffice. The three decades of Kádárism were characterized by a strange contradiction. On the one hand, in a compromise with the populace whose revolution they had crushed, the leaders tolerated, even promoted, a certain degree of superficial modernization, primarily in the form of consumerism and tourism in Western countries. On the other hand, it is sociologically relevant to describe the long Kádárist period as the rule of Hungary's conservative middle class, which, although its members detested communist ideology and "internationalism," joined the regime not just out of sheer opportunism but also because it was the rule of "order and authority" with an iron fist but without "excesses." This decidedly old-fashioned style dominated life under Kádár ideologically (except when the interests of "Marxism-Leninism" were concerned), which accounts, for example, for the style of the Hungarian prime minister's condemnation of an "immoral" paper by two critical Marxist authors in 1973.[23] In this atmosphere, the theoretical proposals of a part of Hungarian critical Marxism, as utopian as they may have been, served the need for the modernization of the lifestyles of the younger generations of Hungary's urban middle class.

But on a number of crucial issues, signs of the inadequacy of the critical Marxist framework had already been gathering in the seventies, and its inability to articulate the problems of transition from totalitarianism to democracy was widely felt in the eighties. The major issue involved here was the impossibility of reformulating a theory of modernity on the basis of a preserved Marxian grand narrative with its dichotomy of "capitalism" versus "socialism." Similarly, from the premise of the very meager political theory of critical Marxism, the proper strategy and the adequate organizational forms of citizens' resistance to totalitarianism simply could not be designed. Even when critical Marxist theory did not get in the way of the democratic initiative outright, as it indeed did in the case of Hegedűs's misconceived thesis of "power" versus "domination" (whose exclusive function was to find a justification for single-party rule, coupled with a degree of tolerance for dissenting opinion),[24] the blueprints generated from critical Marxism were meaningless for the emerging forms of dissidence. The objection made by Judt to the "rights language" (adopted by the opposition in the eighties), in terms of which the loss of a holistic framework facilitated the erosion of the Enlightenment component in the dominant theories of Eastern Europe, may have a certain theoretical relevance. But it certainly misses the functional significance of the change in language, which stemmed from the increasing inadequacy of the Marxian grand narrative, preserved by the critical Marxists.[25]

Least of all was critical Marxism capable of expressing the spirit of the nation. In this regard, the populists have always been in a superior position. On a certain level, the issue at stake is "organic" versus "contractual" patriotism (the latter coupled with a degree of cosmopolitan leanings that finds an easy accommodation in the "European context" these days), and the conflicts have spread over to present-day posttotalitarian politics. But on another level, the difference boils down to one of "political instinct" which is always sharpened or blunted by the dominant ideology of a particular political actor. And there is no doubt that the populists have a far sharper instinctive feeling of the concerns of Hungarians qua Hungarians.

Was the collective abandoning of the critical Marxist scenario an opportunist move, or, on the contrary, the sign of a higher and newly acquired philosophical wisdom, or simply a must for those who wanted to remain public actors? Was it gain without losses or self-fragmentation? And, finally, how can the retrospective bottom line of the decades spent in Marxist opposition against "Marxism-Leninism" be drawn? Was it a cul-de-sac, a false detour of life, has it remained part of the continuity of the theorist's life, or was it a disease from which the theorist had to be cured?

The first question can be answered firmly with the voice of critical Marxism's founding father, Lukács, and his answer would be an unambiguous condemnation. The great philosopher, who had chosen Marx as an antidote to the cynical relativism of his age (the declining nineteenth century), would now see himself confirmed in his devastating opinion of the modern intellectual's capacity for quick readjustment. However, a powerful argument, more important than references to the obvious internal drama of so many former critical Marxists—which would be a shallow psychological motivation in any case and as such a mere excuse for Lukács—could be contrasted with the accusing shadow of the founding father. It was Marx, it can be argued, not his critics and enemies, who made his theory into a "philosophy of praxis," the truth of which ultimately depends on the realization of philosophy in an emancipated ("unalienated") new world. And that world, which has carried Marx's name for more than seventy years (no matter, rightly or wrongly), was not a confirmation but rather a devastating refutation of any philosophy worthy of this name. It has been a world of mass graves, slave labor, general lack of freedom, the cheapest kind of materialism, and universal banausis. Weighed by the standards of "Marxist" society and using Marx's own methods, Marx's theory historically proved to be a mere "ideology," the ideology of a ruthless and ultimately bankrupt industrial revolution. Shedding its tenets was, therefore, at once a philosophical and a personal emancipation for the critical Marxist.

Notes

1. The Hungarian Communist Party, Magyar Szocialista Munkáspárt (MSzMP), split into two factions during its last congress while in power, in October 1989. Its majority, led by the reformist leaders—Imre Pozsgay, Rezső Nyers, and others—who accepted the legitimacy of the process of the democratic revolution, renamed the party the Magyar Szocialista Párt (MSzP). The unreconstructed Stalinist minority retained the name and the ideology of the old party. It was from their ranks that the so-called Marx Károly Társaság (Karl Marx Society) for the cultivation of orthodoxy has been formed. Its chairman is József Szigeti, one of the most ominous figures in the ideological history of communism in Hungary. Once a personal disciple of Lukács, Szigeti first made his name known in Hungary during the 1949 "Lukács debate" when, in an unsolicited act of "self-criticism," he betrayed his master and poured accusations on him. See J. Szigeti, "Self-criticism" in *A Lukács-vita (1949-1951)* [The Lukács Debate] (Budapest: Músák Közmüvelödési Kiadó, 1985), 249-63. After the crushing of the 1956 revolution, Szigeti, as a deputy minister of culture, was the Stalinist purger of Hungarian academic and cultural life. His feats in the field of ideology consist not of books but of destroyed careers, betrayed friends, and venomous denunciations.

2. The Polish group of "critical" or "humanist" Marxists, Leszek Kołakowski, Zygmunt Bauman, Bronisław Baczko, Włodimierz Brus, Maria Hirszowicz, and others, are too well known to need characterization and are discussed in chapter 5. It has to be mentioned, however, that while personal contacts between the Hungarians and Poles were minimal until the end of the 1960s (when the Warsaw critical Marxists were forced into emigration), their works were steadily circulating among the critical Marxists of Budapest. A somewhat different story evolved between the Hungarian and Yugoslav critical Marxists. Yugoslav critical Marxism, as it appeared in Hungarian awareness, was tantamount to the Zagreb group of *Praxis* and the Belgrade philosophers and sociologists (Mihailo Marković, Svetozar Stojanović, Zagorka Golubović, and others). They enjoyed the privilege of being the de facto theorists of Tito's rebellion against Stalinist orthodoxy. They were thus in the position of disseminating and commenting upon heretical texts of the Marxist tradition that were practically unavailable in Hungary. This mediating role, more than the Yugoslavs' own theoretical activity, was crucial for the Hungarian critical

Marxists. From the mid-sixties onward there was regular contact between the Hungarians and the Yugoslavs, particularly in the form of participation in the Korčula seminars, organized by the *Praxis* group.

3. Lukács, a natural "school founder," had several generations of disciples after 1945 in Hungary. His "first school," created in 1945, consisted of future leading Stalinists, József Szigeti, István Király, Imre Lakatos. (It is another story that Lakatos became internationally known after 1956 as a major Popperian philosopher and a rabid anticommunist.) Years later, the Lukács school consisted of István Hermann, Agnes Heller, Vilma Mészáros, István Mészáros, Miklós Almási, and István Eörsi. New faces began to appear around Lukács in 1954-55, but the major shakeup only happened after his return from internment in Romania in 1957. From this time onward, that particular group was gradually emerging which Lukács himself termed his "Budapest school" in a posthumously published article ("The Budapest School," *Times Literary Supplement*, 11 June 1971, p. 5). Its members were Agnes Heller, György Márkus, Mihály Vajda, and Ferenc Fehér. However, still in Lukács's lifetime (around the middle of the sixties), a new, young generation joined the Budapest school whose members were György Bence, Géza Fodor, János Kis, Mária Ludassy, Sándor Radnóti.

4. The most important critical economists of Hungary (all of them Marxist initially), who grew critical of Marx, too, not only of the actual functioning of a command economy, were, at various intervals, János Kornai, György Péter, István Zádor, Ferenc Jánossy, András Bródy, Tibor Liska, Mária Augusztinovics, Márton Tardos, and Tamás Bauer. Their respective curricula embrace the history of Hungarian communism from the underground years between the world wars to the final break of the Hungarian intelligentsia not only with communism but also with socialism of milder sorts. These days, almost all of them embrace a social-liberal position.

5. Sociology had a stormy history in Hungary. Banned by two dictatorships, the conservative prewar regime and Stalinist communism alike, it was resurrected only from the late fifties onward. András Hegedűs played a key role in its reorganization as well as in its critical orientation (which was always meant as "criticism from within"). His most important titles, written individually and together with Mária Márkus, with whom he formed a critical Marxist team in the 1960s, are A. Hegedűs, *A Szociológia. Egy Tudomány Lehetősége és Határai* [The Potentials and Limits of Sociology] (Budapest: Akadémiai Kiadó, 1966); A. Hegedűs, *A Szocialista Társadalom Struktúrájáról* (Budapest: Akadémiai Kiadó, 1966) and *Változó Világ* (Budapest: Akadémiai Kiadó, 1970) (the last two were published together under the title *The Structure of Socialist Society* [London: Constable, 1977]); A. Hegedűs, *Socialism and Bureaucracy* (London: Allison and Busby, 1976); A. Hegedűs and M. Márkus, *Ember—Munka—Közösség* [Man, Labor, Community] (Budapest: Közgazdasági és Jogi Könyvkiadó, 1966); A. Hegedűs and M. Márkus, *Sviluppo Sociale e organizzazione del lavoro in Ungheria* (Milan: Feltrinelli, 1975).

6. A formal faction of inner-party opposition was formed around Imre Nagy in late 1954. Its most important members were in part leading—and disillusioned—communist writers, in part similarly disillusioned party journalists of the central newspaper of the Communist Party, *Szabad nép*. The most important of them were Miklós Molnár and Péter Kende, as well as a few academics and younger intellectuals, for example, Gábor Táncos, the latter secretary of the oppositional Petőfi circle. Neither of them was, or even regarded himself as, a social theorist. The documents of the most ambitious theoretical

character stem from Nagy himself. They consist of his memoranda, addressed to the party membership and providing an ever deepening criticism of the Stalinist regime. They were collected posthumously in Imre Nagy, *A magyar nép védelmében—Vitairatok és beszédek* [In Defense of the Hungarian People—Pamphlets and Speeches] (Paris: Cahiers Hongrois, 1984).

7. The short episode of Hungarian Trotskyism boasts several distinguished protagonists. Francois Fejtö, these days the doyen of moderate Hungarian socialism, was attracted to Trotsky's doctrine for a short period of time in the mid-thirties, while a student in Paris. Fejtö initiated the only great poet Hungarian communism ever had, Attila József, into the forbidden charm of Trotskyism, stemming from a dual—conservative and communist—anathema. Pál Justus, a young radical intellectual, later not entirely accidentally one of the chief defendants of the show trial against Rajk in 1949, wrote an original Trotskyist interpretation of Lukács's *History and Class Consciousness* in Hungary during the war years. The young Trotskyists found temporary asylum in the Social Democratic Party, mainly because of the ideological provincialism and indifference of the party's leadership. But this strange cohabitation came to an end after the war; so also did the short intermezzo of Hungarian Trotskyism.

8. The refusal of self-criticism of any kind by Imre Nagy following the March 1955 condemnation of his policies in a Stalinist revival was not merely a daring act but, viewed in retrospect, the actual prelude to his heroic death. This example gave strength to many others after him. When in the process of purge the members of the Budapest school were summoned to a collective ritual of self-criticism and they refused to participate in it, formally challenging the party's authority, they simply copied, under much less dangerous circumstances, Nagy's example. At the same time, this challenge naturally sealed their fate.

9. See the analysis of the role of Kádárism's tacit self-advertisement as the only Khrushchevite country in a post-Khrushchevite atmosphere in "Kádárism as the Model State of 'Khrushchevism' " in A. Heller and F. Fehér, *From Yalta to Glasnost* (Oxford and Boston: Basil Blackwell, 1990).

10. In the early seventies, Kádárism passed through one of its regular and recurring inner-party crises, for various reasons. Kádár had been compromised in the eyes of Brezhnev for his complicity with Dubček, whose regime Kádár had clearly wanted to save. For the domestic neo-Stalinists, the experiments with the economic reform, much as they were inconsistent, appeared dangerous, and the neo-Stalinists were plotting against Kádár. In this atmosphere, Kádár resorted to Khrushchev's old trick, but with greater success. When Khrushchev was cornered, for the nth time, in the early 1960s by his neo-Stalinist colleagues, he decided on a futile attempt to sacrifice the heads of rebellious intellectuals in order to appease his Stalinist colleagues. Kádár's similar predicament was the real background of the purge against the Budapest school, conducted in the first half of 1973, which ended with their complete expulsion from Hungarian cultural and social life. See *Filozófus-per, 1973* [The Trial of Philosophers] (Budapest: *Világosság*, special edition, 1989).

11. See Lukács's speech, launching an appeal for a "return to Marx and from Marx to 'reality' " on 15 June 1956, in *A Petőfi Kör Vitái* [The Debates of the Petőfi Circle], ed. András B. Hegedűs (Budapest: Kelenföld Kiadó—ELTE, 1989), 67-74.

12. György Bence and János Kis (under the pseudonym Marc Rakovski), *Le marxisme face aux pays de l'Est* (Paris: Savelli, 1977) (English-language edition: *Towards an East*

European Marxism [New York: St. Martin's, 1978]); György Konrád and Iván Szelényi, *The Intellectuals on the Road to Class Power* (New York: Harcourt Brace Jovanovich, 1981); Ferenc Fehér, Agnes Heller, and György Márkus, *Dictatorship Over Needs* (Oxford: Basil Blackwell, 1981); Mihály Vajda, *The State and Socialism* (London: Allison and Busby, 1983).

13. Hegedűs and Márkus, *Ember, munka, közösség* [Man, Work, Community]; Hegedűs, *The Structure of Socialist Society*.

14. The best critical analysis of the systemic irrationality of a command economy by a Hungarian critical economist can be found in the classic work of János Kornai, *A hiány* [Scarcity] (Budapest: Közgazdasági és Jogi Könyvkiadó, 1980). The book operates with an Aesopean "theoretical model" of command economy in seemingly abstract terms, which provides a more devastating criticism of the system than any "empirical" study amassing a wealth of data.

15. György Bence, János Kis, and György Márkus, *Lehetségese kritikai gazdaságtan?* [Is Critical Economy Possible?] (manuscript). The manuscript was completed in 1972.

16. The first draft of a moral criticism of "real socialism" can be found in the university lectures on moral philosophy given by Agnes Heller as early as 1957-58 at the Lóránd Eötvös University of Budapest. The guardians of party orthodoxy grasped very quickly the politically hostile nature of the abstract theoretical analysis. A venomous polemic against—or rather, a lengthy denunciation of—Heller's moral philosophy was published in 1958 in the central theoretical journal of the Communist Party, *Társadalmi szemle*, by two arch-Stalinist authors, Tamás Földesi and Mária Makai. In good Stalinist fashion, "criticism" meant no attempt at a theoretical refutation of a particular system of moral philosophy, rather an inventory, made with sharp political sense, of the implications, hostile to the rule of the nomenklatura, inherent in this "counterrevolutionary" ethics. An updated version of Heller's 1957-58 lectures on moral philosophy was published during a short period of relaxation of Kádárist censorship, *A szándéktól a következményig* [From the Intention to the Consequences] (Budapest: Magvető, 1971).

17. György Lukács, *A demokratizálódás jelene es jövője* (Budapest: Magvető, 1988). The manuscript was written between September and December 1968 on the solicitation of this author, who convinced Lukács that he was almost duty bound to react theoretically to the invasion of Czechoslovakia. The pamphlet had an ironic fate. In Lukács's innermost circle, the "Budapest school"—which was at that time already embarking on a course of overt opposition having abandoned all hopes of an internal reform of the regime—generated disillusionment, communicated to the author in respectful but emphatic terms. On the other hand, the "outspokenness" of the pamphlet shocked the ruling party circles, who—equally respectfully but in no less uncertain terms—asked the author to refrain from its publication abroad "for a while." For more than fifteen years after Lukács's death in 1971, the manuscript was a carefully protected secret document in the party archives. When it was finally published in Hungary, the time of Kádárism was already running out. The pamphlet, which could have been a sensational event in the mid-seventies, turned into an obsolete piece of memorabilia by the end of the 1980s.

18. A systematic analysis of the revolution of 1956, written from a position that was no longer "critical Marxist" in nature in the sense of the 1960s but bore some resemblance to this position, can be found in A. Heller and Ferenc Fehér, *Hungary, 1956 Revisited (The Lessons of a Revolution After a Quarter of a Century)* (London and Boston: Allen and Unwin, 1982).

19. György Márkus, "Viták és irányzatok a marxizmusban" [Debates and Trends within Marxism], *Kortárs*, August 1968.

20. Ivan Szelényi and György Konrád, *Az új lakótelepek szociológiai problémai* [Sociological Problems of the New Housing Developments] (Budapest: Akadémiai Kiadó, 1969).

21. Hungarian Maoism had a short, but interesting, history. In the second half of the sixties, parallel with and in reaction to the first attempts at an economic reform, a group of young intellectuals and students embraced Mao's doctrines and, after establishing contact with the Chinese embassy, which was under strict police surveillance, they began to distribute leaflets giving voice to an egalitarian criticism of Kádár's regime. Much as the participants now want to bury this episode of their lives in oblivion, and despite the fact that the Maoist propaganda did endorse a ridiculous criticism of any concern for democracy, the documents contained an acute sense of the apparatus planning to use the reform, together with the technocracy, for its own selfish reasons. The Maoists were persecuted by the Kádárist secret police in 1970-71, and in turn defended by the emerging democratic opposition. This gesture laid the foundations for a future alliance, and some of the ex-Maoists, most notably Miklós Haraszti, later emerged as leading figures of the democratic opposition in Hungary.

22. Several works by Agnes Heller, written in the late sixties and the seventies, growing out of her theoretical inquiry into "everyday life" and the European and North American sociology of culture, attested to an acute theoretical interest in the "revolution of forms of life." See *A morál szociológiája vagy a szociológia morálja* [The Sociology of Morals or the Morals of Sociology] (Budapest: Gondolat Kiadó, 1966); "Die Revolution des Alltagslebens," *Praxis* 5, no. 1 (1968). These writings echoed New Left trends in Western Europe and the United States.

23. Agnes Heller and Mihály Vajda, "Családforma és kommunizmus" [Family Forms and Communism], *Kortárs*, 1972, no. 1. Jenö Fock, then prime minister of Hungary and a member of that "iron guard" of communism that had crushed the revolution of 1956, commented on the "immoral" authors of this paper in the March 1973 session of the Hungarian Parliament, when the expulsion of the Budapest school from Hungarian cultural life was already well under way, in the following manner: "We shall take the pen out of their hands." He lacked the erudition to know that he was just paraphrasing Dr. Joseph Goebbels.

24. See A. Hegedűs's Weberian distinction between "power" and "domination" as applied to "real socialism" in "A társadalmi fejlődés alternatívái" [The Alternatives of Social Development], *Kortárs*, 1968, no. 6.

25. Tony Judt, "The Language of Opposition," in *Crisis and Reform in Eastern Europe*, ed. Ferenc Fehér and Andrew Arato (New Brunswick, NJ: Transaction, 1990).

4

The Significance of Marxist Dissent to the Emergence of Postcommunism in the GDR

Leslie Holmes

Introduction

In October 1989 Erich Honecker, East German leader since 1971, was forced to resign. This symbolized not only the end of a particular leader's regime but also, and far more significantly, that the increasingly visible crisis of East European communism was now reaching what had long been seen as one of the most stable and self-assured of all communist regimes. Honecker's successor, Egon Krenz, lasted only until December. By this time, another major symbol of East German communism, the infamous Berlin Wall, had—metaphorically speaking at least—come tumbling down. The GDR was in flux. As other countries of Eastern Europe underwent transformations that can only be described as revolutionary, it became increasingly difficult for Krenz's successor, Gregor Gysi, to maintain communist power in the German Democratic Republic. As elsewhere, there were various identifiable stages in the transformation from old-style communism to the diverse phenomenon we are currently, for want of a better term, calling "postcommunism." Thus, in the early stages, the new communist leaderships attempted to acquire some legitimacy by blaming their predecessors for numerous problems in the country. Having done this, many members of the former leadership were accused of corruption. Subsequently, as part of a bid to emphasize the move toward the rule of law, the role of the secret police (the infamous Stasis) was substantially reduced; indeed, the Stasis were all but abolished as an institution in December 1989. Yet another development in common with the general East European move to postcommunism was the abandonment in December 1989 of the concept of the "leading role" of the Communist Party (Socialist Unity Party or SED). This was followed by a renaming of the party (mid-December) and its abandonment of certain key tenets. But—again as

57

elsewhere—this was insufficient to save it. From September 1989 on, there emerged a number of new political organizations and parties in the GDR to challenge the SED. Moreover, some of the minor parties that had coexisted with the SED since the 1940s underwent major transformations in the latter half of 1989–early part of 1990. In several cases there were new leaders (e.g., G. Hartmann replaced H. Höhmann as head of the National Democrats; Lothar de Maizière replaced G. Gotting as head of the Christian Democrats). Even more important, some of these parties now began to distance themselves from the SED far more than they had ever previously attempted. There was a feeling in many quarters that communist power was doomed, and it was in this situation that the new leaderships of "old" parties sought to take advantage of the crisis of communism by emphasizing how different their parties were both from the SED and from their own former selves.

Eventually—once again, in a manner similar to that in other countries of Eastern Europe—the East German population was permitted to vote in the first really free national elections since the 1940s; these were held in March 1990. The East Germans—like the Poles, the Czechoslovaks, the Hungarians, and others—revealed at the polling stations that a substantial majority of them had had enough of communist rule. In April 1990 the leader of the Christian Democratic Union, Lothar de Maizière, announced the formation of a new government, in which the communists would play no role.[1] The GDR had reached postcommunism. But the revolution did not stop there. In October 1990, the GDR ceased to exist as a sovereign entity—an entity that had for all but a few months been a communist one. Not only did the GDR cease to exist, but it was integrated into what the communists had long perceived as their archrival, the Federal Republic of Germany. In this sense, the collapse of East German communism was more complete than the collapse of communism in any other country of Eastern Europe.

The main question to be addressed in this chapter is that of the *significance* of Marxist dissent to the collapse of communist rule in the GDR. However, there are other ways in which the significance of East German Marxist dissent can be considered. For instance, one can consider the *originality* of East German Marxist critiques; here, significance is being analyzed in terms of the contribution of dissident writing to the general field of post-Marx Marxist theory. Was there anything in East German dissident Marxism that will be as durable as the writings of Gramsci or Habermas, or, arguably, Althusser? How well known were the dissidents in the West? Did East German dissidents succeed, where others have not, in adapting Marxism for an analysis of their own society in areas in which classical Marxism seems singularly ambiguous and/or inappropriate and/or deficient (e.g., the question of class and class structure)? Much of this *first* aspect of significance is difficult to answer, and it will be addressed only briefly. This said, the conclusions will include some consideration of the uniqueness of East German Marxist dissidence. Some aspects of this relate directly to significance; others do not, but slot better into this part of the analysis than elsewhere.

A *second* approach to significance is in terms of the perceived *validity* of Marxist dissidence. The focus here is on the proximity of critical writing to what other analysts have perceived as the salient features of GDR reality in recent years. In attempting to answer this question, we will inevitably slide into the *third* and, for the purposes of this chapter, most important aspect of significance—its *political relevance*. How many dissidents were there, and did numerical strength or weakness signify anything in itself? How cohesive were the dissidents, and can one talk of there having been a dissident "movement"? What was the impact of the dissidents on the masses, and was there any serious linkage between the two groups? Was the linkage between dissidents and the masses the most important one anyway, in terms of political importance? If not, which relationship(s) was/were *more* important? How did the former (communist) East German leadership react to the dissidents, and what does this tell us about the latters' significance? Above all, what role did East German Marxist dissidents play in the collapse of the communist system in 1989-90?

Although the above list of approaches to the question of "significance" is far from exhaustive, it will already be clear that any attempt at analyzing significance will necessarily produce a multifaceted response. Before attempting to reach such a complex answer, the meaning of the term "dissidence" will be considered, a brief historical overview of East German dissidence to the 1980s will be provided, and then recent writings of those who may be considered to have been the most interesting and potentially "significant" of the Marxist dissidents will be analyzed. This will be followed by a brief analysis of the treatment of dissidents and the conclusions.

Dissidence Defined

The word dissidence derives from the Latin words *dis*, meaning "apart," and *sedere*, "to sit," so that a dissident is someone who sits apart from something. As applied to the communist world, it is generally accepted that the dissident "sits apart" from the regime. What is less widely appreciated—although it is a very important issue—is that a dissident might not be close to the views of the masses either. Clearly, in terms of the "significance" of dissidence, especially in the third sense being used in this chapter, this meaning of dissidence cannot be omitted. Given our inability to conduct acceptably rigorous surveys of popular attitudes in communist states, any answer to the question of resonance between dissidents and the masses has necessarily to be intuitive and speculative; but it will be addressed in the concluding section.

Of course, the notion of "sitting apart" is both too vague and too weak to serve as anything more than a starting point for a definition of dissidence, and a fuller, more satisfactory definition is provided by Roy Medvedev:

A dissident is someone who disagrees in some measure with the ideological, political, economic, or moral foundation that every society rests on. . . . But he does more than simply disagree and think differently; he openly proclaims his or her dissent and demonstrates it in one way or another to compatriots and the state. In other words he doesn't just complain in private to his partner or close friends.[2]

The distinction drawn by Schapiro, Reddaway, and others[3] between dissent (which is used here interchangeably with dissidence) and opposition is a useful one on a conceptual and comparative level but is probably of marginal relevance to the East German situation. This is because the bulk of major dissident writing in the GDR has been, at least on the surface, concerned with improving the existing system rather than fundamentally opposed to it. This said, one has to acknowledge that the line between dissidence and opposition is often a very fine one, and that some of the dissidents, as well as the authorities, have themselves talked of their opposition; this is mostly used only in a loose, everyday sense, however.

The application of the label "dissident" also raises problems. In one sense, any person who is prepared publicly to criticize any aspect of the regime or its policies is a dissident if in doing so they run the risk of state reprisals. This would therefore include anyone who participates in an unofficial peace demonstration, for instance. But such an interpretation is broader than the one that will be employed here. Somewhat arbitrarily, only individuals who have written broad critiques of the communist system in the GDR will be included, those van der Will presumably has in mind when he refers to "high-profile dissent";[4] people who have only spoken against the system or its policies, or who have written on only one issue—such as the position of the churches—would be excluded from this.[5] This said, the following section locates the dissidents among other overt manifestations of political dissatisfaction in the GDR. Another problem is whether to include dissidents who did not live in the GDR in the later communist period. It could be argued that such people should be included if they were still analyzing and commenting on the GDR and if their views were filtering back to the GDR and being discussed there, albeit unofficially. Thus the views of Rudolf Bahro from the time he left the GDR in 1979 *are* included in this chapter.

An Overview of East German Dissidence

The notion that Marxist dissidence first emerged in the GDR in 1956 is not entirely accurate.[6] Already in the 1940s there were communists in the Eastern zone of Germany—a prime example being Wolfgang Leonhard[7]—who were concerned at the way in which their country/zone was developing. However, according to Leonhard, such dissidents at that time revealed their views only to a small number of friends and acquaintances in so-called "conversations among ourselves'' (*unter uns Gesprochen*); in this sense, this does not qualify as dissidence for the purposes of this chapter. The first really overt dissident voices in the GDR were heard in the mid-1950s, after the brutal suppression of rioting citizens in June 1953. By 1956, with both this and the Soviet leadership's condemnation of Stalin and Stalinism in mind, a number of intellectuals felt that the time had come to speak out. Some of these people were calling for relatively specific reforms. For instance, Werner Dorst was concerned that the educational system should promote the most intelligent and gifted students, not those declaring the most overt political loyalty. Fritz Behrens and Arne Benary were concerned primarily with making the economy perform more efficiently, although their suggestions on how this should be achieved, especially their calls for industrial organization along the lines of Yugoslav ''self-management,'' had profound implications for the distribution of power in society and were therefore political.[8] But the most overtly critical and significant voices were those of a group centered on Wolfgang Harich. Harich, a lecturer in philosophy at the Humboldt University in East Berlin, was the chief author of a document which appeared in 1956 and came to be known as the ''Harich Program.'' Some indication of the importance of this is seen in the fact that, as late as 1970, one Western commentator described it as ''the only consistent formulation of East German reform communism that has come to be known outside the GDR.''[9] Among the many proposals made by Harich were the following: there should be a real choice in elections; the state legislature (*Volkskammer*) should be a genuine discussion forum and independent of party control; forced collectivization of agriculture should be stopped; and workers' self-management in industry, along the Yugoslav lines, should be introduced. However, Harich and his coauthors did not stop at changes in the organization of the state and society, they also advocated major change within the party itself. For instance, they called for the expulsion of all Stalinists—who were seen as essentially ''fascist''—from the party, and for more power to the rank-and-file membership at the expense of the party apparatchiks. Moreover, in line with similar aspirations in other parts of Eastern Europe in 1956, the Harich program called for a specifically German road to socialism; the time for blind and often inappropriate emulation of Soviet theory and practice was over. Given that the communist leadership in the GDR was never particularly liberal in comparison even with some other communist leaderships, it was hardly surprising that Harich was arrested in November 1956; the following March he received a ten-year prison sentence, of which he served seven years before being released.

Several supporters of Harich were also tried and imprisoned in 1957, and this clampdown led to a relatively quiet period in the history of East German dissidence. At this stage (late 1950s), those who felt too strongly about the system could in any case always leave it without too many difficulties. But with the erection of the Berlin Wall in August 1961, it became much more difficult to escape from the GDR.

Ironically, the East German leadership appeared to become somewhat more liberal following the construction of the Wall. This change was most obvious in the introduction of the New Economic System (NES) in January 1963. NES envisaged a certain amount of decentralization of decision making in industry and was interpreted by some as a sign that the leadership, feeling more self-assured now that skilled workers and peasants could no longer flee, was prepared to place more confidence in the citizenry. It was in this atmosphere that the man who was to become one of the best known of all the East German dissidents, the chemist Professor Robert Havemann, produced a trenchant (but again Marxist) critique of the regime in a series of lectures delivered at the Humboldt University in the 1963-64 academic year. In these lectures, Havemann called for a more humane form of socialism, in which people would be free to make constructive criticisms aimed at building a better society. He denounced the authoritarian nature of the regime and was particularly critical of the interference of what he saw as party dogma in the development of natural science; on this point, at least, his views were somewhat akin to those of Sakharov.[10]

Any notion that the East German leadership had become more tolerant toward political criticism was dispelled soon after Havemann's lectures. The chemist lost his chair at the university and his party membership. Admittedly, he was not imprisoned, but his enforced retirement was a serious blow. Nevertheless, Havemann continued to criticize what he saw as the authoritarian, even Stalinist, aspects of the GDR's political system, usually in articles or books smuggled to and published in the FRG. Havemann praised the political experimentation of the Prague reformers in 1968 and later argued that East Berlin would one day have its own "Spring."

One of Havemann's most frequent criticisms was that the political leaders, despite their adoption of the NES, did not recognize that most East Germans had accepted the basic tenets of socialism; from this premise he further argued that they (the leaders) should now demonstrate more faith in the masses and permit them a greater role in the running of their own society. A typical article was one that appeared in the West German newspaper *Frankfurter Rundschau* in December 1973 entitled "The Government Should Show Confidence in Its Own People." Here Havemann argued that there was no dictatorship of the proletariat in the GDR, only a "dictatorship of a clique of party functionaries." In line with his view that most East Germans basically accepted socialism, he argued that "the sole threat to socialism is the present form of the state that rules here."[11] However, like Harich, he also believed that change away from "bureaucratic" socialism and toward a humane variant should come from above; the basic reason for this is that such change would then be more secure than one induced by rioting mobs.

In the autumn of 1976 the GDR authorities emulated their Soviet counterparts, deciding to deal harshly with the dissidents before the latter had much opportunity to organize themselves for monitoring their government's adherence to the 1975 Helsinki agreement. The balladeer Wolfgang Biermann was expelled to West Germany, while Havemann was placed under house arrest. Eighteen months later a relatively new, but highly influential, dissident, Rudolf Bahro, was also imprisoned; he was soon released and left for the FRG. Bahro's analysis, though Marxist, called for a much more liberal and decentralized communist society than, most notably, Harich's. In his book *The Alternative*, published in West Germany in 1977, Bahro accepted that an authoritarian state is necessary in the immediate aftermath of a revolution but felt that the party-state complexes in Eastern Europe had outlived this justification for their role and should start transferring more power to the ordinary people (i.e., more in line with Havemann's ideas). He maintained that the events in Czechoslovakia in 1968 demonstrated very clearly the validity of his argument that the East European party-states had become reactionary and were hindering the development of genuine socialism and communism in that part of the world.

Despite the large number of expulsions in the late 1970s, the "grand old man" of East German dissidence, Havemann, remained in his native country and continued to criticize the regime, despite harassment. Toward the end of his life (he died in April 1982), Havemann became closely involved in what developed into the most sensitive issue in East German politics in the early 1980s—the unofficial peace movement. The background to this event is that the intensified repression of the late 1970s, plus the deteriorating East–West relationship, was accompanied by a marked increase in the militarization of East German life. In particular, school children were required to undergo elementary weapons training, which led to tensions between the church (predominantly Evangelical in the GDR) and the communist authorities. By 1981, and encouraged by the peace movement in the West, Havemann and various church leaders were becoming increasingly critical of this militarization of their society. They advocated a "social peace service," whereby young people would be given the option to perform peaceful social work for two years rather than the eighteen-month military conscription required by existing laws. Toward the end of 1981, Havemann and others sent a letter to Leonid Brezhnev in the USSR, calling on the Soviet leader to work harder for peace.[12] This movement thus had narrower aims than any of the earlier dissidents (including Havemann himself) had had. On the other hand, the adoption of a more specific and tangible target appears to have attracted a large number of followers, particularly young people. Although the authorities attempted to suppress this movement, they were in a very embarrassing and ambivalent position, since it was the official policy of the GDR to work for peace. Until the late 1980s, this peace movement, though coming under strong pressure from the authorities, was the most important unofficial political movement to have emerged in the GDR.

Major Dissident Writing of the 1970s and 1980s

This section presents an analysis of the more recent works of Bahro and Havemann, plus Harich's *Communism without Growth*—which has perhaps been insufficiently publicized and analyzed in the English-language literature, a point borne out by the fact that Roger Woods's generally excellent study of East German opposition makes no reference either to the book or even to Harich himself[13]—primarily in terms of the three writers' views on a number of issues to which they have all addressed themselves. This has been done principally to render the analysis as comparative as seems reasonable. However, the attempt has also been made to demonstrate the different emphasis each writer places on a given issue, and to highlight those aspects of each writer's work that are unique, or at least of more concern, to that writer than to the others. The main issues focused upon are:

general attitudes toward the GDR;
attitudes toward Marxism and communism;
views on the source of revolutionary change;
attitudes toward technology and environmental issues; and
attitudes toward feminism.

It should be noted that this sequence has not been rigidly adhered to if and when it seemed appropriate to consider the issues in a different order. It should further be noted that Bahro's *The Alternative* has been excluded from this part of the analysis, largely because it has already been analyzed extensively elsewhere; there will be occasional references to the book, however, when appropriate.

Bahro

The Alternative was written while Bahro was still living in the GDR. He was imprisoned there because of it. Bahro subsequently moved to the FRG, where he lectured and wrote extensively until returning to the GDR in 1990; three sets of his speeches and writings appeared in English in the 1980s, and it is primarily with his views on the GDR as revealed in these that this section is concerned.[14]

Contrary to what might be supposed, by the 1980s Bahro was not particularly critical of the GDR in his writings. He argued that *The Alternative* contained all the major criticisms he wished to make of the "actually existing socialism" of Eastern Europe and that, had he stayed on in the GDR, he would not have continued to confront the authorities. This is not to say that he did not still criticize *some* aspects of the GDR—he certainly did. For instance, he argued that the GDR's economy was a "second-class" version of capitalism, which did not perform as well within the capitalist frame of reference as did the FRG's. He also felt there was far too little say for the working masses and described the East

German system as "factory despotism" at the level of society, hardly a complimentary term.[15] And he complained about the severe housing shortages in the GDR. But on the other hand, he argued that the GDR had broken with the militaristic tradition of the Nazis (something with which many East German unofficial peace activists would have taken issue), and that, despite their complaints, most East Germans were basically supportive of the system. In fact he went so far as to say that the majority would stay in the GDR were the Wall to be dismantled.[16] He criticized those sections of the Western media that portrayed him as an East German dissident and asserted that thinking at the topmost levels was more advanced in the GDR than in the FRG.[17] He even went so far as to claim that his views were very close to those of most SED members and that, on balance, he had been loyal to and supportive of the regime. Does this mean that Bahro regretted moving to the West? Bahro was ambiguous on this, claiming both that he felt he could be more useful to the critically thinking Left in the GDR from his position in the West (he claimed that many of his comrades in the East came to endorse this position) and that, had he foreseen the development of the "eco-pacifist" movement in the GDR, he might well have tried to stay on in his native land.[18]

There was a certain ambiguity, too, in Bahro's views on Marxism. In the collection published in English in 1984, he made it clear that, if he were to be permitted to use Marxism selectively ("reconstruct" it) and update it when this seemed necessary, then he was still a communist and a Marxist. On the other hand, he also felt that in the West these terms implied a certain rigidity and adherence to virtually everything Marx wrote. Because he did not wish to be associated with such unquestioning loyalty to the ideas of a nineteenth-century theorist, he felt it would be more appropriate not to label himself a Marxist. Instead, he considered himself an eclectic, who could both reconstruct Marxism to fit the late twentieth century and add to it ideas from elsewhere that he thought were missing in Marxism. Thus he felt that Marx did not place sufficient emphasis on the psychological and spiritual aspects of human needs and organization and so wanted to include Freud, Fromm, Christ, Buddha, and others in his analysis of the human condition and how to improve it. In particular, Bahro favored a cultural revolution (i.e., a revolution of consciousness), seeing this as more important than and embracing political and social revolution; he argued that too much emphasis on purely economic factors, and too narrow a conception of materialism, was a flaw in Marxism.[19]

Bahro's strong condemnation of capitalism—he blames it for all the major problems in the world, such as the arms race, hunger, depletion of natural resources, pollution, and most generally, "exterminism" (a term he borrowed from E.P. Thompson, although he has used it in a much broader way than does the British academic)—makes it absolutely clear that Bahro remained a socialist. But what *kind* of socialist is less readily answerable. He has seen the ecological issue as the most serious and urgent in the modern world, and in this sense was (and is) a Green. In a number of other ways, and continuing the theme of the last paragraph, he was always a very unconventional Marxist. For instance, he did not accept that the proletariat of the advanced industrial states could be the main motor of the kind of revolution he was advocating, and which he wanted to call a populist revolution. Rather, he looked primarily to what Toynbee has called the "external proletariat," the marginalized masses of the Third World. This said, he did not completely discount *any* revolutionary role either for the metropolitan proletariat or for the communist world.[20]

Bahro's views on the kind of society that would follow a revolution were still blurred in his more recent writings (i.e., as they were in *The Alternative*). On the one hand, he condemned centralist political parties and state bureaucracies and frequently advocated "self-reliant" small communities.[21] On the other hand, he stated explicitly that he favored centralized social planning, and that this was one aspect of the "actually existing socialism" of Eastern Europe that should not be abandoned.[22] He even *appeared* to favor Jacobinism in a somewhat obscure statement toward the end of *From Red to Green*.[23]

As for the immediate tactics for the ecological movement in Germany, Bahro was quite unambiguous about favoring a form of historic compromise. He strongly condemned factionalism and internecine strife (a feature he considered far more typical of the Left than of the Right), arguing that this only delays the emergence of the cultural revolution and so aids capitalism in its strides toward global suicide.

Two final aspects of Bahro's thought concern technology and the feminist movement. Again, it is not entirely clear what Bahro really thought about technology. He explicitly claimed to be a utopian socialist, but he did not wish to abolish technology. Instead, he wanted to subordinate it and use it to the benefit of humanity rather than fetishize it and trust that it will solve all our problems. The feminist issue has concerned Bahro much more than either Harich or Havemann. This is perhaps reflective of the fact that he was living in West Germany, where the issue has been much more alive in the past ten to fifteen years than in the GDR. He has been highly critical of patriarchy and in this sense is antisexist. On the other hand, he has also argued that feminism is the last great bourgeois political movement and that the issue is not *as* pressing as the environmental one.

Harich

When one first reads Harich's major work of recent years, *Kommunismus ohne Wachstum* (1975), one could be forgiven for wondering why this onetime philosophy lecturer was ever seen as a dissident by the authorities. Whereas Bahro was highly critical of a number of—though, as we have seen, by no means all—aspects of "actually existing socialism," Harich not only emphasized frequently that the GDR is superior to the FRG (for instance, in terms of the quality of life), but even claimed that there was genuine socialism in the Eastern bloc, and that power was exercised by the working class, albeit via a Communist Party.[24] He accused Havemann of being an opponent of the East German system and claimed that he was not.[25] Indeed, Harich maintained that he had always been "loyal to the official line" (*linientreu*);[26] that he was unquestionably an orthodox Marxist; that he believed in the need for a powerful, centralized communist government; and that he sympathized with many of the dilemmas facing the GDR leadership. It thus seems very strange that the East German communist leadership treated Harich as a dissident (the reasons for this are more appropriately dealt with below, in the conclusions). For now, it is sufficient to note that the answer may be closely related to Harich's views on economic growth.

In his 1975 book, Harich very explicitly advocated zero growth. The reason for this, basically, was that he, like Bahro, had been very influenced by ecological arguments. Harich claimed to have become interested in ecological matters as far back as 1948 but only really focused on them from the early 1970s, after having read and been enormously impressed by books such as Gordon Rattray Taylor's *Doomsday Book* (1970), the English publication *Blueprint for Survival* (1972), Schumacher's *Small Is Beautiful* (1973), and various publications of the Club of Rome. It was in the light of his reading of this literature that he rejected some of the major tenets of his earlier writing, such as his views on leadership and the state as expressed in *Zur Kritik der revolutionären Ungeduld*.[27]

Harich remained more clearly a Marxist than Bahro, although, as the latter explained, this could primarily be a function of the fact that Harich continued to live in the GDR, and did not feel as tied to classical ideas as many Western Marxists are alleged to be. Harich certainly *was* prepared to jettison aspects of Marxism that he felt had become redundant. One of the most significant examples was Harich's rejection of what many have interpreted as Marx's positive orientation toward growth of the productive forces. Harich claimed that Marx himself was ambiguous on this issue, sometimes favoring growth, at other times being more concerned with the quality of life (notably in *The German Ideology*). Harich also argued that he was not being a dissident to adopt this approach and cited a number of Soviet natural scientists and even a Soviet social scientist (the economist Medunin), who, he maintained, adopted a basically similar approach to his own.[28]

The other major concept of classical Marxism rejected by Harich was the (specifically Engelsian) concept of a "withering away of the state." This was seen by Harich as utopian anarchism in the modern world; far from wanting a withering of the state, Harich essentially advocated an all-powerful *world* state. He argued for a highly centralized, powerful world economic council that would issue global economic plans based on the needs and resources of the various peoples and parts of the world.[29] He also called for a powerful dictatorship of the proletariat in the immediate aftermath of the overthrow of the world capitalist system. In his faith in the proletariat, Harich was much more of an orthodox Marxist than Bahro ever was. This said, Harich also argued the need for a coalition of all forces (classes and strata) other than the monopoly capitalists to bring about the revolution he wanted. Thus, although Harich was less ambiguous than Bahro, there were gray areas and contradictions in his argument, too. One of the strangest is in his attitude toward working-class activity under capitalism. Although he clearly believed just as strongly as Bahro did that the ecological issue required urgent resolution—he even allowed his book to be published before he felt it was ready, on the grounds that he was ill and did not know how long it would be before he would feel strong enough to resume work on it—he did not, apparently, feel that it overrode all other political issues. Thus, in a way Bahro would not do, Harich argued that the working class should never be moderate in its demands of capitalists *even on ecological grounds.*[30]

Another ambiguity in Harich's writing can be found in his views on technology. On the one hand, he accused Sakharov of being a Western-oriented "technocratic type" who venerated technology. Yet on the other hand, he himself appears to have had a naive faith in the ability of computers optimally to allocate goods on a worldwide basis. Indeed, despite his pleas for a proletarian dictatorship, he also argued that science should override the views of the masses.[31] Given Harich's desire for strong, centralized government and his acceptance of the need for Jacobinism and authoritarianism—he even revealed some admiration for Stalin and appeared to justify both the Berlin Wall and the GDR authorities' treatment of himself[32]—plus the aforementioned faith in computers, it would seem that Wolfgang Biermann's phrase to describe the GDR system, "computer Stalinism," would be a fitting summary of much of Harich's argument. The irony here becomes acute when one remembers Harich's 1956 arguments.

One final ambiguity in Harich's views is on the origin of the revolutionary transformation to communism. Sometimes, Harich appeared to believe it would be in the developed capitalist world (the so-called First World), at other times he looked to the communist countries (the Second World). If it were to start in the former, Harich again felt that Marxism needed to be modified, in that, he argued, the capitalist countries could proceed directly to communism (i.e., avoiding the lower stage, socialism). Exactly how this was to be compatible with the dictatorship of the proletariat is also unclear.

Harich never had the interest in the feminist issue that Bahro had. But in the only reference to the gender question in his book, Harich argued that a woman's right to orgasm is greater than her right to procreate; this, too, is very much in line with his highly socialistic approach, in that the production of new human beings has social (and environmental) ramifications. Orgasm, on the other hand, is a personal matter.[33]

In addition to those already indicated, major weaknesses in Harich's approach include a failure to address the questions of *control* of the omnipotent world planners (a power elite to end all power elites?), and of who is to decide what people *really* need (i.e., he appeared to be insufficiently aware of the complex problem of need being a socially determined concept).[34]

Havemann

In his last writings (e.g., *Berliner Schriften*, 1977; *Ein deutscher Kommunist*, 1978; and *Morgen—Die Industriegesellschaft am Scheideweg*, 1980—although the 1982 edition is used here), Havemann displayed an interest in, and often a similar approach to, many of the problems that concerned both Bahro and Harich. Thus he made it clear that he, too, was particularly concerned about the ecological issue and, like the other two, frequently referred to the writings of the Club of Rome. Like them, he had a sense of urgency about the ecological problems facing humanity. In his last major work, for instance, he cited various data from the Meadows report (for the Club of Rome) concerning what are widely held to be the most optimistic forecasts on how long reserves of a number of basic raw materials (e.g., oil, coal, iron, gas) will last; the figures range from 29 years (gold) to 173 years (iron).[35] Also in line with Bahro and Harich, Havemann argued that the logic of capitalism was such that it could not avoid an ecological crisis; indeed, capitalism, with its drive for production and profits, was seen as the single most important factor leading to this crisis.[36] However, he also accepted that "actually existing socialism" could not solve the problem either, largely because in its competition with capitalism, the kind of system existing in the GDR and elsewhere in Eastern Europe had actually adopted goals, methods, and even structures (economic monopoly) similar to its opponent. This is not to say that he did not, for instance, perceive any fundamental differences between the FRG and the GDR; he did, and he considered the GDR the better society. He argued that it provided many more of the basic requirements of life to the citizenry than did the Bonn system. Moreover, he implied that the infighting among the various left-wing groups in the West was essentially destructive and pointless and stated unambiguously that the future of socialism would be decided in his own country rather than in the FRG.[37] For this reason, he always insisted on staying in the GDR and was disappointed when Bahro decided to remain in the FRG.

His attitude toward the GDR was not invariably positive, however. The main target of his attack was the party apparatus, which he, in line with most other dissidents, perceived as constituting the major hindrance on the road to true socialism and ultimately communism. He argued that there were a number of charlatans who had attained high office in the GDR, either within the party-state complex's apparatus or with its support (e.g., industrial managers), and that these opportunists and careerists often blocked the promotion of real specialists, with all the negative repercussions for East German society that this entailed. He continued to argue that the political leadership at the various levels should place more faith in the masses and permit citizens to express their views and criticisms openly and publicly.

So far, the focus has been on those aspects of Havemann's ideas that were basically similar to either Harich's or Bahro's. But there were some important differences, too. In *Ein deutscher Kommunist*, for instance, Havemann identified explicitly the areas in which, despite his overall support for Bahro's *The Alternative*, he took issue with the former economist and manager.[38] The point he emphasized most was that he disagreed with Bahro that the masses needed a much better standard and level of education in order to understand the complexities of modern society and life generally. For Havemann, universities are useful for teaching technical skills but are not invariably so and are certainly not necessary for teaching people about political and social problems. He criticized the mystificatory analyses of many social scientists and argued that many such specialists in fact see the wood (as distinct from the trees) less well than many less highly educated people. He maintained that the really important problems of society can be grasped by most if put across simply, though not simplistically. His criticisms of charlatanism in East German society mentioned earlier fit in with this general point about mystification and false claims to a right to rule in the GDR. Another important area in which he felt Bahro was being too precipitate was in the latter's call for the dissolution of the SED and its replacement by a new, uncorrupted League of Communists. Havemann believed that this was a good idea in principle and in the long term, but that in the situation of the 1970s and 1980s it would be preferable and more effective to adopt an incremental approach. The kinds of measures he advocated included the introduction of much freer forms of discussion in the SED, the FDGB (the trade-union organization), and other official organizations; an open and freer press; and more meaningful discussion in the *Volkskammer*.

These pleas were all part of Havemann's strategy for a move toward what he called the "second step" on the path to communism, namely, the real democratization of society and the abolition of the party dictatorship.[39] In this, his position was quite different from Harich's. Harich really seems to have had little faith in the masses, whereas Havemann saw the future in them. Whereas Harich saw the "withering away of the state" as a utopian and outdated concept, Havemann continued to see it as a long-term goal while acknowledging that it would be inappropriate in current conditions. And whereas Harich placed a great deal of faith in a world government ruling by computer, Havemann was fearful of the state's use of "secret electronic data banks," which conjured up for him the frightening images contained in Orwell's *1984*.

Like Bahro, Havemann believed in coalitions for overthrowing capitalism. However, presumably because he did not emigrate from the GDR, Havemann devoted less attention to this sort of question than did the younger critic. But he did agree that revolution was needed in all three worlds and that revolutions in East and West would have to interact and mutually endorse each other.

Havemann devoted more attention than did the other two critics to his vision of a desirable and feasible future society. This said, there is considerable agreement in the views of the three men. The society would be one in which quality of life is far more important than material wealth; people would have time to appreciate art rather than to work so much, for example. In all three writers, there was a marked strain of *puritanism*—all condemn private cars, for instance, and only partially for environmental reasons—although this is possibly more marked in Havemann than the other two. He only reluctantly accepted that people might be able to enjoy an alcoholic beverage, for example (there is little doubt that he would have supported Gorbachev's efforts to reduce alcoholic consumption and abuse in the USSR).

Toward the end of his life, much of Havemann's time and energy was devoted to the unofficial peace movement. Harich had maintained in the mid-1970s that peace was only part of a much larger problem, and he does not appear to have played a role in this movement (although this might well be as much because of his state of health as because of his view that it was of marginal significance).

Like Harich, Havemann never *fully* appreciated why the authorities treated him as a dissident. Certainly, he frequently declared his loyalty to the GDR, and his oft-repeated commitment to Marxism and communism was surely genuine. He also criticized Westerners who tried to use his writings in propaganda attacks on the GDR; he often made the point that he would have preferred to have published his works in the GDR, and that it was the authorities who had forced him to publish with Western publishing houses, thereby making him appear to be disloyal to his own country.

Other Dissidents

Most of the other people usually cited by Western analysts as GDR dissidents were less overtly so than the three men already considered. They included a number of writers—e.g., Stefan Heym, Rudolf Schneider, and possibly even Christa Wolf (she was critical of both superpowers in her 1983 novel *Kassandra*), whose writings were frequently metaphorical or allegorical. Many of such writers' works could unquestionably be considered as dissident if by that all we mean is that their allegories and metaphors could have been seen to have cast aspects of the GDR's political system in a negative light. Heym's *Collin* (1979) and Schneider's *November* (also 1979) are good examples.

However, the "horse's mouth" itself sometimes revealed—to Westerners who were objective enough to listen—that its works were not invariably intended to be as political as they had sometimes been interpreted. This emerged, for example, in an interview with Stefan Heym conducted by Hans Wolfschütz in the early-1980s; in response to Wolfschütz's question "Can one say that, for you, writing is politics by other means [*mit anderen Mitteln*]?" Heym answered, "Not so directly. I do not write in order to engage in politics—I am not some prevented or frustrated politician. But it has always turned out that that which I have written always has a political effect on others."[40] On the one hand, it could be argued that if Heym knew his works could have this effect, and if he was correct in arguing that he was the most popular writer in the GDR,[41] then he was being a dissident by publishing them. On the other hand, such indirect and partially unintended "dissidence" is also supposed to be open to varying interpretations and is in many ways *so* allegorical that, given Heym's own statement above, one would have to be desperate for proof of dissidence in the GDR to make very much of such writing. Moreover, most of these writers were not clearly Marxist and in this sense fall outside the scope of the present chapter. This all said, the point should be made that *some* of these writers' views were more clearly anti-GDR than those of the mainstream Marxist dissidents.

Treatment

The communist authorities in the GDR used an extensive range of methods for dealing with dissidents, although they do not appear either to have made much use of psychiatric hospitalization (in contrast to the USSR) or to have pursued and possibly executed dissidents once they had left the GDR (compare this with allegations about Bulgaria and Romania). The methods used by the East Germans included imprisonment; fines (often for "illegally" publishing abroad and acquiring hard currency—this applied to both Havemann and Heym in May 1979); house arrest; exile abroad; media campaigns designed to discredit "dissidents";[42] deprivation of SED membership (especially during the 1979-80 exchange of party cards); and general harassment. The last point would include job demotions, above-average difficulties in acquiring better living accommodations, and the problems children of dissidents could face in entering higher education. The East Germans tightened up the criminal code in 1977 and in June 1979,[43] and this enabled the authorities to deal more harshly with dissidents should they so wish.

The reasons for the authorities' treatment are several. Since these have been dealt with at length elsewhere,[44] they will only be listed here. They would include: historical traditions (political culture); Marxist-Leninist ideology; bureaucratic conservatism; leadership fears; and responses to particular events and developments.

Conclusions

Having considered in some detail the arguments of leading East German Marxist dissidents in recent years, it is now appropriate to return to the question of the significance of such dissent, with particular emphasis on its role in the collapse of the East German communist system.

It will be recalled that the first form of significance considered above related to the *originality* of East German Marxist dissent. From this perspective, the dissident writing considered here seems to score quite well. First, the East German dissidents were highlighting ecological issues rather earlier than most Marxist dissidents in Eastern Europe; indeed, they were not far behind the leading Western environmentalists in their warnings and analyses. The reasons for this are several but would include the relatively greater exposure of East Germans generally to the Western media and ideas; the higher living standards in the GDR than elsewhere in Eastern Europe, so that there was somewhat less concern with real basics, such as feeding and housing oneself, in East Germany than in Poland, Romania, or the USSR; related to the last point, the fact that East Germany was more highly industrialized than other communist states, so that pollution was higher;[45] and, finally, the fact that the GDR made increasing use of its own energy resources from the 1970s on. The significance of the last point is that the GDR was rich in only one source of energy, lignite (brown coal), a particularly inefficient and polluting source of energy. Second, Harich's views in particular might well be considered prescient in the twenty-first century. His argument that the scale and technology of the modern world have rendered the "withering away of the state" redundant is an interesting revision of classical Marxism, and one suspects that his arguments in favor of a powerful world government may yet be widely discussed. The utopianism and anticonsumerism of the major East German dissidents may not seem very relevant to the East German population at the beginning of the 1990s, as the latter—with some foreboding—experience the consumer "paradise" of the FRG. But it seems highly probable that the anticonsumerist arguments of all the major dissidents will return to the agenda by the mid- to late 1990s as certain harsh realities of the consumer society begin to be better appreciated by both many East Germans and others. The European world, at least, might well be searching for a new morality by the end of the present millennium.

In concluding this section on originality, it is worth noting that one reviewer of Bahro's book *The Alternative* hailed it as "the most important book on socialist theory to have appeared since the Second World War." Although the reviewer, Ken Coates, writing in *Tribune*, could well be accused of exaggeration given the likely long-term impact of writers such as Marcuse, Habermas, Althusser, Poulantzas, Djilas, Elster, and others, his statement nevertheless testifies to the originality and intellectual impact of at least some of the writing of one of the dissidents analyzed here. This said, it could be objected that *all* contemporary Marxist writers are working more or less within a paradigm created by Marx himself and in this sense cannot be seen to be making as original a contribution as some. Expressed differently, their originality is less than that of someone who tries to create a quite new way of looking at the world, such as a Freud or a Foucault. On the other hand, it would be naive not to acknowledge that all writers operate to some extent within their intellectual and cultural traditions and milieu, so that this kind of distinction can be misleadingly stark. Thus the fact that a writer is working more or less within a preexisting theoretical framework does not per se signify that that writer is less important or even original than another who is less overtly operating within an identifiable tradition.

In terms of the second interpretation of significance—the *validity* of the criticisms—the Marxist dissidents do not score particularly well. To be sure, the charges of authoritarianism and dictatorship by a clique of party functionaries found great resonance among the masses in 1989-90. Bahro's suggestion that the GDR had a "second-class" version of a capitalist economy also had some truth to it. While it can be debated whether or not the GDR's economy was "capitalist," the authorities themselves acknowledged by late 1989 that the GDR's economy was certainly second class in comparison with most Western economies, especially the FRG's. Surely the strongest piece of evidence to support this point is the fact that East Germans had by mid-1990 virtually handed their economy over to the West Germans to run, with no suggestion of a reciprocal arrangement.

But it should be noted that the Marxist dissidents were also off target in some of their predictions, or at least are likely to have been for the foreseeable future. For instance, Harich's and others' early faith in Yugoslav conceptions of self-management have proven largely ill founded. By the beginning of the 1990s, Yugoslavia was in as much crisis as any other East European state, with its unique "self-management" system almost totally discredited. By many criteria, and despite many problems of its own, the West German concept of *Mitbestimmung* (codetermination) has had a more impressive record.

Another area in which the Marxists presently seem to have been out of line is in their faith in macroeconomic planning. This, too, has been largely discredited. The reasons for this are several and complex, and this is not an appropriate place to elaborate them. Suffice it to say here that among the many reasons why central planning has fallen into disrepute are the practical problems of trying to run any complex economy—ultimately, necessarily located in the vagaries of the world market—from a single source, and the political problems of the overconcentration of power that planning entails.

Perhaps the major area in which the dissidents *may* have misperceived East German realities is in their common belief that most East Germans were *basically* supportive of the system, even if they were critical of individual regimes (i.e., leadership teams). We shall never have a definitive answer to the question of how legitimate the GDR was, not only because of problems in obtaining reliable empirical data on East German values but also, inter alia, because the question itself is problematical. The level of legitimacy may very well have varied over time, for instance. Certainly, some surveys conducted in the past have strongly suggested that the East German masses were more positively oriented toward the West, including the FRG, than the Marxist dissidents claimed,[46] and there was probably considerable justification for Sodaro's conclusion in the early 1980s that it was "legitimate to assume . . . that the vast majority of East German citizens, if allowed to express themselves, would probably voice a strong preference for what may be called 'consumer values' with respect to the economy, and for some form of democratic political regime that would guarantee fundamental civil liberties."[47] However, one must be careful not to reach too hasty a conclusion on this issue. At least three factors urge caution: First, the dissidents' perceptions may have been more accurate at the time they were writing than they would be as of 1989-90. There are good grounds for arguing, for instance, that Gorbachev's "revolution" in the USSR led to some fundamental questioning of the communist system in the GDR not only by ordinary citizens but also by officials. Moreover, there were *some* signs in the 1970s that capitalism might be in crisis itself. By the mid- to late 1980s, however, it had become clear to the majority of people in both Eastern and Western Europe that capitalism had emerged from any crisis it might have been in, while communism was the system that had lost its way.[48] This all said, it should not be overlooked that, even by the time of the March 1990 election, the new version of the Communist Party (it became the Socialist Unity Party—Party of Democratic Socialism in December 1989) was still able to secure a respectable 16.4 percent of the vote in the GDR as a whole and over 30 percent in East Berlin; the PDS also did remarkably well in several East German cities in the May 1990 local elections.[49] This suggests that socialism had not been as discredited and rejected in the GDR as in many other East European states, especially the other so-called "Northern Tier" states.

The score is much lower where the third aspect of the significance of East German Marxist dissidence is concerned: its political relevance and relationship to the 1989-90 collapse of communism. None of the three leading dissidents played any meaningful role in the mass unrest of 1989. Throughout the 1980s, the East German unofficial peace movement played a far more obvious role in raising political consciousness among the East German masses than did the intellectual dissidents. Indeed, the term "movement" cannot be applied to the East German Marxist dissidents. Their numbers were always minute, and, significantly, there was nothing that could seriously be termed an "organization" linking them. There was never any East German equivalent of "Charter 77," nor even a common samizdat forum, such as the *Chronicle of Current Events*. The "Manifesto of the Opposition" that was published in *Der Spiegel* in 1978 was never satisfactorily authenticated,[50] and in any case was a one-off document that does not appear to have had any follow-up. And the so-called "Berlin Appeal" of 1982, which *was* authenticated, could not be classified as a political platform in any of the usual senses.[51] By the mid-1980s, not only were many of the leading dissidents either dead, sick, absent, or subject to the state's clampdown, but there was also a growing self-doubt among many leading critical intellectuals. These doubts arose partially because many writers felt distant from the masses of the population, a distance some felt was to a certain extent explained in terms of the authorities' behavior toward them. Some regime critics pointed out that the authorities were quite prepared to use the putative consumerism and anti-intellectualism of the East German masses to undermine their position. But the authorities were in a sense only exploiting a situation that already existed. Bahro, for instance, expressed fears that his ethically based, somewhat utopian vision of communism was perceived by the masses as unrealistic. Harich, as indicated above, acknowledged that his version of a new society would be unacceptable to most East German citizens. And Havemann on at least one occasion stated openly that he was unsure of just how typical his views were of the East German population generally.[52] Moreover, most of the Marxist critics seemed to lose faith in the inevitability and "scientific nature" of Marxism; the clear-cut, dogmatic, and self-assured structuralist approach of some of the French Marxists found little resonance in the GDR. The self-doubt relates also to the approach adopted by the East German Marxist dissidents toward change. Calls for a fundamental change of the political system in the direction of Western-style pluralist democracy were conspicuous by their absence in at least two (Harich and Havemann) of the three major dissidents' works. Partially for this reason, East German dissidents have in the past been classified as "reform communists" by analysts such as Lippmann and Timmermann.[53] The Marxist dissidents' calls for change from above went largely unheeded, at the same time as they marginalized the dissidents vis-à-vis the masses. This was in spite of the fact that the dissidents had been treated by the authorities as true oppositionists.[54] In sum, then, the Marxist dissidents were not only treated as such by the authorities but they largely "sat apart" from the masses, too.

It would be difficult to argue that the revolutionary change the world witnessed in the GDR in 1989-90 bore much resemblance to the nature, direction, and extent of change advocated by the dissidents; it was more comprehensive and rapid, and it involved the masses far more than certainly either Harich or Havemann ever advocated. Even more importantly, it moved the GDR very much in the direction of the West, both politically and economically. In this sense, the writings of the Marxist dissidents were of very little relevance to the collapse of communism.[55]

Moreover, it must be acknowledged that, at least on the surface, the *final* collapse of East German communist rule was far more closely related to factors outside the GDR—notably, the ramifications of Gorbachev's domestic and foreign policies and the domino effect of communist collapse in Eastern Europe—than to specifically internal aspects of the East German system. The *long-term* build-up to 1989 relates very much to the internal dynamism of the East German system, of course, but here, too, Marxist analysis is grossly inadequate. A full analysis of the dynamics would be too long and complex for a chapter of this sort, but a few comments are appropriate here.[56] The East German authorities, like many others in Eastern Europe, attempted from the 1950s to move toward the exercise of power more on the basis of legitimation than of coercion. With the apparent failure of teleological legitimation, the authorities turned to eudaemonism. Such legitimation typically focuses above all on economic performance, and the adoption of the New Economic System in January 1963 was a major symbol of the new orientation.[57] This economic reform was less successful than had been hoped for by the leadership, among several other reasons because it was unfavorably compared by many with the West German "economic miracle." By the 1970s the authorities were turning to official nationalism as a new form of legitimation in the GDR. But this was at best a two-edged sword in that it tended on one level to highlight the commonality of tradition between the two Germanies. Thus, both eudaemonic and official nationalist legitimation were being used by the authorities in the 1970s, and both were proving to be problematic. Despite this, the East German authorities were not prepared to experiment with the radical alternative of zero growth; the conditions simply did not seem right for that. It was in this context of legitimation problems that Harich's proposals were an embarrassment and unacceptable to the East German authorities. Subsequently, the East German leadership sought to move toward a form of legal-rational legitimation, as did others in the communist world. But this is ultimately incompatible with the communist form of rule,[58] which was one of the underlying factors explaining the legitimation crisis of communism in the 1980s that eventually became general crisis and collapse. By this stage, moreover, many of the "old believers" in the East German hierarchy, like their peers in other East European states, began seriously to question their own values and right to rule as their once reliable role model (i.e., the USSR) itself moved deeper into an identity crisis. This delegitimation among the GDR's leaders and staffs also helps to explain the collapse of communism.

The argument presented here in highly abbreviated form is much closer to Weberian than to Marxist analysis. The collapse of communism is not explained in this approach in terms of class struggle—at least not in any classical Marxist sense. Marxist ideas and, as a corollary, many of the ideas and concerns of the Marxist dissidents are, in short, considered here to be unsatisfactory for explaining the East German events of 1989-90. Whether or not this implies that Marxism generally is redundant is a moot point. There are certainly good grounds for arguing that the collapse of communism in the GDR and elsewhere demonstrates fairly conclusively that attempts to avoid capitalist, "bourgeois" development and engage in a highly voluntaristic, top-down construction of socialism/communism are doomed to eventual failure. But it is argued here that this disproves Lenin's theories rather more than Marx's, on some of whose methodology (notably historical materialism) the jury is still out.

But this huge question of the validity of Marxist theory goes beyond the brief of the present chapter; even if Marx's own writings may still be worth debating, the fact is that a perfectly adequate analysis of the collapse of East German communism and the emergence of postcommunism can be made without any reference to the East German Marxist dissidents. To do so, however, would be to impoverish one's understanding of the culture and development of a unique, and now defunct, entity.

Notes

1. For details on and short biographies of the members of the new government, see "Die Mitglieder der neuen DDR-Regierung," *Deutschland Archiv* 23, no. 6 (1990): 983-86.
2. Roy Medvedev, *On Soviet Dissent* (London: Constable, 1980), 1.
3. L. Schapiro, "Introduction," in *Political Opposition in One-Party States*, ed. L. Schapiro (London: Macmillan, 1972), esp. pp. 2-3; P. Reddaway, "The Development of Dissent and Opposition," in *The Soviet Union Since the Fall of Khrushchev*, ed. A.H. Brown and M. Kaser (London: Macmillan, 1978), 122.
4. W. van der Will, "The Nature of Dissidence in the GDR," in *The GDR in the 1980s*, ed. I. Wallace (Dundee: GDR Monitor Special Series, 1984), 38.
5. On religious dissent, and particularly the relationship between the churches and the peace movement, see inter alia P. Ramet, "Church and Peace in the GDR," *Problems of Communism* 33, no. 4 (1984): 44-57; J. Mushaben, "Swords to Plowshares: The Church, the State, and the East German Peace Movement," *Studies in Comparative Communism* 17, no. 2 (1984): 123-35; L. Holmes, "The State and the Churches in the GDR," in *Religion and Politics in Communist Countries*, ed. R.F. Miller and T.H. Rigby (Canberra: Australian National University, 1986), 93-114; and J. Sandford, "The Church, the State, and the Peace Movement in the GDR," *GDR Monitor*, 16 (1986-7): 27-54.
6. This section relies heavily on an earlier overview produced by the author. See L. Holmes, *Politics in the Communist World* (Oxford: Oxford University Press, 1986), 258-62.
7. W. Leonhard "Die frühe Opposition in der SED (1946-49): Errinerungen und Erfahrungen," in *Ein Marxist in der DDR*, ed. H. Jackel (Munich and Zurich: R. Piper, 1980), 20-43.
8. On all this, see M. Janicke, *Der dritte Weg* (Cologne: Neuer Deutscher Verlag, 1964), esp. pp. 104-106.
9. H. Lippmann, "The Limits of Reform Communism," *Problems of Communism* 19, no. 3 (1970): 16.
10. For Havemann's 1963-64 lectures, see R. Havemann, *Dialektik ohne Dogma* (Reinbek bei Hamburg: rororo, 1964); for Sakharov's views, see A.D. Sakharov, *Progress, Coexistence and Intellectual Freedom* (London: Andre Deutsch, 1968).
11. R. Havemann, "Die Regierung soll dem eigenen Volk Vertrauen schenken," reprinted in *Deutschland Archiv* 7, no. 1 (1974): 47.
12. For a complete English translation of the letter, see *Communist Affairs* 1, no. 3 (1982): 725-27.
13. R. Woods, *Opposition in the GDR under Honecker 1971-85* (Basingstoke: Macmillan, 1986).
14. R. Bahro, *Socialism and Survival* (London: Heretic, 1982); R. Bahro, *From Red to Green* (London: Verso, 1984); R. Bahro, *Building the Green Movement* (London: Green Movement Press, 1986). Other books have been published in German only, notably, *Logik der Rettung* (Stuttgart: Thienemanns, 1987 and 1989); however, since these are

only marginally concerned with the GDR, it would be inappropriate to analyze them here.

15. Bahro, *From Red to Green*, 99.

16. Ibid., 104.

17. Bahro, *Socialism and Survival*, 12.

18. Bahro, *From Red to Green*, 97 and 226.

19. On all this, see, e.g., ibid., esp. 214-23 and *Socialism and Survival*, 134-5. Many of these ideas, particularly the concept of cultural revolution, were initially expounded in R. Bahro, *The Alternative in Eastern Europe* (London: Verso, 1978), esp. 251-453 (the retitled English-language edition of *Die Alternative* misleadingly gives the impression that the book is only concerned with Eastern Europe). One can question the notion that mass consciousness can ever change fundamentally in a "revolutionary" (as distinct from evolutionary) way.

20. See, e.g., Bahro, *Socialism and Survival*, 128-33.

21. Ibid., 60.

22. Bahro, *From Red to Green*, 101.

23. Ibid., 218.

24. W. Harich, *Kommunismus ohne Wachstum* (Reinbek bei Hamburg: Rowohlt, 1975), 135.

25. Ibid., 172.

26. Ibid., 146.

27. W. Harich, *Zur Kritik der revolutionären Ungeduld* (Basel: etcetera, 1971).

28. Harich, *Kommunismus ohne Wachstum*, esp. 77-78.

29. Ibid., 41-42, 161, 165-67. The reader is reminded that Harich was citing Soviet writers in a distinctly "preglasnost'" era.

30. Ibid., 113.

31. Ibid., 114, 145, 167-68, and 192.

32. Ibid., 139-40 and 172.

33. Ibid., 47.

34. This is perhaps surprising, given Marx's own awareness. On this, see A. Heller, *The Theory of Need in Marx* (London: Allison & Busby, 1976).

35. R. Havemann, *Morgen—Die Industriegesellschaft am Scheideweg* (Frankfurt am Main; Fischer, 1982), 13.

36. See, e.g., ibid., 28-35.

37. E.g., R. Havemann, "Antwort auf Zwei Fragen," in Jackel, *Ein Marxist in der DDR*, 196.

38. R. Havemann, *Ein deutscher Kommunist* (Reinbek bei Hamburg: Rowohlt, 1978), esp. 93-98.

39. See, e.g., R. Havemann, "Zehn Thesen zum 30. Jahrestag der DDR," in Jackel, *Ein Marxist in der DDR*, 201.

40. H. Wolfschütz, "Gesprach mit Stefan Heym," *GDR Monitor*, no. 8 (1982-83): 14.

41. Ibid., 1.

42. For a good example, see R. Woods, "East German Intellectuals in Opposition," *Survey* 28, no. 3 (1984): 111.

43. For a translation of the June 1979 version, see *Documents in Communist Affairs—1980*, ed. B. Szajkowski (London: Macmillan, 1981), 280-98.

44. See Holmes, *Politics in the Communist World*, 279-81.

45. In 1989, the GDR enjoyed the dubious honor of being identified as the world's most polluted country.

46. For a range of assessments of legitimacy in the GDR and some survey data, see, e.g., M. McCauley, "Official and Unofficial Nationalism in the GDR," *GDR Monitor*, no. 5 (1981): esp. 18; M. McCauley, "Legitimation in the German Democratic Republic" in *Eastern Europe: Political Crisis and Legitimation*, ed. P. Lewis (London: Croom Helm, 1984), esp. 61-64; G. Eckart, ed., *So sehe Ich die Sache* (Cologne: Kiepenhauer and Witsch, 1984); P.C. Ludz, *Die DDR zwischen Ost und West* (Munich: Beck, 1977), esp. 224; G. Gaus, *Wo Deutschland liegt* (Hamburg: Hoffman and Campe, 1983).

47. M. Sodaro, "Limits to Dissent in the GDR: Fragmentation, Cooptation, and Repression," in *Dissent in Eastern Europe*, ed. J. Leftwich Curry (New York: Praeger, 1983), 94.

48. For a full, theoretical analysis of this, see L. Holmes, *Crisis, Collapse and Corruption in the Communist World* (Cambridge: Polity Press, 1991).

49. For details on and an analysis of the March election, see P.J. Winters, "Zum ersten Mal frei," *Deutschland Archiv* 23, no. 4 (1990): 497-501; on the May elections, see P.J. Winters, "Die CDU liegt auch in den Rathäusern vorn," *Deutschland Archiv* 23, no. 5 (1990): 641-43.

50. See *Der Spiegel*, 2 January 1978, pp. 19-24 and 9 January 1978, pp. 17-32.

51. The appeal was published in *Frankfurter Rundschau*, 9 February 1982. See, too, W. Buscher, P. Wensierski, and K. Wolschner, eds., *Friedensbewegung in der DDR—Texte 1978-82* (Hattingen: Scandica Verlag, 1982), esp. 288.

52. See A. Mytze, ed., *Berliner Schriften* (Munich: Verlag Europäische Ideen, 1977), 22.

53. Lippmann, "The Limits of Reform Communism," and H. Timmermann, *Reformkommunisten in West und Ost: Konzeptionen, Querverbindungen und Perspektiven* (Cologne: Bundesinstitut für Ostwissenschaftliche und Internationale Studien, 1980).

54. On this, see Woods, "East German Intellectuals."

55. It is not argued here that there *could* not have been a revolution from above, since it seems to me that the Hungarian transition to postcommunism testifies to such a possibility. Rather, the argument is simply that this did not occur in the GDR and that the revolution was in any case in a different direction from that predicted and advocated.

56. For a much fuller exposition of my views on this, see Holmes, *Crisis, Collapse*, esp. chaps. 1 and 8.

57. On this, see T. Baylis, "Economic Reform as Ideology: East Germany's New Economic System," *Comparative Politics* 3, no. 2 (1971): 211-29.

58. For an early argument to this effect, with particular reference to the GDR, see W. Seiffert's review, "Die DDR—ein Rechtsstaat?" *Deutschland Archiv* 13, no. 7 (1980): 765-66.

5

Marxist Critiques of Political Crises in Poland

Raymond Taras

Unique among the former European Leninist party-states, postwar Poland was repeatedly shaken by politically destabilizing events. This chapter considers the explanations offered by Marxists for Poland's postwar political crises. These writers—party ideologues, social scientists, philosophers, the cultural intelligentsia—were expected to provide analyses of these crises so as to relegitimate the regime during the postcrisis normalization process. Yet many of these analyses employing the Marxist paradigm pointed to the urgency of political liberalization as a way out of cyclical crises. Through such critiques, liberal party leaders, critical Marxist philosophers, and revisionist ideologues and social scientists contributed to the erosion of the communist dogma that served as the cement of the political order, and this at a time when no other voice of dissent could be heard. It will be argued in this chapter that the influence and utility of Marxist-based critiques were time-urgent. That is, they accurately reflected the broader social consciousness of a particular epoch (the nagging discontent with Stalinism, Gomułka's little stabilization, Gierek's repressive socialist tolerance), but they just as quickly became the false consciousness of subsequent epochs (the exhilaration of the Solidarity period, the decade of the autonomous second culture, the policy of glasnost' and perestroika). Revisionist Marxism may, therefore, have served as a necessary, if insufficient, stage in the transition from Stalinism to postcommunism.

For heuristic purposes, three types of social challenges to the communist authorities of People's Poland will be distinguished: (1) the overt, sometimes violent, mass demonstrations that occurred, as in Poznań in 1956, Warsaw in 1968, Gdańsk in 1970, and Radom in 1976; (2) the social and perhaps authentically revolutionary (or, for the authorities, counterrevolutionary) movements that emerged, as during the legal existence of Solidarity in 1980-81, then its underground networks throughout the rest of that decade; and (3) the amorphous sociopolitical discontent that, in Dostoevsky's terms, produced "fire in the minds of men" and, in the case of postwar Poland, burned more fiercely as the decades under communism accumulated. In aggregate, these phenomena seemed to corroborate Marx's prophecies about how social formations come to an end. The paradox was, of course, that the beleaguered social order in question was it-self purportedly socialist—a paradox particularly obvious to thinkers schooled in Marxist dialectics.

Employing the convenient terminology of Marxism, therefore, we can say that a series of specific events based on collective protest activities, together with a gradual evolution in social consciousness, which might be termed a quiet revolution, made it seem that "real socialism" in Poland and elsewhere in the Soviet bloc, and not the advanced capitalism of Western Europe, had fashioned the noose with which it would eventually hang itself. And true to the Marxian paradigm, a social order under such pressure did indeed collapse, in 1989.

Who Were the Polish Marxists?
Toward a Typology

When observers of contemporary Poland think of Marxists, it is likely they will identify regime (or official, orthodox) Marxists who were employed in the ideological state apparatus of People's Poland. Such Marxists obviously did not interpret the causes of the cycle of political crises in the way described above. It is precisely the part played by these Marxists in doctrinally defending the socialist order that proved particularly nefarious over the years, and it was precisely this group of Marxists that was responsible for the brutal repression of liberalizing, democratic socialist ideas. How Communist Party ideologues fought a rearguard battle over the years to defend the Polish variant of socialism is described in another work.[1] To summarize those conclusions, by the 1980s the famous "Polish road to socialism"—programmatically launched by Gomułka in the late 1940s, then ineptly implemented by the administration he came to head a decade later—had come to signify something very different from the promises it held out when Gomułka was accused of heretic dilettantism by Stalin in 1948. By the 1980s the Polish road had taken on negative connotations not just for dogmatic Marxist purists (that is, the old-guard Stalinists who were originally offended by the concept); it had become equally repugnant to centralist- and efficiency-oriented factions in the Kremlin, which saw in it not only a break from the Soviet "socialist citadel" model but also a bungled and muddled program deleterious to socialist development everywhere. In short, by the late 1980s the Polish road had become the worst road to socialism for neo-Stalinists and neoreformers alike, for it had become equated with both deviation and destitution.

Among the Marxist explanations offered by regime ideologues for Poland's political crises, failure in the party's ideological work, which resulted in the inability to transform social consciousness and thereby create a new socialist personality, was most frequently cited. Old ideas, traditions, and conventions had not been combated with sufficient energy by party cadres, so that in the end transformations in superstructural elements lagged far behind changes in the mode and relations of production. Invigorated socialization campaigns, such Marxist ideologues predicated, could restore consonance between base and superstructure and improve Polish socialism without recourse to systemic or structural reforms.

Even more conservative party ideologues were reticent to pin responsibility on the hegemonic and presumably largely infallible party in even such a circumscribed way. Instead, their Leninist Marxism suggested the continued existence of petty-bourgeois, and even counterrevolutionary, tendencies within Polish society. According to this view, the authorities' toleration of religious practice and of the leading role of the Catholic church in Polish society, their acquiescence to private farming as the bulwark of the country's agricultural system, their inability to undermine the persisting cultural and intellectual proximity with the West (abetted by the ease of travel by Poles to the West), and their complacent and indulgent attitude toward the emergence of "groupuscules" of political opposition in the late 1970s (themselves allegedly supported financially by Western imperialist intelligence agencies) engendered the intensification of class struggle between socialist elements and ancien régime supporters, which culminated in the Solidarity explosion of 1980.

It can be argued that the crisis explanations offered by party ideologues do not constitute Marxist critiques of Polish socialism. First, they were not critiques but rather apologia for the functioning of the existing political system. Second, they were not Marxist because, like the system they set out to defend, they represented an aberration of authentic Marxism. It was in all likelihood this form of official Marxism that the former Polish Marxist philosopher Leszek Kołakowski had in mind when he wrote, "There is probably no part of the civilized world in which Marxism has declined so completely and socialist ideas have become so discredited and turned to ridicule as in the countries of victorious socialism."[2]

If, then, we should discard official or state Marxism from our analysis, the question arises whether we should equally ignore those critiques undertaken by writers such as Kołakowski who, at a certain point, were no longer Marxists nor members of Polish society. If we do consider their work, we confront the dilemma that emigré, oftentimes anticommunist, writers from Poland better represented the authentic Marxist current than any group of thinkers within the country. Yet if we ignore such writers, we are suggesting that the sole repository of Polish Marxist critique had to be Poland itself; more specifically, Marxist critiques could only be located on the periphery of the Polish political system since they were clearly at odds with state Marxism. We may even encounter the charge that Polish Marxist critical thought was by definition an impossibility: If we adopt the first option—a focus on emigré Marxist thought—it could be argued that such thought was not Polish, for it was not the logical intellectual product of living under the existential conditions of contemporary Poland. Choice of the second option—examination of critical thinkers in Poland—risks the rejoinder that they could not be Marxist by virtue of the fact that the state had fully usurped this particular ideological space.

In this chapter, Polish writers based in the country as well as abroad are considered, since the decision about where to live and work was not always left to the individuals concerned. Further, the most important criterion to use in selecting illuminating representatives of critical Marxist thought, it seems, is whether their analyses are based on a Marxist paradigm as a point of departure. In many instances the Marxian analytical legacy is made expressly clear in the works of Polish writers, either by its critical acceptance or by a conscious search for an alternative. At the same time it is important to recognize when a writer has decided to reject altogether a Marxist-based analytical approach and therefore not to impute critical Marxist ideas to someone who has already become an anti-Marxist. Such fine distinctions are, of course, difficult to maintain, and what is aspired to here is the attempt to make such distinctions in a conscious, if necessarily at times arbitrary, way.

Who, then, are the critical Marxists to be considered in this chapter? They have been divided here into four separate groups of writers. The first were the *dissident Marxists* who employed Marxian analytical categories to condemn real socialism as not socialism. Some of these were political activists whose careers began in the Communist Party and ended in dissident organizations, while others were committed to the socialist project while not becoming political actors. What marked them off from other groups was a strong commitment to Marxist ideals and an equally strong revulsion against existing socialism when they wrote their critiques. Their shared objective was the achievement of an authentic form of Marxism in Poland.

The second group were *reformist* (or liberal) *Marxists*, mainly academics who maintained links with the political rulers and who, using Marxian analysis, espoused structural adjustments in the system of real socialism. They were distinguished by their faith in the reformability of the socialist order. Initially at least, these writers sought to effect change from positions within the ruling Communist Party. Their commitment to ''revising'' Marxist doctrine frequently led to their marginalization in, and even expulsion from, the party.

A third category of writers undertaking a critique of Poland was characterized by the deliberate effort to place philosophical, and even some epistemological, distance between their analyses and classic Marxian thought. Even though some openly renounced their Marxist training, in large measure their critique was consistent with the spirit, if not the letter, of Marxian analysis. To describe such thinkers, the unhappy term *Marxologizers* is used, which, partially in defense of its use here, is a word translated from Polish. Their common goal was to develop theoretical alternatives to classic Marxism rather than to bring about change in the system.

As a *lagniappe* to this analysis, a fourth group of Marxists has been included who examined recent Polish political developments from a neo-Stalinist perspective. While not taken seriously by any other group of Marxists (including the conservative party ideologues), their argumentation is worth presenting. This group is limited to the views of a Polish student club and of an Albanian observer. Let us refer to this approach as the search for *Marxist purity*. Its principal concern was the revival of socialist idealism and utopianism that it located in an earlier Stalinist epoch.

From this typology it becomes obvious that a more inclusive understanding of critical Marxism than commonly accepted in the West has been opted for here. Regardless of the objectives involved, use of the tools of Marxism was the criterion qualifying a particular writer as a critical Marxist. An additional point of clarification is that the degree to which the writers examined here explicitly applied their analyses to the case of Poland differed: several of the works were purely theoretical, having application to various social orders; others specifically addressed Polish circumstances. What is important from our point of view is the explanatory value they possess for understanding existing Polish socialism and its failures.

The Dissident Marxists

Perhaps dissident Marxism was launched in Eastern Europe with the publication of Milovan Djilas's *The New Class* in 1953, but some historians might hold it was already latent in the uneasy merger of workers' and social-democratic parties throughout the region around 1948. It is clear, however, that within a decade, ''fellow travelers'' of Djilas emerged in a number of countries in the region: future members of the Budapest school,[3] the Czechoslovak reformers,[4] and the *Praxis* group in Yugoslavia.[5] In Poland, reformist Marxism openly emerged within the Communist Party after Gomułka took power in October 1956. One of its advocates was Kolakowski, who increasingly became identified with the call for a ''second stage'' to the Polish October: building upon the de-Stalinization achievements of the first stage, this additional stage would restore political pluralism, human rights, and social justice. By 1966 the Warsaw University philosopher had moved beyond reformism (or revisionism, as Gomulka preferred to stigmatize this tendency) and had associated himself with the dissident Marxism of two university students, Jacek Kuroń and Karol Modzelewski. He was removed from the party and, following the March 1968 student disturbances, forced to leave Poland. In the West he decided upon the fundamental unreformability of Marxism and left Marxism behind altogether.[6]

The tract published by Kuroń and Modzelewski, which led to their first imprisonment and Kołakowski's subsequent party expulsion, was called *An Open Letter to the Party*. Written in 1964, it was influenced by New Class theories and by workers' self-management practice, both originating in Yugoslavia where they had formed part of the Titoist heresy some fifteen years earlier. Its Marxian form of analysis was very evident: "It is the relationships of production that are decisive; we must, therefore, examine more carefully the productive process and the relationships in that process between the working class, which is the basic creator of the national income, and the central political bureaucracy, which collectively has at its disposal the means of production."[7]

For Kuroń and Modzelewski, the Polish worker was exploited by the central political bureaucracy to which he was compelled to sell his labor and which confiscated the surplus product in order "to support the apparatus of coercion (army, political police, prisons, etc.) which perpetuates the present economic and social relationships."[8] For the authors, the solution to this travesty of socialism was public or social (as opposed to state) ownership of the means of production, to be operationalized by establishing genuinely independent workers' councils. This emphasis on the distinction between social and state ownership had already been crucial to the theories of Polish economists such as Oskar Lange and Włodzimierz Brus, and it remains to this day an important heuristic category for undertaking a critique of any socialist order.

In addition to a Trotskyist-type critique of the bureaucracy under socialism, Kuroń and Modzelewski also, interestingly, lashed out at the nature of technocracy under socialism: "Today, the technocracy has become a stable stratum conscious of its own interests. It enjoys the privileges of high consumption and is in conflict with the working class in its daily supervisory function and in its hankering for a form of 'managerial socialism.' "[9] This line of argument (which followed on from Djilas and James Burnham) anticipated later analyses conducted by Jürgen Habermas and Nicos Poulantzas.[10] In a second respect *An Open Letter to the Party* was ahead of its time. In its methodical dissection of power relations in Polish society, the document served as an incisive account less of past political crises than of future ones. When reread after the 1970, 1980, or 1989 events, its etiology of crises remains highly convincing, if not exhaustive.

A third anticipatory aspect of the tract, which gave it legitimate status as a classic of critical Polish Marxist thought, was its forecast of revolution. In their conclusion, the authors diagnosed the emergence of a revolutionary situation in the socialist Poland of the early 1960s. Although it need not be violent, "the revolution that will overthrow the bureaucratic system is a proletarian revolution."[11] Only such a revolution, the authors held, could serve as the essential precondition for further socioeconomic development in Poland. While there are various interpretations of the nature of the Solidarity movement created in September 1980, the most convincing to this author is as a revolutionary movement of the industrial (especially highly skilled) working class on whose bandwagon other social groups subsequently jumped. If this view is correct, then it follows that the Kuroń and Modzelewski thesis of proletarian revolution was vindicated by the events of 1980.

Finally, Kuroń and Modzelewski argued that the antibureaucratic revolution was not a purely Polish affair: ''The economic and social contradictions we have analyzed appear in mature form in all the industrialized bureaucratic countries: in Czechoslovakia, the GDR, Hungary and the USSR.'' Nor was it to be limited to the socialist bloc: ''The bureaucratic system, passed off as socialism by official propaganda in both East and West, compromises socialism in the eyes of the masses of developed capitalist countries. . . . The antibureaucratic revolution is, therefore, the concern of the international workers' movement and of the movement for colonial revolution.''[12] Without distorting the nature of the 1989 events in Eastern Europe, we can recognize that the authors' general belief in the need for a unified bloc effort to overthrow the incumbent ruling class of Eastern Europe appears confirmed by recent political changes.

In his 1989 autobiography, Kuroń maintained the validity and predictive capacity of the Marxian approach he had adopted in his *Open Letter* of twenty-five years earlier. By focusing on fetishization of production under real socialism, ''the Marxian schemata proved to be useful in analyzing real socialism in that it allowed us to discover the most general mechanisms of crisis in this system, and even to predict coming crises.''[13] Not surprisingly, Kuroń disavowed part of the framework he used in the *Open Letter*, in particular, two central concepts of Marx: class struggle and the primacy of the working class in creating wealth in a society. Yet he defended the idealism inherent in his earlier program from critics such as Kołakowski who had argued that idealism was the starting point of totalitarianism, and he also pointed to the value of revisionism at the time he wrote. ''The '*Open Letter*' was for us, though we had not intended it, the beginning of Marxist revisionism, and it is most difficult precisely to begin thinking on this subject.''[14] In contrast to many other Marxist-trained dissidents, therefore, Kuroń accepted his Marxist past and even underscored its utility in his intellectual development.

If the period of social contestation in Poland had begun with the Poznań events of June 1956, then the Kuroń and Modzelewski letter marked the beginning of systematized dissident Marxist analysis in the country. Oddly, little more such thought was articulated until the mid-1970s and the establishment of the Workers' Defense Committee (KOR) by Kuroń and others.[15] There were several reasons for this. First, after the 1968 disturbances a number of prominent intellectuals of Marxist bent, such as Kołakowski, the sociologists Zygmunt Bauman and Maria Hirszowicz, and the economist Włodzimierz Brus, were forced to emigrate. In England, where they settled, critical Marxism often gave way, quite naturally, to oftentimes innovative but fundamentally non-Marxist axiological approaches. Second, a variety of factors combined to thrust the mantle of socialist opposition away from the intellectuals into the hands of the working class. While workers may have been badly served in a workers' state, the scale of their dissatisfaction, and the growing sense of their political savvy and organization, only became apparent in the strikes and demonstrations of 1970, 1971, and 1976. In a sense, the industrial proletariat had appropriated from intellectuals the leading role of societal dissent in this period. At the same time, it did not engage in creative Marxist thought—largely to its credit—and Marxist critique of the Marxist state was seen exclusively in industrial action initiated in the shipyards of Gdańsk and Szczecin and the factories of the Warsaw periphery (Ursus, Płock, and Radom).

In short, the 1970s marked a period of political *practice* in which theoretical considerations took second place. Apart from the outright challenges issued to the incumbent authorities, a number of opposition groups were organized in these years, most notably, KOR in 1976 and ROBCIO (Movement for the Defense of Human and Civil Rights) in 1977. The church played an increasingly more subtle political role under the leadership of cardinals Wyszyński, Wojtyła (later John Paul II), and Macharski and was able to attract many intellectuals to its ranks. KIK (the Clubs of Catholic Intelligentsia), founded in the late 1950s, were also reinvigorated. More often, petitions, appeals, and public statements addressed directly to the authorities were undertaken. One crucial episode was, for example, the constitutional amendment crisis of 1975-76.[16] The Flying University was set up to offer courses on Polish history and other related subjects, frequently from a critical Marxist perspective. The proliferation of underground periodicals and publishing houses also was an example of political practice; there were few systematic Marxist-grounded critiques published by them as the intellectual search beyond Marxism had begun in earnest. The poverty of critical Marxism was also associated with the fact that, as Kołakowski noted, Marxism had by this time become nothing more than "mummified remains suddenly exposed to the air."[17]

An exception to the dearth of dissident theoretical Marxists at that time was constituted by the towering figure of Adam Michnik. Like Kuroń, this historian's pedigree was irreproachably communist, and he appeared to inherit the combativeness and determination that marked postwar Polish Communist Party members like his parents. It was all the more remarkable, therefore, that Michnik gave up the charmed life that he could have expected as one of the "children of communism" in order to undertake a long and personally costly struggle against authority generally, and the country's ruling party in particular. In *The Left, the Church: A Dialogue*, published in 1977, he first offered a theoretical justification for the somewhat unusual coalition of dissident Marxists and secular leftists (to which he belongs to this day) on the one hand, and the Catholic intelligentsia and Christians generally on the other.[18] But already in his often-cited piece called "A New Evolutionism," written in 1976, he characterized the historical roots of the two emerging coalition partners. "The revisionist concept was based on a specific intraparty perspective. . . . In the long term, the actions of the revisionists seek to allow enlightened people with progressive ideas to take over the party."[19] In their number Michnik counted Kołakowski, Lange, Lipiński, Hirszowicz, Brus, Pomian, and Baczko and, among literati, Kazimierz Brandys, Ważyk, Woroszylski, and Bocheński. The other orientation was termed neopositivist: it included Catholic activists led by Stanisław Stomma who, while rejecting Marxist doctrine and socialist ideology, were willing to participate in the socialist order in the hope that there would be "positive evolution in the party, to be caused by the rational policies of wise leaders, not by incessant public pressure."[20] Michnik argued that revisionism died in the aftermath of the March 1968 student disturbances, while the Znak group of Catholic deputies turned from conciliation into outright capitulation over time. Rallying the survivors of these two orientations, the historian proposed giving up the idea of seeking concessions from the authorities and called for the evolution of a popular nationwide movement. In a phrase that sums up the successful strategy of Poland's opposition from 1976 to 1989, Michnik urged that "a program for evolution ought to be addressed to an independent public, not to totalitarian power."[21]

Michnik thus provided the formula that ensured the successful transition from totalitarianism to posttotalitarianism.[22] Revisionism had its time and place, he argued, and evolutionism—the simultaneous accepting and ignoring of the communist order by society—had likewise a transitional role. But his constant conciliatory approach to the Left had, by 1990 when the communist government had been removed, aroused the suspicion of newly empowered anticommunist leaders, one of whom called Michnik a "crypto-communist." The legacy of having started out as a dissident Marxist seemed difficult for the historian and journalist to shed completely in the new times.

If the 1970s were, with the exception of Michnik, dominated by the politics of practice, it is possible to view the 1980s as a period of intense political praxis. Not only were a series of self-governing independent organizations set up (chief among them Solidarity), but extended critical analyses of both a Marxist and non-Marxist kind were carried out. As representative of dissident Marxist analysis of the period, studies by two Polish sociologists shall be examined: one based at Poznań University who wrote under the pseudonym of Stanisław Starski; the other, Jadwiga Staniszkis, based at Warsaw University.

The Marxian category at the center of Starski's analysis of Poland at the time of Solidarity was implicit in the title of his work, *Class Struggle in Classless Poland*. Indeed the young Poznań sociologist returned to New Class theory (citing Konrád and Szelényi, and Gouldner, among others) and began his study by establishing a link between Polish statism of the interwar period (largely influenced by Piłsudski) and the making of a class of state owners in the postwar period (the product of the communist takeover). The cycle of political crises in People's Poland was interpreted as the result of the growth of an "antistatist" movement, which according to Starski was based on a loose (and never clearly spelled out) amalgam of intellectuals (up to and including the 1968 protests), a specific generation (that of the late 1960s; for them, "Instead of class a new concept organized a sense of group identity—the generation"),[23] the traditional working class (on the Baltic coast in 1970-71), an alliance of the classless (in 1976), the emergence of a new working class (in the summer of 1980), and the making of an antagonistic class opposing the ruling class (with the creation of Solidarity). He therefore saw less of a unilinear evolutionism in the development of an opposition to communism than did Michnik.

The one constant variable that appeared in Starski's analysis was, predictably, the ruling class. Borrowing a typology from his mentor, the philosopher Leszek Nowak (whose work is discussed below), Starski identified a tripartite ruling class made up of a political dictatorship, an economic proprietor of the means of production, and a spiritual monopolist in matters of ideological, educational, and cultural values. The author seemed to imply that the establishment of a free trade-union movement in 1980 signaled the beginning of a new phase of class conflict in Poland: its intensification and institutionalization. The question left unanswered was which specific actors were locked in this new class struggle; it can only be assumed that Starski wanted to include all parts of the ruling class and all elements making up the new antagonistic class. Subsumed in the latter category were such differentiated groups as "the church of the oppressed," an amorphous women's movement, and, for good measure, an even less identifiable ecological consciousness. This view of class struggle was a long way from Marx, and it hardly appeared as rigorous analysis at all.

In fact, Starski's primary concerns were both the process and outcome of class struggle (central to Marx), as well as the evolution and goals of the antistatist movement (crucial to Lenin's views set out in "The State and Revolution"). Thus the major achievement of the Polish August was that "Solidarity provides a huge stimulus to all those spontaneous social energies and forces which aim at the de-state-ization of society and the dismantling of the absolute domination of the ruling class over the working masses."[24] For the author, class conflict and antistatism were part of the same struggle.

In his assessment of Marxism's role in raising class consciousness in a period of heightened class struggle, Starski again appeared inconsistent. He asserted, "The young marxists have also noticed that marxism itself did not play any direct and simple role in raising class awareness in Poland."[25] The function of Marxism was, instead, quite different: "The ruling class used marxism without Marx to ideologically obscure the actual aims and means of class struggle. The working class used a marxian inspiration without marxist rhetoric in order to articulate demands and execute their fulfillment."[26] Yet while correct on the first count, he also ascribed an "unorthodox Polish workers' approach toward Marxism" in launching the slogan in Gdańsk "Workers of all enterprises unite."[27]

Starski's dissident Marxism put a favorable gloss on the contribution of the

1980 events to Marxist political development. By contrast, Staniszkis clearly recognized the un-Marxist turn in the emergence of Solidarity. In a number of articles and in her book *Poland's Self-Limiting Revolution*, Staniszkis described some of the paradoxical "dialectics" (more bluntly, series of errors and readjustments) that characterized the functioning of socialist societies. Her provocative, and not always persuasive, central thesis was that the polity followed a pattern of regulation through crisis. In the earlier crises of 1956 and 1968, according to Staniszkis, "forms of social protest began with a stage of artificial negativity, in which opposition was constructed from above in order to permit the political system to introduce the necessary changes."[28] But by the late 1970s artificial negativity had gotten out of control and been displaced "by a corporatist form of interest articulation that was transformed in August 1980 into a class form of protest in which the exploited and powerless opposed those in power who were at the same time the controllers of the means of production."[29]

Like Starski, Staniszkis drew a linkage between prewar Polish society and its contemporary version: "Lack of a developed market, both in the economy and in politics, the prototraditional legitimacy of power, and a strong status order built on distance and exclusiveness seemed . . . to be the main features of a social system in Poland, locating it closer to traditional than to modern societies."[30] Staniszkis went even further to label the pre-Solidarity political system "neofeudal," with its constellations of personal influences, its segmentation of problems, solutions, and even interest articulation, and the polymorphic character of institutional power where the Communist Party and state administration were characterized by low specificity. These systemic features became the targets of Solidarity's reform thrust. More specifically, the Communist Party was compelled to adopt a power-segmenting strategy: in exchange for sharing responsibilities with other groups and ending its grip on all social and political institutions, the party could simultaneously halt its slide toward bureaucratization, depoliticization, and, ultimately, disintegration. The deconcentration of power was also functional, at least initially, for the independent trade-union movement.

As a dissident Marxist at the time, the author also addressed the questions of class and class conflict in socialist Poland. In 1970 workers "used the term 'class' legitimacy in their protest. They imitated the Marxist semantics to make their protest more efficient and safer."[31] However in 1980, when workers "had created real class representations, they rejected such semantics as a prosthesis no longer needed. Paradoxically, they acted as a class but did not label themselves in class terms."[32] We noted that Starski made much the same point. But Staniszkis explored this paradox further and identified three barriers holding back the development of working-class consciousness in a socialist state. They were: (1) the limited semantic competence of workers because of the state's appropriation of Marxist categories; (2) the reification of extant power relations so that workers feel no other power hierarchy is possible; and (3) an antipolitical

political culture and a self-limiting self-image that were based on "monistic tendencies linked with a moralistic conception of movement legitimacy, one-dimensionality in perceiving the external world ('we' versus the ruling group), an ahistoricism understood as an inability to generalize the logic of the movement's development, a lack of middle-range aims . . . and a rough and tumble, mostly reactive policy."[33]

We have already remarked on Staniszkis's view of the crisis-oriented philosophy of ruling, by which political authorities used, provoked, and ritualized crises so they would serve as regulatory mechanisms. Accompanying this process in the 1970s was the phenomenon of detotalization from above, that is, decentralization of decision making and the creation of "lame" (or artificial) pluralization. Interest articulation, blocked by the country's authoritarian-bureaucratic system, was now to be simulated, though not represented. Repressive toleration of opposing points of view was introduced under Gierek. As well, state activity and political life generally were deideologized: "Ideology acted mainly as the lowest denominator of the coalition and had little impact on its choices and decisions."[34] Limited detotalization, by which the rulers sought to escape from traps they had themselves built, went hand in hand with submission to the totalitarian temptation.

The Polish August transformed this political process in three important ways. The lame pluralism of the 1970s became "almost-responsible" pluralism under pressure from Solidarity. A quasi-legal social contract was established by the August agreements, giving the regime a new form of legitimacy. Finally, a new stage in the system's feudalization occurred: central government was weakened, a barter economy developed, and the weak absolutist state was able to control only those processes it had generated, not real life. Despite the rigorous depiction of the dialectical model of socialist society, Staniszkis was at a loss to foresee the introduction of martial law. Like a good Marxist, however, she made recourse to dialectics (the *deus ex machina* of Marxism) to argue that anything was possible in the future: "The dialectical process of attrition of forms of domination (as well as forms of protest) and the development of the system's contradictory logic are full of the unexpected and ambiguous."[35]

From this survey of dissident Polish Marxist thought it becomes evident that the analyses could be theoretically sophisticated yet largely tentative when formulating iron laws; they were rooted deeply in empirical research but differed profoundly in the interpretation of events; and they mainly addressed the issue of why Polish socialism had failed while implying that, with corrections, it could be salvaged. The refinement of Marxist theory and method was limited, and class conflict in particular remained a largely unmodified organizing concept. In its ability to provide innovative explanatory paradigms, Polish dissident Marxism compared unfavorably to Western neo-Marxist and post-Marxist schools, and it generally remained at a lower level of abstraction. Even when compared to the dissident Marxism in the rest of Eastern Europe, one is struck by the relative poverty of philosophy emanating from dissident Marxist circles in Poland.[36] On the other hand, Kuroń and Modzelewski's magisterial work borrowed from earlier New Class theory but also helped to develop it. Michnik was prophetic in concluding what type of social movement was best prepared to overcome totalitarianism. Starski's focus on the persistence of both class struggle and statism under socialism reflected long-standing concerns of Marxist thinkers. Staniszkis's examination of power relations in a socialist society suggested how communist elites first confiscated it from its rightful possessors, the industrial working class, then sought to retain it through a variety of convoluted devices.

The attention of all critiques was drawn to the level of social consciousness, the forms of political organization of the masses, and the ideological state apparatus. Perhaps the most distinctive characteristic of this body of dissident Marxism, however, was its self-consciousness and self-doubt and its resulting lukewarm commitment to promoting such a version of Marxism as a realistic option in Leninist party-states. We can detect an implicit assumption of the "unreformability" of the system of real socialism, with a concomitant implication that only on the basis of a tabula rasa could authentic socialism take root. In sum, Polish dissident Marxism appeared more committed to critique and constituted less of a Marxist *engagement* than the reformist Marxism discussed below. This thrust allowed its proponents to be able to function successfully in the type of posttotalitarian society Poland is today.

The Reformist Marxists

Up to 1989, critical Polish Marxists were confronted with a basic choice of whether to take their version of Marxism into the corridors of power and join liberal, reformist party factions, or into opposition circles and become dissidents. To select the first option meant, implicitly, becoming part of the shadowy ranks of the loyal opposition, understood as party factions that could reasonably hope to exercise power at some later date and propagate a liberal, even social-democratic, brand of Marxism. The chief feature of such reformism was ideological acquiescence to the basic structural components of real socialism. There could be no theses concerned with the new class, statism, or confiscated power. The argument could not be made that real socialism was an incurable aberration or deviation from the socialist doctrines propounded by the founding fathers. Rather, reformist Marxists sought to fine tune the existing system and adapt it to the functional imperatives of a late industrial society—an area left in some obscurity by Marx and later generations of his followers.

In their defense from the criticism that they effectively served as regime collaborators, we can cite Michnik's evaluation of the part played by the reformist Marxists of the late 1950s: though they may have been naive in seeking to reform Marxism from the inside, nevertheless it was "the same revisionist ex-Stalinists who created and spread amongst the intelligentsia the attitude and pattern of opposition which permitted the rebirth of civil life in the difficult conditions of Poland.''[37] To show that revisionism was not a dated political activity, we can invoke the conclusion drawn by an astute Western observer of Poland's politico-cultural life, Jeffrey Goldfarb, who in his 1989 book *Beyond Glasnost* argued, "In the post–martial law period, present-day revisionism and neopositivism are necessary. Someone has to use official ideology and Newspeak to free officialdom from its confines." Furthermore, if "outright opposition seems to be naive, moralistic, and politically inconsequential," it follows that "expanding the breadth of what it is possible to say with official acceptance is more important than speaking freely unofficially."[38] Who is to say that, with the hindsight of the 1989 events, it was not this process of eroding the fabric and solidity of the official ideology by reformists that did most to effect the self-destruction of the Polish Communist Party and usher in the Mazowiecki government?

In this section we look at some representative examples of Polish reformist Marxism. While the following is a criterion that is difficult to apply rigorously, those revisionist writings whose target audience was, above all, the highest political authorities have been selected to make this study manageable. We have chosen not to consider the larger philosophical-sociological school that, according to the Solidarity newspaper *Tygodnik Solidarność*, "played such a significant role in the history of Polish culture," and whose representatives included Kołakowski, Stefan Morawski, Jerzy Szacki, Andrzej Walicki, and Krzysztof Pomian.[39] Before "classical Polish revisionism" is examined, "latter-day revisionism"—the reports of a discussion club, the "Experience and the Future" group (DiP)—will be analyzed.

The DiP discussion club was established in 1978 by a group of reform-oriented intellectuals, many of whom were university professors and the majority of whom were party members. As with *An Open Letter to the Party*, DiP carried out a comprehensive analysis of the state of Polish society and forwarded the two reports it completed before the summer 1980 crisis (in May 1979 and May 1980) directly to the political leadership. Two other reports were published during the Solidarity and martial-law periods. Their general character was greatly shaped by academic empirical sociology, but the normative structure of classic Marxian analysis was also evident.

Perhaps the most fundamental category borrowed from Marxist analysis that can be found in the reports is the role of social consciousness. Although Marx himself minimized the part played by such consciousness in his historical materialist interpretation, later generations of Marxists (in Poland, Kelles-Krauze in particular) attached far greater significance to it. Postwar Polish Marxist sociology, largely shaped by the pioneering work of Stanisław Ossowski,[40] treated consciousness as a critical social force, and DiP adopted this perspective. "The state of public consciousness is just as real a fact as the existence of social classes. People's acts, opinions, and aspirations are equally produced by the content of consciousness.''[41] This approach had important implications for the perceived legitimacy of the political process and political institutions. The first DiP report argued, therefore, that "social consciousness is no less important than the objective state of things. No less important than actual participation is people's awareness that they share in collective governance, collective decisions, and cooperation."[42]

But social consciousness was also influenced by a number of negative social phenomena appearing in society's economic base. DiP documented the growing inegalitarianism and hierarchical nature of Polish society and the resultant antagonism between individuals and social groups. Accordingly, in May 1979 DiP concluded, "Perhaps precisely this troubling moral state of society—which reveals itself in ever more unsatisfactory relations between individuals, dishonesty, indifference to matters of common concern, and the collapse of social ties—is the greatest threat we face."[43]

The reformist solutions envisaged by DiP appear modest in light of the subsequent more radical proposals put forward by various groups in the Solidarity period. The reform measures, elaborated in greater detail in DiP's second report, "Which Way Out?" included clearer division of power between the party and the administrative, economic, and legal apparatus, a broader role for elected bodies (such as the Parliament), increased autonomy for self-government organs, a more impartial legal system, and institutional guarantees for safeguarding civil rights.

While DiP's contribution is easily lost in the flurry of change—new political actors, movements, parties, ideas, quarrels—which occurred in Poland in 1989, the importance of the programmatic spadework that DiP carried out in charting Solidarity's self-limiting revolution and its advancement of the concept of a self-governing republic should not be underestimated. Even less obvious may be the policy links between "Which Way Out?" and the Jaruzelski administration's later economic reform package. DiP placed considerable stress on comprehensive economic reform of the system and recognized the dilemma Jaruzelski and Mazowiecki were later to face: "Without change, we face calamity. Even if, on the other hand, changes are made, we can expect nothing good for quite a while."[44]

A report produced by a very different body under very different circumstances but that came to very similar diagnostic and prescriptive conclusions underscores DiP's influence on a liberal party faction. In 1981 the Communist Party Congress recommended setting up an official commission of enquiry to look into the sources of postwar Polish crises. Headed by a Politburo liberal, the Kraków sociologist Hieronym Kubiak, the commission issued its final report in 1983. In contrast to its earlier drafts, where bad government was given as the source of political crises, the final official version identified two general causes of crisis: (1) the socioeconomic contradictions originating in the mistaken policies of successive leaders; and (2) the gap between a fairly advanced social consciousness (where the public had internalized the basic principles of socialism) and the ossified institutions of interest representation. The reformist Marxism underlying the Kubiak commission was most clearly apparent in its series of recommendations that aimed at the introduction of socialist democracy in Poland.[45] But the fate of DiP, the Kubiak commission, Kubiak himself, and reformist Marxism generally was similar under Jaruzelski's normalization of the 1980s: they were marginalized and rendered irrelevant.

If we return to the halcyon days of revisionism—the two or three years after Gomułka's accession to power in October 1956—we may appreciate the extent to which reformist Marxists were successful over the decades in "expanding the breadth of what it is possible to say with official acceptance," as Goldfarb put it.[46] Let us look at the works of three of the "founding fathers" of revisionism, all of whom were closely associated with the party in the early Gomułka years: Wiladysiław Bieńkowski, Adam Schaff, and Bronisław Baczko.

Bieńkowski served briefly as minister of education before falling out with Gomułka, but his admiration for Marxism was still much in evidence in his underappreciated major study, *Theory and Reality*, published in 1981. An opening statement makes clear his sympathies: "The criticism of marxism is a constant proof of its vitality, a confirmation that its value does not lie in those areas where Marx was mistaken."[47] The vitality of Marxism as a general social theory was its focus on "explaining *not* how society is constructed nor even how it functions, but how it changes and develops, and how the moving forces of this development operate."[48] In his analysis of the socialism of Soviet-type societies, Bieńkowski suggested that "the meaning of the concept has become blurred and in some respects we have returned to the kind of situation which prevailed before Marx: since rational laws have failed us, we entrust our dreams to the future."[49] Socialist ideology, and Leninism in particular, became institutionalized and took on a dynamic of its own, independent of human will. As a result, "socialism ceased to signify the next 'higher' stage of development; it could, at the most, signify *another road* to this stage" or, citing Joan Robinson, it could become "a substitute for capitalism."[50]

Bieńkowski identified a number of factors that conspired to distort socialism in the USSR: Russia's traditions, the complete isolation of the Bolsheviks from external influences, and the establishment of a police dictatorship and of censorship. His treatment of Stalinism was eclectic: "Stalin fulfilled the role of a long-range missile in space travel. On achieving a given velocity the long-range element is released and condemned to destruction in the atmosphere; the space craft is already travelling in the desired direction."[51] His approach to bureaucracy was also unusual: in the Soviet Union the creation of a modern, Weberian-style bureaucracy was impossible given the ideological criteria employed to appoint cadres and the regular intervention of the police apparatus in all stages of "bureaucratic" procedures. Bieńkowski further spoke in an unorthodox way of the coming to the USSR of "dual power": a real system based on the unlimited power of the party apparatus, and a decorative one that served propagandistic functions and produced a "quasi-theocratic state," but which also engendered "an endless and complicated game of appearances, and creates a fictitious world in which half of internal political life takes place 'as if,' in a complete sham."[52]

Several other paradoxes of real socialism were noted by Bieńkowski. Contrary to what Marx had envisaged, in such systems productive forces initially grew while, simultaneously, the political superstructure became increasingly backward. *Theory and Reality* was written before the birth of Solidarity, and it would be interesting to learn whether Bieńkowski might have devised a later stage of socialist development to describe Eastern Europe of the 1980s, in which productive forces are fettered and decline while the political system is given a modernized appearance. At the time of writing, the author was critical about the long "history of systemic 'non-adaptation' "[53] in the region. Finally, in referring to social tensions that become thrust into the social subconscious, where they continue to influence all areas of life, Bieńkowski made clear that this was the essence of a dictatorial regime: "The fundamental characteristic of a despotic, dictatorial regime is that it has (by definition) to feel threatened by its own society. . . . The factor of threat is an inexhaustible source of energy which forces the institutions of the regime to escalate their activity."[54]

In Bieńkowski's sociological tract, written in emigration in the West, we have found enough commitment to Marxism, and enough of an attack on the existing socialist order, to classify the work as a major treatise of revisionism. The philosopher Schaff provides a second exemplification of early Polish revisionist Marxism. In *A Philosophy of Man*, ostensibly a defense of Marxist humanism against an existentialist offensive, the author advanced the thesis that man was the starting point of Marxism.[55] This view seemingly lacks controversy until we recall that this period still assigned primacy to the role and interests of the proletariat as a social class, to which the individual took second place. Schaff dramatized the significance of human activity by claiming that, with Marxism, "man takes the place of God and, indeed, surpasses God."[56] But this was not all: Schaff's revisionism exhibited a sharp-edged practical side when he pointed to how "we are rather inclined to delay the process of democratization than to hasten it."[57] He demonstrated how "narrow practicalism is a danger to the building of socialism . . . because whenever any individual right may be infringed because of the practical exigencies of some particular political situation, this infringement may come to be regarded as quite normal and may be perpetuated."[58] A careful reading of this defense of Marxism would also find Schaff urging the public to rebel: "Is there any justification for the inner revolt of people who feel more strongly about evils in a socialist society than in the previous society? Yes and no. Yes, if it is a question of feeling the need to oppose evil. . . . [T]he protest against social evil should be stronger, and the struggle against it more determined, under socialism. Resentment against evil in socialist society is a truly sacred resentment."[59]

If the body politic had not noticed Schaff's insurrectionary exhortation, the political leadership had. His next book, titled *Marxism and the Human Individual*, was criticized by the party Central Committee itself. In it the philosopher repeated the view that "the key to Marx's view of the world should be sought in his theory of man.''[60] Yet in their application of Marxism, socialist states had inevitably concentrated on organizing the macrostructure of a society and, correspondingly, tended to neglect the individual as individual. Socialization work took on a mass character, with the result that the attempted inculcation of a general socialist consciousness was superficial and even counterproductive.

Consistent with the rediscovery in that period of the young Marx who, in Schaff's words, was a "militant humanist," the Polish philosopher emphasized the importance of happiness as the prime objective of humanist Marxism: "The militant character of Marxist humanism is closely connected with this aspect of happiness: it calls for an uncompromising struggle against the causes of human misery as a mass phenomenon—and thus versus its social roots."[61] But socialist systems had not been particularly successful on this front. Schaff again posed a revisionist Marxist question: "Is it true that private property is at the basis of all alienation? And, consequently, does the end of capitalism mean the end of all alienation? Is alienation impossible under socialism?"[62] He responded with categorical no's. Alienation continued to exist under socialism, fostered by both the machinery of power and the division of labor. Adopting a no less pessimistic view of the future, he prophetically observed that the "elimination of the social sources of unhappiness that existed in the past does not at all mean that there might not be new causes of an even greater unhappiness in the future society."[63]

Schaff also examined the role of the state and, following Marx, argued that it should not be the state that shaped the existence of private individuals pursuing their own interests; on the contrary, it should be civil society that conditioned the state. While Schaff was, politically, a long way from Kuroń or Michnik, he partially agreed with New Class theory in recognizing the existence of privileged groups under socialism. In his analysis of state administration, he again urged that a struggle be waged not against bureaucracy itself but against "bad, unreasonable, incompetent, top-heavy" bureaucracy.[64] Schaff's humanist Marxist ideas and his earlier practical efforts to humanize the country's political system earned him the opprobrium of the party leadership even before the Czechoslovak version of humanist socialism was established. Concerned more with the metaphysical than the political level of reformist Marxism, Schaff was soon expelled from the party's Central Committee for revisionism but remained a party member up to the mid-1980s.

Bronisław Baczko is the last in our trio of founding revisionists. Perhaps because of his focus on French intellectual history, he is less well known in his role as a Marxist revisionist than Schaff or Bieńkowski, and indeed his writings since leaving Poland show little interest in seeking to build upon the existing socialist order in Eastern Europe. However, for many Polish intellectuals he is closely identified with early revisionism in the country.

Influenced markedly by the French school of new history, Baczko has studied the part played by utopian thought, the social imagination, collective historical memory, socially constructed symbols, rituals, and myths, and the collective mind generally in both revolutionary movements and the upholding of social orders. Disagreeing with the ideas advanced by theorists like Bieńkowski who stressed the centrality of a study of the past and present in Marxism, Baczko pointed to the fundamental utopianism inherent in Marxian thought. His manifesto for a future society included the end of exploitation, a planned and classless society, the withering away of the state and its administrative appendages, an internationalism that would end war, and distributive justice based on the principle to each according to need. Citing Marx, Trotsky imagined how "the average man would reach the height of an Aristotle or Goethe." For Baczko, such utopianism contained the potential for the destruction of Marxism: "For the authorities, utopia could become a reference point from which to question reality." In this way, "revisionism inevitably began with the question, 'is this socialism?' "[65] Moreover, the monopoly on the construction of utopian vision held by the totalitarian system became itself a source of disagreement.

Applying his analysis to Poland, Baczko stressed the importance of the past generally and of the struggle between the communist authorities and the rest of society over collective memory. Until Solidarity reconfiscated national memory, "the party, as the repository of the true doctrine, would communicate directly with History"[66] and define society's past itself. For Baczko it was significant that throughout its existence in 1980-81, Solidarity organized commemorations of a series of anniversaries and events that helped define a collective identity apart from that hitherto propagated by the party. It followed that the reappropriation of a collective memory by society was liberating, integrating, and at the same time "accusatory," unmasking the party's own brutal part in the fashioning of recent history. Baczko's revisionism was concerned above all, therefore, with the epiphenomenal in Marxian theory, which, he contended, had to reflect accurately the interests of the collectivity rather than of its purported vanguard.[67]

By contrast Jerzy Wiatr, a Warsaw University political scientist and member of the Kubiak commission, was concerned primarily with the logistics of the socialist order. Avoiding the fate of the 1950s and 1960s revisionists who were forced to emigrate from Poland, Wiatr remained committed to a party career and, especially in the difficult years of Jaruzelski's normalization, he sought to liberalize policy while avoiding marginalization. In his writings of the 1980s, he spoke of the "alienation of government" in Poland that precipitated the August crisis, and "the opposition between the 'governing' and the 'governed' " that was a hallmark of the postwar political system. Such problems could be overcome, he argued, by limited structural reforms, which would provide for input into the political process by social groups other than the party. Such institutional reform was perceived by conservatives as a surrender of the party's hegemonic role in society, and in the Jaruzelski administration Wiatr, too, lost standing in the party hierarchy.

Wiatr was always concerned with the thorny question of the role of the state in socialist society. We observed earlier that antistatism was the basis of dissident Polish Marxism, and in the West, too, there has been a spirited revival of the Hegelian dichotomy of the state and civil society.[68] The reformist Marxists in Poland were inevitably confronted with this issue, and Wiatr's response was one of the most illuminating.[69]

He began his analysis with Marx's criticism of the Hegelian view of the state: the state is not the creation of civil society but, according to Marx, represents the interests of the ruling class. Thus the Marxist tradition was established of rejecting the cult of the state. But Hegel and Marx also took diametrically opposed stances on the part played by the administration of the state: for the former, state bureaucracy was the apotheosis of rational administration; for the latter, it had at all times to be submitted to effective control by society if it was not to run amok. Wiatr claimed that Marx was wrong in his belief that the state would wither away, and he added that the task facing the socialist state, which by the very logic of social ownership had more functions to carry out than its nonsocialist counterparts, was to ensure society controls it.

At this point the reformist Marxist thesis becomes apparent. Societal control over state administration could only be exercised effectively if collective interests had an independent outlet for articulation and remained autonomous from the state. For Wiatr this meant the establishment of trade unions, professional associations, self-management bodies, religious institutions, and other social groups that were truly independent of the state. Wiatr called such a society in which interests could be differentiated (and subsystem autonomy was the fundamental principle) a "contemporary socialist civil society." Its distinctive feature was the autonomy of social, as opposed to political, relations, which remained free from state interference. As he asserted, "Socialism is not and should not be equated with the liquidation of all social linkages that are autonomous from the state; the totality of such autonomous linkages, which can be termed a new civil society, exerts a significant influence on the conditions in which the state functions."[70] In this way, the state was not an antagonist of civil society but, rather, its political fulfillment. The argument was similar to Schaff's and even appeared to sanction the "evolutionism" that Michnik had advocated.

On the other hand, Wiatr's socialist civil society was not the civil society Jacques Rupnik had in mind in tracing the growth of dissent in Poland after 1968. For Rupnik, like Michnik, political opposition was the crucial activity: as dissent of all kinds increased, society could claim more political space for itself and could ignore state power with greater abandon. Wiatr's conception was more Gramscian, and he referred explicitly to the notion of political hegemony—a linkage of an ethical kind between the state and society in which the former accurately expresses society's collective identity, while the latter lends it active support. If Rupnik and Wiatr differed over the political process that led to civil society, both accepted the fact that independent social activity was "the beginning of a long journey aimed at progressive transformation of relations between state and society in Poland."[71]

Finally, Wiatr turned to the problem of bureaucracy in a socialist state that had also interested Kuroń, Modzelewski, and Bieńkowski. He argued that only with autonomous and active social organizations could bureaucratization be combated. Furthermore, not only should the Communist Party itself be free of bureaucratic tendencies, its leading role in society provided a unique opportunity for it to act as an antibureaucratic force. Wiatr's concern with the practical mechanisms of societal control, autonomy, and differentiation can be interpreted as recognition of a conflict of interests under socialism. Indeed he signaled that the creation of a socialist civil society—where class divisions and antagonisms were largely eliminated but differentiated interests persisted and were promoted—was not one of total harmony. In fact social conflict was likely to persist into the final stage of communism: "Nothing in Marxist theory and methodology suggests the view that the type of development generated by the appearance and resolution of contradictions will end with that historical phase in which humanity finally moves on to communism."[72] Wiatr was therefore ominously concluding that Poland's 1980s problems might not vanish at some higher stage of socialist development, and the task of reformist Marxism was to make clear the difference between pathological and normal developmental difficulties.

This survey of reformist Marxism, necessarily selective and longitudinal, has indicated the persistence and wide-ranging concerns of this Marxist current in Poland. We found that reformist Marxism could be pointedly humanist as well as methodically practical, and normative as well as prescriptive. It sought to resolve some perennial problems of Marxism but also addressed the current dilemmas of socialist practice. Above all, it was the proving ground of subsequently more liberal Marxist orthodoxy, which by 1989 proved unsustainable. Strangely, therefore, the political fate of the revisionists was crueler than that of the dissident Marxists. Unable to place sufficient distance between themselves and the prevailing orthodoxy of the party, identified in the public mind as belonging to "them" rather than "us," revisionists who had fought the good fight against totalitarianism and were, it could be argued, indispensable in the transition to Poland's posttotalitarian polity could not find a place in the country's new political order.

The Marxologizers

A small group of Polish thinkers involuntarily found themselves in a double-bind situation in the 1980s. The more they publicly rejected Marxism as a

normative system, the more apparent it became that their Marxist epistemological foundations were not withering away. It would be as inaccurate to call such
thinkers Marxist as it would be to claim that they were fully emancipated from
Marxist influence. Obviously the open disavowal of Marxism by a scholar in a
socialist state would have done little for his career. That is the case with three
eminent Marxologists to be examined in this section: the Kraków University
sociologist Piotr Sztomka, the philosopher Leszek Nowak, and the sociologist
Zygmunt Bauman. While pointing to their respective contributions to the conscious development of post-Marxist theory, it should be added that their studies
are not explicitly empirically grounded in Polish sociopolitical development.

Thus Sztomka's intellectual activity has been confined mainly to
epistemological questions—a strong, if overlooked, subfield of Polish sociology.
His major objective in the 1980s was to synthesize Marxism with functionalism.
In his view, their basic affinity lay in the adoption of systemic models of society,
but if their methodological approach was similar, their normative structures
were not. As examples he juxtaposed three sets of values: exploitation–
reciprocity, conflict–consensus, and development–stability. While Marxian analysis underscored the first value in each set, functionalism emphasized the second. Sztomka concluded, therefore, "They speak about the same, but say different things." At the same time, he added that the controversy was surmount-
able and that "taking sides is neither a matter of taste nor intellectual predilec-
tions, but rather a matter of fidelity to historical and sociological evidence."[73]

In his earlier writings Nowak was primarily concerned with clarifying certain
Marxist categories which remained largely fuddled. These included the exact
components making up the economic base and the institutional superstructure
and the precise relationship between material conditions and social consciousness.[74] By 1980, however, he completed an extended work entitled *Property
and Power*, whose objective was the development of a "non-Marxian historical
materialism."[75] This stemmed from his contention that "the poverty of the
theory of socialism expresses the poverty of our understanding of the modern
world in general."[76] His ambitious goal was to "surpass Marx," whose emphasis on such social mechanisms as class struggle had become of secondary importance in contemporary societies, and whose ideological dimension was "quite
erroneously expedient for the dominant social forces of our times."[77]

For Nowak, the overriding Marxian ambiguity undermining his historical
materialism was stress at some times on the contradiction between productive
forces and the relations of production as the motor force of history, and at other
times the primacy accorded to class struggles. Both praxistic and nomological
approaches to Marxian social theory succeeded in "disambiguating" this in-
consistency. Only the orthodox interpretation, which for Nowak formed an un-
fortunate theoretical basis for the official ideology in socialist countries, continued the process begun by Marx of a "mechanical joining of both Marxian
motifs."[78] The Poznań philosopher sought to develop a historical materialism

that would fall outside this dualistic tradition but that would still adopt Marxian methodology, conceptual apparatus, and dialectics.

Basing his model on the Polish Marxist Rosa Luxemburg's analysis of surplus value, Nowak contended that there was one crucial factor that engendered the growth of demand under capitalism, which in turn produced enlarged reproduction: it was the "surprisingly simple" answer of growth of consumption by owners. Put another way, "the luxury of the owners in some historical conditions plays an equally indispensable role for economic development as the work of the direct producers."[79] Stimulated by such a drive, the ownership class sought to maximize a specific form of surplus value, that of the fund of luxury. This consumption motor, which had to lie within and not outside a given society, had shown itself to be the engine of history from the time of slavery to that of real socialism.

There was more to Nowak's model. He went on to examine the peculiarities of feudalism and traced the rise of a "dual society": in addition to the old class division, a class of new owners and new direct producers had emerged. "And so, new disposers of the productive forces (or, new owners) maximize the (new) surplus value exploiting the new direct producers not less than the old producers."[80] A unitary society was split into two subsocieties with a pair of antagonist classes each. If this was reminiscent of Marx's analysis of productive forces being fettered by existing relations of production, so was Nowak's next thesis: the two subsocieties produced revolutionary disturbances (class struggles), which eventually effected unification of society through rivalry.

Nowak then adopted a quasi-Keynesian perspective to resolve the quintessential dilemma of the succeeding capitalist social formation. With commodity production spurred on by new technological forces outstripping demand, the class of owners eventually had to allocate part of the technical surplus to the class of direct producers so they could reduce the "dead surplus value," that is, the enlarged production. In this way the exploiters come to the aid of the exploited.

A further aspect of the non-Marxian model of historical materialism, as it applied to capitalism, was what Nowak identified as a "formational cycle" in which increasing alienation of work produced revolutionary disturbances, which then led to decreasing alienation. The capitalist business cycle followed this outline: "The phase of the depression (the diminishing of effective demand but with some surplus of the 'consumptive motor' over the sum of wastages of the variable capital) corresponds to that of the increasing alienation of work, the phase of crisis to that of revolutionary disturbances, and the phase of prosperity to that of decreasing alienation."[81] The correspondence of the cycles was due, according to Nowak, to the identity of social mechanisms at work, that is, class struggle.

Nowak's attempt to develop a Marxist theory of power was based on a schema similar to that applied to ownership of the means of production. Disposal of the means of coercion was, in the political sphere, the equivalent of such economic ownership, and the resulting political hierarchization of rulers and citizens corresponded to the economic one. Civic alienation and political class struggle also occurred in this sphere, and the familiar cycle of increasing alienation (of a civic kind) and revolutionary disturbances followed by constraint was duplicated. Nowak concluded that property and power relations were in many respects analogous, though the interests of owners and direct producers could more quickly be harmonized than those between rulers and citizens.

One final aspect of Nowak's model was the material momentum found in each society. There were three possible momentums: economic production, political production, and consciousness production. Nowak classified societies according to the number of momentums driving them and found, after a complex analysis of various forms of struggle, statization, and totalitarianization, that real socialism represented one-momentum society. What were its principal characteristics?

> Decisions concerning the use of all three types of material forces of society are put into the same category of people. The same people decide, then, what is to be produced, what is to be allowed and what is to be put into the minds of the remaining people. The same category of people plays, then, the role of owners, rulers and priests. That society is divided into the two triple classes—that of the triple tyrants (owners–rulers–priests) and that of the triply tyrannized (direct producers–citizens–faithful). . . . The class tyranny reaches its apogee in such a society, whatever its ideological self-identification would be.[82]

Nowak then noted, "Evidently, the best self-presentation is as a classless society."[83]

Nowak's model was shaky, perhaps the inevitable product of the effort to construct a non-Marxian theory of social formation using such explicitly Marxian categories as production relations, classes, alienation, struggle, and the unity of opposites. Certain *sensu stricto* non-Marxist concepts, such as the consumption drive or the property and power analogy, were hardly novel. Finally his imputations of specific features to various stages, which were to engender new phases of social formation, represented a cruder form of historical determinism than Marx ever could be charged with. His thesis that a Marxian society inevitably produced the one-momentum, triple-class despotism was as epistemologically spurious as his final statement: "The way to achieve a classless society leads through the most class-ridden form of society which is deceitfully called socialism. This system of the three-rule is a historical necessity, as historically necessary as its fall and the rise of a new social formation: at any rate, in the East, in societies which are ahead of the historical process in the post-Marxian epoch."[84] Still, one can understand such a utopian thrust on the part of a Polish philosopher experiencing the Polish political events of the 1980s.

Let us look briefly at the work of a third Polish Marxologizer. In *Memories of*

Class, Bauman explored the genesis of class-based society which finally coalesced in the early nineteenth century. For the author, economic issues (such as control of the surplus product) were less important in class formation than the struggle to construct social institutions that provided group status and individual security. Historical memory of that class-based and class-conflictual society, Bauman continued, largely mystified the present nature of societal dynamics. In particular, the enhanced role of the state in affecting the social totality was, for a long time, not fully understood. For the state set the rules of the game and the parameters for group and individual activities and, over time, it evolved into a corporatist state that was now beyond the bounds of class contention. In short, class conflict was of little significance in state-regulated capitalism. The state redistribution of resources aimed at mediating deprivation and served to nullify the emergence of contradictions based solely on class.

In late capitalist society, therefore, social disorder was caused not by class politics but by "the growing pressure of the consumer role, coupled with the slow disappearance of the producer roles, still remembered as the sole entry to the game of distribution." Furthermore, "Contradictions which haunt the sociopolitical system are explicable as the incongruence of the state-managed defense of the production-oriented power structure, rather than as a reflection of the antagonistic class interests."[85] That is, they stemmed from the very nature of the corporatist system.

But Bauman observed that over the long term this set of problems, which was often depicted as technological or economic, would become perceived as political because "it concerns above all the type and the distribution of social power."[86] The crucial question would again become the organization of social life. Thus, "the field of politics would come into its own; it would cease to be—as it has been increasingly throughout the history of industrial society—'economics by proxy,' "[87] that is, group competition over the allocation of goods. To this may be added that in Bauman's scenario political science, too, would move away from its pretentious role as "economics by proxy." Bauman concluded, "Politics would become instead more directly political—i.e., concerned with the organization of social life, self-management, restitution and preservation of human control over the ways in which human bodily and spiritual potential is developed and deployed."[88]

Following Alain Touraine[89] and other theorists of social movements, Bauman believed that participation in the resuscitated politics would cut across social-class and group identities. It would be about control over cultural reproduction in society rather than over surplus product. Yet he lay no claim as to the fit of such a model to a disintegrating socialist society and did not view the emergence and objectives of Solidarity in the supraclass, noneconomistic categories he proposed in his model. If the absence of class conflict was for Bauman as central a characteristic of late capitalistic society as its presence was for orthodox Marxist thought, then his analysis of the sources for Poland's move to posttotalitarianism excluded the concept of class—whether present or absent—altogether. Instead Bauman employed such vague terms as "sectional interests" and "the Polandization of communist rule," such prosaic ones as "elite circulation" and "national communism," and such banal a deduction as "No one seems to *want* what everyone seems to *need*" as his conceptualization of Poland's transition.[90]

The introduction of viable non-Marxian theses standing in opposition to Marx, as seen in the works of Nowak and Bauman, may suggest that social theory engaged in a dialectic with Marxism (with the latter serving as the antithesis) may indeed arrive at fruitful explanatory models of late industrial, and even socialist, society. However, the inability to apply any part of such models to explain the historic social events occurring in Eastern Europe in 1989 and after—as in the case of Bauman—might also suggest that the theoretical struggle against Marxism can produce the same cul de sac as Marxist social theory itself.

The Purist Marxists

In addition to the Marxist-oriented perspectives discussed above, the purist approach (sometimes depicted as neo-Stalinist) should not be ignored. Admittedly in intellectual terms it is a weak current and attracts few converts. But because it searches for a long-lost purity, supposedly to be found in Marxian thought and then reconstructed, it can hardly be dismissed as an ideological aberration, though it may indeed constitute a political one. Two adherents of this school are examined in this section: the Sigma Club of Warsaw University, and the study of an Albanian ideologue.

Probably the most sophisticated and controversial representatives of the purist Marxist school in Poland were the members of the little-known Sigma Club based at Warsaw University. In their analyses of Polish crises, not only did its activists (largely students and young workers, with a few university professors and a sizable number of party members included) take the pre-Solidarity political system to task, they also were highly critical of the August agreements and of Solidarity's goals. Their objections were voiced in Bolshevik categories. The lessons of August 1980 were, for the Sigma Club, that workers remained capable only of trade-union consciousness, for they simply desired to put fetters on economic management rather than to eliminate it. Solidarity aimed solely at putting social democratic limitations on Poland's state capitalism; moreover, it was willing to collaborate with the existing state bureaucracy and party apparatus rather than seeking to abolish them.

Even prior to the birth of Solidarity, the club's journal, *Colloquia Communae*, advanced the thesis that Poland was passing through what Marx described as the accumulative phase of state capitalism. In order to pass to the next stage, the dictatorship of the proletariat, the working class would have to use violence to liquidate the entrenched bureaucracy, together with those members of the intelligentsia, in particular the technocrats, who served it. In this period Sigma activists condemned liberal Gierek administration policies and the liberal opposition (such as the Flying University) alike. There were clear neo-Stalinist tendencies in the club's advocacy of a return to crude principles of equality, to class criteria for selecting leadership cadres, and to the rigidity of Marxian dogma.

Yet it would be inaccurate to view the Sigma Club as a fiercely independent group of Marxist mavericks striking out, like the old-guard Maoists of Albania, on their own. In the Solidarity and martial-law periods they soon fell victim to party intrigues that pitted various anticentrist factions (such as the Toruń forum—the horizontalist movement within the party—and the Katowice forum—composed of pro-Soviet party conservatives) against each other. Ultimately their autonomy and credibility were undermined. But a decade later they might have interpreted the 1989 events as evidence that their critique of liberalized totalitarianism had been justified; for this totalitarianism was itself swept away with Sigma-type orientations.[91]

The last Marxist critique of Poland to be examined was not carried out by a Polish thinker either in the country or abroad. It was an ingenious, generally well informed, if largely implausible account by an Albanian writer, Spiro Dede, and carried the imaginative title, *The Counter-Revolution Within the Counter-Revolution*. It is of interest to our study precisely because it contained an attack on all manner of critical Marxist thought such as we have explored in this chapter.

The central thesis of the study was that post-1956 Polish politics was characterized by a protracted struggle between two wings of revisionism: "On the one side stand the forces of the revisionist counterrevolution linked with the Polish United Workers' Party, the present Polish government, and Soviet social-imperialism, i.e., the forces of modern revisionism in Poland. Confronting them stand the forces of ultrareaction linked with Western capital and the Vatican."[92] While we should by now be aware of the reasons why Albanian Marxist ideologues might have discovered revisionism in Poland's ruling Communist Party, the reasons advanced for labeling the Solidarity movement as revisionist are more intriguing: (1) it was completely devoid of Marxist-Leninist ideology and characterized instead by "a conglomerate of syndicalism, anarcho-syndicalism, Titoite theories of self-administration, all-round pluralism, etc.";[93] (2) it was lacking a vanguard detachment, a true Marxist-Leninist party, to spearhead demands for change; (3) Solidarity's demands were aimed only at strengthening and making more efficient the revisionist-capitalist system in existence in Poland since Gomułka's takeover, not overthrowing it; and (4) the movement "was inspired by the aim of replacing the dependence on the social-imperialists [the USSR] with dependence on the Western imperialists."[94]

How did such a "counterrevolution within the counterrevolution" (Solidarity) differ from the "revisionist peaceful counterrevolution" (the Polish Communist Party)? Invoking the official resolutions of the Eighth Congress of the Party of Labor of Albania, Dede identified five dissimilarities: (1) whereas the Communist Party sought gradual counterrevolutionary change, Solidarity aimed at rapid such change; (2) the peaceful counterrevolution wished to maintain a socialist facade, in contrast to the counterrevolution within the counterrevolution; (3) the August 1980 counterrevolution aimed at replacing the Russian yoke with the Western yoke; (4) the incumbent revisionists had a vested interest in existing political institutions and processes whereas the new revisionists did not; (5) it was the 1980 counterrevolution that more greatly increased the ideological deception and degeneration of the working masses. For the Albanian ideologue,

> the "independent trade unions" in Poland never were or could be independent organizations. They were as little "independent" as the existing order in Poland is "socialist." The only difference between these two deceptions lies in the fact that, while the interests of the revisionist clique in power and its social-imperialist allies are linked with the deception about "socialism," the deception about the "independence" is linked with the interests of the Polish ultracapitalist reaction, Western imperialism, and the Vatican.[95]

Some of the critical Marxists we have discussed who were engaged in party struggles in Poland might now find the purist Marxist analysis charitable and flattering. For Dede, two revisionisms struggled with each other within one system, a capitalist one. It was not, therefore, either a class struggle or a conflict between rival systems but rather different groups of the bourgeoisie and local reaction vying with each other for changes in the capitalist system, the counterrevolutionary clique in power, its ideology, and the external imperialist-revisionist patrons it would have. The Polish bourgeoisie was divided between two main tendencies: one oriented toward the revisionist East, the other toward the capitalist West. However, when they were confronted with a threat posed by a third force—the genuinely revolutionary-conscious proletariat—both revisionisms collaborated: "More than a million Polish 'communists' were 'militating' shoulder to shoulder with the counterrevolutionary forces which guided and inspired the movements of the years 1980-1981 . . . , with such rabid anticommunists and antisocialists as the Mysznicks [sic], Kuroń, Bujaks, and Wałęsas, shoulder to shoulder with the Catholic clergy."[96]

The purist Marxist analysis of Poland's crises is, paradoxically therefore, supported by evidence in this chapter. While the revisionist Communist Party managed to survive a series of political crises in Poland, it had been at some cost: each time the counterrevolution within the counterrevolution gained more freedom in its ability to organize and function, to implement economic "reforms," to establish more links with the capitalist West and with the Vatican. Dede's final conclusion was not one, however, that the present historical era appeared likely to substantiate: that only the entry of the Polish proletariat into politics as an independent force, not one under the leadership of other interests, could guarantee the restoration of a Marxist-Leninist political order.

The purist Marxist critiques presented here were neither academic treatises nor politically realistic in character, even if their analyses were deeply grounded in Marxian categories and methods. They represented views, however, that Lenin and Stalin both advanced in their time: that the only good revolution was one that could defend itself, and that class struggle had to be intensified given the two-camp nature of national and international politics. Official Marxism proved unable to defend itself in the face of critical Marxist thought, and revisionists had not sided with the orthodox camp, thereby hastening the end of communist systems. This was the important function played by critical Marxism in shaking the superstructure of the totalitarian order and, inadvertently, making it susceptible to overthrow.

Conclusion

This survey covered a variety of forms of Marxist critique: orthodox (the perspective of the ruling elite), dissident (neo-Marxist), reformist (party liberal), Marxologising (academic post-Marxist), and purist (dogmatist). While sharing Marxian terminology, its analytical framework and, perhaps most importantly, teleological concern—the restoration of or movement toward a genuine communist order—their diagnoses and ideological programs differed sharply. Although Kołakowski doubtlessly had other forms of ideology in mind than Marxism, he was right in arguing that in Eastern Europe "the main battle in the realm of ideology is to restore hope, to burst out of despair, and to combat the mendacity built into the power system as an instrument of rendering people hopeless and mentally disarmed."[97] All types of Marxist critiques sought this effect.

At the same time we should put Polish Marxist critique into proper perspective. Generally it was not as systematic, creative, innovative, or captivating as forms found elsewhere in the region. Dissident and reformist Marxism was undistinguished (even if some of its proponents were), the Marxologizers were inventive but largely irrelevant, while the purists were anachronistic. Poland did not produce a Lukács this century, or a Budapest school, or even an isolated Bahro. When compared to Western intellectual debates about Marxism (which involved such formidable scholars as Jon Elster, John Roemer, Gerald Cohen, Louis Althusser and the French structuralists, Göran Therborn, and the Frankfurt school), the Polish debate paled into insignificance. What the Poles did better than virtually anyone else was political practice. In this way, collective action distinguished the Polish Left more than its theoretical elaboration or exegesis did.

Finally, not only from the practical but also from the theoretical perspective, perhaps this is the way it had to be if Poland was to pioneer the road to a posttotalitarian society. Ideological self-destruction may have been a necessary condition anticipated by Marx himself in the search for a higher social formation. The sociologist Jorge Larrain claimed that ideology of any kind had no place in Marx's utopian vision: "Inasmuch as Marx defines ideology in relation to social contradictions, there can be no doubt that overcoming contradiction in practice entails the disappearance of ideology."[98] Associated with this, in Larrain's argumentation, was that

> thought is inevitably ideological in so far as it stems from a contradictory society. A non-ideological consciousness is only possible in the future but not in the present. On the other hand, the future can be conceived not as a mere negation, but as the realization and fulfillment of elements already existent in present society by means of a conscious practice of transformation. This practice and its comprehension justifies the claim to a non-ideological thought in the present.[99]

Many observers of Polish politics would agree that efforts undertaken by various politicized groups represented, over the decades, the conscious practice of transforming Polish society. The diverse examples of Marxist critique we examined focused on the struggle to eliminate contradictions in state and society, yet by failing to resolve them and even dramatizing them, they foreshadowed the breakdown of ideological patterns that such contradictions fostered. In Poland today hardly any political group claims it is ideological, and there is a real opportunity for the emergence of nonideological thought, at least for a time and in spite of lingering social contradictions.

Notes

1. Raymond Taras, *Ideology in a Socialist State* (Cambridge: Cambridge University Press, 1984).
2. Leszek Kołakowski, *Main Currents of Marxism*, 3 vols. (Oxford: Oxford University Press, 1978), vol. 3, pp. 473-74.
3. For a representative work from the Budapest school, see Ferenc Fehér, Agnes Heller, and György Markus, *Dictatorship Over Needs* (New York: St. Martin's Press, 1983).
4. Vladimir Kusin, *The Intellectual Origins of the Prague Spring* (Cambridge: Cambridge University Press, 1971).
5. Gerson Sher, *Praxis* (Bloomington, IN: Indiana University Press, 1977).
6. Kołakowski's earlier work, when juxtaposed with his ideas in *Main Currents of Marxism*, traces his intellectual evolution away from Marxism. See his *Toward a Marxist Humanism* (New York: Grove Press, 1968), and his *Marxism and Beyond* (London: Pall Mall Press, 1968).
7. Jacek Kuroń and Karol Modzelewski, *An Open Letter to the Party* (London: Socialist Review Publishing Co., 1968), 8.
8. Ibid., 14.
9. Ibid.
10. Jürgen Habermas, *Toward a Rational Society* (Boston: Beacon Press, 1971); Nicos Poulantzas, *Political Power and Social Classes* (London: New Left Books, 1973).
11. Kuroń and Modzelewski, *An Open Letter*, 52.

12. Ibid., 67-68.
13. Jacek Kuroń, *Wiara i Wina* (Warsaw: Nowa, 1990), 197-208.
14. Ibid.
15. For a history of KOR, see Jan Józef Lipski, *KOR: Workers' Defense Committee in Poland 1976-1981* (Berkeley: University of California Press, 1985). Zielonka, too, takes up the story of Poland's political ideas from the birth of KOR. See Jan Zielonka, *Political Ideas in Contemporary Poland* (Aldershot: Avebury, 1989).
16. See Peter Raina, *Political Opposition in Poland 1954-1977* (London: Poets and Painters Press, 1978).
17. Kołakowski, *Main Currents of Marxism*, 466.
18. Adam Michnik, *The Church, The Left: A Dialogue* (Chicago: University of Chicago Press, 1990).
19. Adam Michnik, *Letters from Prison and Other Essays* (Berkeley: University of California Press, 1985), 135-48.
20. Ibid.
21. Ibid.
22. For more on these notions and Michnik's role, see Jeffrey Goldfarb, *Beyond Glasnost: The Post-Totalitarian Mind* (Chicago: University of Chicago Press, 1989), 142-57.
23. Stanisław Starski, *Class Struggle in Classless Poland* (Boston: South End Press, 1982), 36.
24. Ibid., 209.
25. Ibid., 188.
26. Ibid.
27. Ibid.
28. Jadwiga Staniszkis, *Poland's Self-Limiting Revolution* (Princeton, NJ: Princeton University Press, 1984), 30. See also her "Ideology in Poland," *Telos*, no. 66 (Winter 1985-86).
29. Staniszkis, *Poland's Self-Limiting Revolution*, 35.
30. Ibid., 58.
31. Ibid., 113.
32. Ibid.
33. Ibid., 168.
34. Ibid., 206-7.
35. Ibid., 338.
36. For a survey of Eastern Europe, see Thomas Oleszczuk, "Dissident Marxism in Eastern Europe," *World Politics* 34, no. 4 (July 1982): 527-47.
37. Adam Michnik, "The New Evolutionism," *Survey* 22, nos. 3-4 (Summer-Autumn 1976): 268-69.
38. Goldfarb, *Beyond Glasnost*, 175, 177.
39. Andrzej Friszke, "Rewizjoniści," *Tygodnik Solidarność*, no. 18(55), 29 September 1989. I need to add a further reservation: the issue of economic reformism is also so vast that it merits separate treatment. Interested readers can consult works written by Oskar Lange, Michał Kalecki, Edward Lipiński, and Włodzimierz Brus. I have considered reformist explanations about the specific issue of postwar Polish crises in "Official Etiologies of Polish Crises," *Soviet Studies* 38, no. 1 (January 1986): 53-68.
40. Stanisław Ossowski, *Class Structure and Social Consciousness* (London: Routledge and Kegan Paul, 1979).

41. "Experience and the Future" Discussion Group, *Poland Today: The State of the Republic* (Armonk, NY: M.E. Sharpe, 1981), 57-58.

42. Ibid., 60.

43. Ibid., 101.

44. Ibid., 184.

45. For abbreviated English versions, see Leopold Labedz, "The Kubiak Report," *Survey* 26, no. 3 (Summer 1982): 87-107; Ewa Celt, "Party Documents Assessed," *Radio Free Europe Research*, SR/7, 7 April 1984.

46. Goldfarb, *Beyond Glasnost*, 177.

47. Władysław Bieńkowski, *Theory and Reality* (London: Allison and Busby, 1981), 12 (emphasis in the original). For his critique of Yugoslav socialist self-management as propounded by Mihailo Marković, see pp. 268-73.

48. Ibid., 31.

49. Ibid., 164.

50. Ibid., 167.

51. Ibid., 201.

52. Ibid., 187.

53. Ibid., 210.

54. Ibid., 191.

55. In keeping with the period in which Schaff was writing, I do not introduce gender-neutral terms to his style. Interestingly, the issue of whether "man was the starting point of Marxism" was heatedly debated in Chinese philosophical circles in the 1980s. See Stuart Schram, *Ideology and Policy in China since the Third Plenum, 1978-1984* (London: University of London, School of Oriental and African Studies, 1984).

56. Adam Schaff, *A Philosophy of Man* (New York: Delta Books, 1963), 87.

57. Ibid., 121.

58. Ibid., 104.

59. Ibid., 97.

60. Adam Schaff, *Marxism and the Human Individual* (New York: McGraw-Hill, 1970), 171. For a later study concerned with the individual in the information age, see Adam Schaff, *Dokąd Prowadzi Droga?* (Szczecin: Wydawnictwo Glob, 1988).

61. Schaff, *Marxism*, 181.

62. Ibid., 108.

63. Ibid., 254.

64. Ibid., 131.

65. Bronisław Baczko, *Les Imaginaires Sociaux* (Paris: Payot, 1984), 135-37. For his study on utopia, see idem, *Utopian Lights* (New York: Paragon House, 1989).

66. Baczko, *Les Imaginaires Sociaux*, 203.

67. Ibid., 233.

68. Zbigniew Pełczyński, ed., *The State and Civil Society: Studies in Hegel's Political Philosophy* (Cambridge: Cambridge University Press, 1980); also Neil Harding, ed., *The State in Socialist Society* (Albany, NY: State University of New York Press, 1984).

69. Jerzy Wiatr, "Współczesne treści marksowskiej teorii państwa," *Studia Socjologiczne*, 1985, nos. 3-4 (98-99): 47-65. See also his English-language article, "The Sources of Crises," *Polish Perspectives* 25, no. 4 (Autumn 1982): 18-21. For a not altogether unsympathetic portrait of Wiatr by a dissident Marxist, see Kuroń, *Wiara i Wina*, 36-37

70. Wiatr, "Współczesne treści," 61-62.

71. Jacques Rupnik, "Dissent in Poland, 1968-78," in *Opposition in Eastern Europe*, ed. Rudolf Tökes (Baltimore: Johns Hopkins University Press, 1979), 103.

72. Wiatr, "Współczesne treści," 65.

73. Piotr Sztomka, "Marxism, Functionalism, and Systems-Approach," in *Polish Essays in the Methodology of the Social Sciences*, ed. Jerzy Wiatr (Dordrecht, Holland: D. Reidel Publishing Company, 1979), 154.

74. See Raymond Taras, "Polish Sociology and the Base–Superstructure Debate," *Philosophy of the Social Sciences* 13, no. 3 (September 1983): 307-24.

75. Leszek Nowak, *Property and Power* (Dordrecht, Holland: D. Reidel Publishing Company, 1983), xxv.

76. Ibid., 15.

77. Ibid., 30.

78. Ibid., 69.

79. Ibid., 88.

80. Ibid., 117.

81. Ibid., 183.

82. Ibid., 226.

83. Ibid.

84. Ibid., 377-78.

85. Zygmunt Bauman, *Memories of Class* (London: Routledge and Kegan Paul, 1982), 180.

86. Ibid., 193.

87. Ibid.

88. Ibid., 197.

89. Alain Touraine, *The Voice and the Eye* (Cambridge: Cambridge University Press, 1981). See also Touraine et al., *Solidarité* (Paris: Fayard, 1982).

90. Zygmunt Bauman, "Poland: On Its Own," *Telos*, no. 79 (Spring 1989): 55 (emphasis in the original).

91. This account is based largely on Staniszkis, *Poland's Self-Limiting Revolution*, 69-70, 176-80, 192-93, and on mimeographed documents obtained by the author from Sigma's offices.

92. Spiro Dede, *The Counter-Revolution Within the Counter-Revolution* (Tirana: 8 Nentori Publishing House, 1983), 9-10.

93. Ibid., 37.

94. Ibid., 43.

95. Ibid., 229.

96. Ibid., 178.

97. Leszek Kołakowski, "Ideology in Eastern Europe," in *East Central Europe: Yesterday, Today, Tomorrow*, ed. Milorad Drachkovitch (Stanford: Hoover Institution Press, 1982), 50.

98. Jorge Larrain, *Marxism and Ideology* (Atlantic Highlands, NJ: Humanities Press, 1983), 228.

99. Ibid., 219.

6

Marxist Critique and Czechoslovak Reform

James Satterwhite

Background

The years 1956-68 witnessed a revival of creative activity in all spheres of life in Czechoslovakia, most notably in the arts. Artists were breaking away from the dictates of "socialist realism" and were beginning to explore new modes of creativity. The task of giving theoretical expression to this revival was facilitated by the emergence of a new understanding of man and his creative role in the world—an understanding that was exceptionally well represented by two Marxist philosophers, Karel Kosík and Ivan Sviták.

The year 1956 was of particular importance for all of the countries of Eastern Europe. Stalin had died three years earlier, and in 1956 his successor, Nikita Khrushchev, denounced Stalin and Stalinism at the Twentieth Congress of the Communist Party of the Soviet Union. Khrushchev's speech sent a shock wave rippling throughout Eastern Europe, giving momentum to a trend that had begun at the death of Stalin—a disorientation and a questioning of basic assumptions. This shock was less immediately felt in Czechoslovakia than in Poland or Hungary; it was the revelation that the 1952 Slánský trials were not what they had been represented to be that most undermined belief in the Communist Party and the system in Czechoslovakia.[1] But throughout the region, an undercurrent of searching for new, more authentic values began.

In Czechoslovakia this search began quietly. It took the form of a desire to gain more flexibility in everyday endeavors—that is, less interference by the party. But the party was still firmly in control in Czechoslovakia and was determined not to participate in the "de-Stalinization" campaign any more than it had to. It resisted any and all questioning of its position and was unwilling to give up any part of its prerogatives in any sphere. Nevertheless, the shock wave set off by Khrushchev's speech had done its damage, and the questioning process that had begun could not be halted.

In the legal profession, the revelation that the Slánský trials were a sham prompted a rethinking of the problem of the nature and role of law in a socialist society.[2] In the sphere of art and culture, the guidelines of "socialist realism" were being more and more loosely interpreted under pressure from artists. Part of the artists' discontent focused on the dictate of "socialist realism" that art play a socially edifying role and build up the character of the new socialist society. In 1956–57 a series of debates on philosophy and culture took place in the newspaper *Literární noviny*. Karel Kosík and Ivan Sviták played a prominent role in the debates, which attracted a good deal of attention and were instrumental in raising public awareness of some of the questions being asked in intellectual circles.[3]

As time passed and more and more people became involved in this process, it became clear that philosophy had a major role to play in providing a coherent expression for the often inchoate strivings in all areas of society, especially in the artistic and cultural sphere. Kosík's and Sviták's tasks were different, but complementary. In his study of the Czech Radical Democrats of the nineteenth century, Kosík sought a clue to understanding the nature of Czech culture. Kosík published *The Dialectics of the Concrete* in 1963. It partook of varied currents of philosophical thought yet transformed them into something genuinely new, and something that was authentically Marxist as well.[4] In *Dialectics of the Concrete* Kosík followed the pattern set by all serious West European Marxist scholars as well as those in Eastern Europe who were committed to a serious study of Marx—as opposed to apologetics—and drew on the main currents of European thought, such as existentialism and phenomenology. He could not have failed to take into account the writings of György Lukács as part of the intellectual heritage of twentieth-century Marxism and most certainly was familiar with the work of his contemporaries in the field worthy of note, whether from Eastern Europe or the West. This is in particular contrast to the approach taken by Soviet Marxist scholars and those connected with the more orthodox view in Eastern Europe, who were characterized by their refusal to come to terms with other philosophical currents in any serious or open fashion. Existentialism and phenomenology were of particular significance to Kosík because they center on man and his activity.[5]

Kosík was important in systematically providing a theoretical foundation for this new understanding of man. Ivan Sviták's contribution lay in building on this foundation with his interest in a philosophy of aesthetics and culture. Sviták's major book in this regard was *The Human Meaning of Culture,* a series of essays written from the early 1950s to 1968 dealing with the problematics of philosophy and art.[6] Sviták helped to formulate a new theory of the role of art based on the concept of man's creative activity in the world, or praxis. His particular genius lay in the way he managed to interpret the new philosophical concepts for the realm of culture. As a philosopher of culture he looks at works of art for their significance and meaning in terms of their portrayal and understanding of man and his world and man in the world.

Sviták's essays were quite controversial, and his career reflects this. He was a member of the Institute of Philosophy in Prague, where his lectures and writings were banned as early as 1955. Almost all of his subsequent writings were originally lectures not allowed into print or confiscated as soon as they were published. During the years 1955 through 1964 he was suspended from and then reappointed to the institute three times.[7] In 1964 he was expelled from the institute and from the party, though the institute's party organization itself refused to fire him, as did the next higher level in the party hierarchy. Nevertheless, in 1966 he lectured at Charles University as part of a series on "Philosophical Anthropology" which was later suspended by the dean of the Philosophic Faculty. During 1968, Sviták came into his own again. His essays and lectures were published in book form, and he participated in public discussions in various newspapers over the course of that year. He completed another book, a collection of some of his newspaper articles and essays under the title *Head Against the Wall,* but the invasion prevented its publication.[8]

Kosík and Sviták both took an active part in the public debate, starting at the time of the Fourth Congress of the Union of Czechoslovak Writers in 1967, that culminated in the Prague Spring. This philosophical activity put into words and gave a theoretical base to the new direction in art and culture. In a certain sense art and philosophy were developing in a parallel fashion. Both strained against the same limits, but philosophy was by its very nature given the task of formulating and expressing the problem theoretically as well.

Foundations of the Philosophical Critique

The new Marxist philosophy of man was at once a philosophical reaction against the Stalinist-inspired orthodoxy and the theoretical expression of and foundation for the struggle. Without it, artists might not have become as self-conscious or have had a clearly formulated idea of why and in whose name they were carrying on their struggle against "socialist realism." A new vision of reality was emerging, one diametrically opposed to the prevailing orthodoxy, and it fell to philosophy to give voice to this vision.

That orthodoxy, Marxism-Leninism, stressed that man was conditioned—indeed, determined—by the social and historical forces arising from the mode of production and production relations: "Man is an ensemble of social relations," said Marx.[9] Only the working class, given its historical position in the declining capitalist system, had the possibility of being the agent of real change, but even this possibility was as much a result of the "objective forces" at work as it was of conscious effort. Hence Lenin's view that it was up to the vanguard of the working class to effect change; this view, too, sprang from a perception of necessity, of historical and social forces at work.[10] The vanguard of the working class, the Communist Party, was to be the interpreter of historical necessity for the working class and for society at large. Under Stalin this role was reduced to a set of formulas. In the end the whole conception served as a legitimation of the party's activities, whatever they were, and thus as a legitimizing ideology for power. The individual had no part to play, for he was simply a product of "objective" social relations over which he had no control. In epistemology this had its corollary in Lenin's concept of "reflection" (*otrazhenie*): there is an "objective reality," and man's task is to mirror it in his understanding as closely as possible and act on this basis.[11] It was from this way of conceiving reality and, by inference, the party's role in society that the whole concept of the socially edifying role of the arts and philosophy arose, and it was against this perception of reality that philosophy and the arts were waging their struggle.

Kosík wrote in an essay on Hegel that philosophy is no longer philosophy if it refuses to investigate reality in its full breadth, in all its internal interconnections, and gives up its revolutionary, critical nature in favor of apologetics (thinking that it is thereby defending socialism and serving the party) or views development from the perspective of the given moment and a given need instead of examining it dialectically in terms of overall development and the contradiction inherent in any given historical situation.[12] According to Kosík, philosophy during the time of the "personality cult," instead of basing itself on arguments to be verified, rather based itself on "revealed truth," to be believed. Philosophy must investigate reality not as a mere collection of atoms that have nothing to do with one another but as an "internally differentiated, developing whole. . . . Why did we view socialism before in a one-sided, dried-out way and only now are coming to conceive of it as a contradictory but rich, concrete, specific reality that grows out of our activity, our work, and our creation?"[13]

"What is philosophy?" Svítak asked, and did it even exist in Czechoslovakia at that time? Beginning his essay "The Art of Philosophy" with this question, Sviták conveyed a certain conception of philosophy and implied that it was, in fact, nonexistent in the Czechoslovak social setting. Philosophy—defined here, for the sake of simplicity, as "love of wisdom"—had become "an aversion to thinking . . . , a system of dogmas based on an emotional bias in favor of socialism."[14] How had this happened? Sviták's answer is both a mockery and a challenge: Isn't social consciousness determined by social relationships? In a discussion of the leading role of the party, Sviták suggests that the nonexistence of philosophy in the true sense of the word was a result of party interference in matters pertaining to science and art—a situation brought about, in Sviták's view, by a misconception as to what the party's "leading" role entailed. "It was thought," Sviták writes, "that party spirit meant serving the interests of the party. . . . We are now abandoning this practice forever and beginning to make room for real theoretical work, laying emphasis on the significance of theory as creative work, as the discovery of the new.''[15] The party had no right to demand something of philosophy that would mean the negation of philosophy, Sviták was saying. To be sure, the party could ask that philosophers disseminate and popularize the basic tenets of Marxist-Leninist philosophy, but this was not the sole function of philosophy, nor should it be subordinated, like the economy, to the rulings of the party. Theory is responsible only to reality, to facts, Sviták said, and not to the party. Thus, the battle was joined.

"Praxis" and Human Creative Activity

The concept of praxis is the key to an understanding of the whole of Marxist humanism. It was the crucial idea in the struggle between orthodox Marxism-Leninism and the Communist Party on the one hand and the proponents of the new Marxist philosophy on the other. The new understanding of praxis as man's creative mode of living in the world, as the recognition that reality is a *human* reality with man as its *subject,* and not only its *object,* is fundamentally different from the Marxist-Leninist view of the world. Man makes his social reality and can therefore change it. For Kosík, "concrete totality" is reality in the form of a structured, developing, and self-creating whole. Any arbitrary or chance fact may be comprehended as part of this whole.[16] True reality is not evident for all to see but must be uncovered, sought out. This is the significance of the dialectics; it is dialectically that the distinction between appearances and actual facts is made. Appearances, or "pseudoconcreteness," the world of everyday phenomena that has been taken by most as the "real" world, has to be transcended if the true nature of reality is to be comprehended.

It is through praxis that we arrive at reality, because we perceive it as our product. Nature can be changed and transformed, but social reality can be changed in a *revolutionary* way, because this reality is man's creation.[17] Reality is not meaningful for man unless he makes it a "thing for himself." It is in this context that the destruction of pseudoconcreteness means revolutionary human praxis, the "humanization" of man. Critical dialectical thought goes beyond appearances to the "thing in itself." Every individual has a part in the creation of his truth, as a sociohistorical being.[18]

In Soviet Marxism the term "ideology" had traditionally been used exclusively with reference to the bourgeoisie, meaning in essence "bourgeois ideology." Later it took on a more general connotation and "class ideology" became a popular concept, the implication being that ideology was bad only when it lacked the proper class base, i.e., anywhere except under socialism.[19] By linking the fetishization in everyday consciousness with what he called "philosophical ideology," Kosík cut through this subterfuge and restored something of the original Marxian content to the understanding of ideology. He drew an important distinction between philosophy and ideology. [20] Kosík defined ideology as the way of thinking that views "categories, ideas, conceptions as something independent, self-sufficient and absolute," rather than as a "theoretical expression of reality," of the "forms of being, the conditions of existence" of reality itself.[21]

Kosík saw three distinct and historically separate definitions of "ideology" at work yet notes that they had become confused. Marx (in the beginning) and Engels (throughout his life) used the term to mean "false consciousness" in the sense of an upside-down, illusory conception of reality"; for Lenin ideology was a "reflection of class conditions in the minds of people"; Stalin in his *Short Course* "talked about the ideological and theoretical principles of the party as if he were talking about two separate matters."[22] Kosík himself favors the first definition, at least by usage. He speaks of Marxism as the philosophical expression of the ideas of the working class, but never refers to this as ideology and always is careful to indicate that while Marxism may encompass this element, it is not only the reflection of working-class ideas of conditions.

Kosík also examines the nature of reason and criticizes the idea that reason is only the "independent reason of the Cartesian man," which in Kosík's view depends on the "reason" of society: the "transcendental" reason of society takes the form of transcendental "regularities," which man fails to see as springing from the social activity of human beings. "Reason" and science thus concern themselves only with discovering these "regularities" and, in the name of freedom as "recognition of necessity," submitting themselves to them.[23] Reason is not, according to Kosík, the "recognition of necessity"—historical, social, or otherwise. "Reason is the reason of an individual, but the reasonableness of his reason is not that it is without presuppositions, but that it *includes reasonable premises as the premises of its own reasonableness*. Therefore, there is no direct evidence of Cartesian reason; reason is communicated by rationally apportioned and rationally created (social) reality."[24] In June 1967 Kosík gave a short speech at the Fourth Congress of Czechoslovak Writers. It was titled "Reason and Conscience" and took its inspiration from Jan Hus. In it Kosík developed the distinction between "false reason" and "true reason" and applied that explicitly to the Czech situation.

According to Kosík, the materialist thesis holding that man is an ensemble of social conditions, without adding that he is the *subject* of these conditions, makes of the "interpretation" of something only a choice as to whether to put the *real* subject into the empty space or to put a mystified subject there—a mystified "ideology" or a mystified "we" for whom the authentic individual is transformed into an instrument or a mask.[25] This is a scarcely veiled attack on what Kosík refers to as "vulgar materialism," meaning the Stalinist legacy in orthodox Marxism-Leninism.

In order for man to be able to discern the truth about alienated "everydayness" and transcend nonauthenticity, he must put a certain distance between it and himself, rid it of all familiarity, and apply a certain "force" to it. Here

Kosík sets the stage for the first real mention of the role art has to play in the world, and what he says on the subject is in diametrical opposition to the concept of "socialist realism." "Into what kind of 'forced' metaphor and likenesses must man and his world be transformed for people to see their own real face and recognize their own real world? It seems to us that one of the main principles of modern art, poetry and theater, graphic arts and film is the 'violence' on everyday reality, the destruction of pseudoconcreteness."[26]

Here Kosík was implicitly making a very strong political statement even though his writing is by no means polemical and the task he set for himself was purely philosophical. "Philosophy" has to be understood here as Kosík would have it understood—not as a "dead" discipline but as a living inquiry into the nature of reality and man's place in it. If reality is both expressed in and hidden by the phenomena of our everyday lives, how do we penetrate it? Through philosophy and through art. "It is for this reason that art and philosophy have such a specific meaning for man and such a special mission. Art and philosophy are in their functions vitally important, irreplaceable, and nothing can be substituted for them. Rousseau would have said that they are inalienable."[27]

This understanding of art and philosophy is distinguished from "sociologism," which replaces the idea of "social being" with "conditions": conditions change and the "human subject" merely reacts to these changes—as if the "subject were merely a collection of mental capabilities. . . . Man becomes a photograph of conditions."[28] He learns to recognize and represent them artistically or scientifically. The stress in Kosík is in marked contrast to Lenin's theory of "reflection."[29] For Kosík, man perceives the world and makes it his own through this sensual activity, but he "discovers the meaning [sense] of things by *creating* a human meaning for them."[30] Otherwise they are indeed "senseless."

Kosík argued that reality could not be conceived of only in terms of "economic factors," viewed as if they were independent of the whole of society and of man and his activity. The true materialist view holds that the "social whole (socioeconomic formation) is created and constituted by the economic structure. The economic structure creates the unity and interdependence of all spheres of social life."[31] Here the economic structure is conceived of by Kosík as "the ensemble of social relations which people occupy in production and in relation to the means of production."[32]

The concept of class struggle is bound up closely with the understanding of the economic structure, but just as "structure" became "factor" in the orthodox Soviet Marxist approach, the whole idea of class struggle was also drastically simplified. From this approach came such ideas as the "class character" of a work of philosophy or of art. Kosík's understanding of "economic structure" undermined this view, clearing the way for any new understanding of culture and artistic activity:

> Marxism is not a mechanical materialism that would reduce social knowledge, philosophy, and art to "economic conditions," and whose analytical activity would then depend on discovering the earthly core of spiritual formations. On the contrary, materialist dialectics shows how the historical subject concretely promises relevant ideas and a complete set of forms of knowledge. Knowledge is not reduced to conditions, but the process by which *the concrete subject produces and reproduces social reality, and in it is simultaneously produced and reproduced,* is brought to the center of attention.[33]

Art, like praxis, makes an indelible mark on all human activity. "Every work of art has a twofold character in an indivisible unity: it is an expression of reality but simultaneously produces reality—the reality that does not exist outside of the work of art or before it but precisely only in the work of art.[34] Thus Shakespeare's plays are not simply "an artistic reflection of the class struggle in the era of primary accumulation."[35] What is expected of art? Must the "reality" that art at once reflects and makes be that which men *assume* to be reality? "How does man know," Kosík asks, "whether this reality that man assumes he knows is not in fact only his *idea* of reality?"[36] But "a work of art is not a representation of *ideas* about reality. As a work of art and as art it represents *reality* and simultaneously *produces* reality, the reality of beauty and art."[37]

To sum up, Kosík and Sviták were key figures in the attempt to redefine philosophy and culture in Czechoslovakia between 1956 and 1968. Their contributions had an enormous impact on all facets of the reform movement, for it was through culture that the issue of political reform was first addressed, but "it remained to be seen whether this authentic Marxism . . . would give birth to more than criticism of the status quo and a pyrotechnical display of ideas dispersed against the dark sky of reality."[38]

Critical Marxism and the "Prague Spring"

In 1968 both Kosík and Sviták became caught up in the tempo of political change, and both tried through their writing and other activity to influence the course of events. In a series of articles entitled "Our Present Crisis," which appeared in *Literární noviny* in the spring of 1968,[39] it is evident that Kosík's thinking changed considerably over the twelve-year period in question and that the practical consequences he drew from his thought became progressively more radical.[40] Kosík begins by saying that what is at question is a search for meaning in the life of the society, the nation. In this search the opportunity exists for transforming society and replacing old forms with new, but also for merely changing one set of circumstances for another, equally bad.[41] In light of Kosík's central idea, praxis, of man as subject as well as object, with the capacity to change social conditions in a radical and revolutionary way, the article was a call to action.

Kosík again attacks "the leading role of the party." "Politicians talk of the 'leading role of the party'," Kosík wrote, "by which they mean . . . the ruling position of a power group."[42] He proposes that "instead of the old obsolete alliance of Party and non-Party members, a new political alliance of communists, socialists, democrats and other citizens might be created. Socialist democracy is either an all-inclusive democracy, or it is not democracy at all."[43] Here Kosík has moved beyond "democratic centralism," even if the party was accorded a "guiding" function, as some had suggested.[44]

Kosík's call for a new alliance, a new "socialist democracy," implied the necessity for social conditions that would allow man to be creative, hence an end to party interference in philosophy and art and the view that their function was to serve the party in its role as edifier of the masses. "Edification" had become "mystification," the creation of a false consciousness. For Kosík, it was precisely the nature of art and philosophy to *de*-mystify, to cut through appearances to the essence of phenomena.

Kosík summed up his view in an interview with Antonin Liehm on the topic of Czechoslovak culture during the period from 1956 to 1968.

> There is another question which intrigues me; namely, why our culture proved so effective, so vital. There was a definite cross-fertilization between literature, art, and philosophy, so that we can truly speak of culture in the broadest sense of the word. . . . There was a particular cultural "common denominator" which emerged during the last few years and which manifested itself especially clearly in our cinema. . . . The fundamental reality of Czech culture hinged on the question: "What is Man?" That is the political, critical, revolutionary essence. . . . The real fundamental polemic of our culture lay in the fact that against the official—one might say "reigning"—concept of Man, it put forth an entirely different concept of its own.[45]

Kosík goes on to explain the "official" concept of man. It is

> a concept of man implicit in the regime's political, economic, and moral functioning, one which was, at the same time, mass-produced by the regime because it required precisely this sort of human being. . . . In dealing with the question "What is Man?" culture naturally formulated its answer quite differently. While the official view saw human characteristics in terms of Man's limits, emptiness, simplicity and lack of dynamism, Czech culture emphasized Man as a complex creature, continually alive, elastic, striving to overcome conflicts, a being irreducible to a single dimension.[46]

Kosík also put forward the contention that Stalinism was not a distortion of socialism but a "full realization of an entirely different conception of socialism."[47] This conception rested on a fundamentally different view of man. Stalinism is characterized by:

> The conception of history as necessity unfolding with the inevitability of natural, scientific law; the self-justification of socialism as both necessary and a manipulable unit; the reduction of dialectics to a few elementary features; the perception of truth as a utilitarian tool—the sum of these ideological presuppositions shows us the source from which the well-known Stalinist period originated.[48]

Kosík saw the significance of the "Prague Spring" and the whole era leading up to it as challenging those involved to a thoroughgoing reexamination of some of its underlying assumptions, both philosophical and in terms of the "social, political, and economic functioning of socialism; that is, of the socialist working model."[49] This was the task Kosík set himself, and one that he fulfilled to an extraordinary degree in *Dialectics of the Concrete*.[50] And it was exactly what Kosík was calling for in his interview with Liehm: a systematic reformulation of the most fundamental philosophical assumptions of socialism, based on a radically new view of man and his world. If the Phoenix was rising from its ashes, this was due at least in part to Karel Kosík. Ivan Sviták, in a sense, served as a bridge between the systematic thinking of Kosík and the realm of art and culture, but he was not simply an interpreter for Kosík. The thought of both men sprang from a common source, the new conception of man which was then emerging in East European Marxist philosophy.

It will be instructive to examine some of the ways in which ideas developed by Kosík and Sviták found expression in 1968—in the official reform program as well as in dissident voices, for in the Prague Spring two movements began to fuse. One of these was outside the party and had been slowly building since 1956. The other was within the party and had taken shape toward the end of 1967, resulting in the ouster of party first secretary Antonín Novotný. From January of 1968 onward the reform movement within the party gained momentum, and under the pressure of circumstances the two movements began to converge. This is not the place to discuss these circumstances; that has been done elsewhere. What is of interest here is to analyze the official program of reform for ideas that can be traced to concepts developed in the Marxist critique of the existing order.

Marxist Critique and Czechoslovak Reform

The best place to begin is with the April 1968 "Action Program" of the Czechoslovak Communist Party. The program was a comprehensive statement of the party's position on reform. It was criticized by many people outside the party for not going far enough, but it is significant for how far it actually did go.

Alexandr Dubček had proclaimed his goal to be "socialism with a human face," and he called the "Action Program" a "first step toward a new democratic model of socialist society."[51] His words recall the discussion of "models of socialism" used by the early reform thinkers to differentiate between the new approach to Marxism and the Marxist-Leninist orthodoxy. In "Our Present Crisis," Kosík had called for socialist democracy, making explicit what had been understood in *Dialectics of the Concrete* and even in his writings from 1957-58. As recently as two weeks before the promulgation of the "Action Program," Sviták, in a speech at Charles University, made a point of distinguishing between "democratization" and "democracy," warning that the former did not necessarily ensure that the latter would be realized.[52]

The official and nonparty approaches to the question of democratic socialism converged also in the person of Zdeněk Mlynář. His 1964 work *State and Man* had been a milestone in the debate on political reform. In that work he had spoken out "in favor of 'a man who is not alienated from himself, a master of truly equal opportunities for a constant development of his creative and active human substance.' This kind of formulation is directly reminiscent of Kosík's *Dialectics of the Concrete,* and the Kafka discussions of 1963."[53]

Following the Thirteenth Party Congress in June 1966, Mlynář headed a team charged by the congress with preparing political reform. He later summarized this process in an article in *Nová mysl,* the party's theoretical journal, where he explicitly called for a "pluralistic socialist system." Rather than a multiparty system, Mlynář proposed a widening of the purview of the National Front (or the restoration of its original intent).[54] This proposal was incorporated into the "Action Program."

The "Action Program" spoke of "the insufficient development of socialist democracy within the Party, an unfavorable atmosphere for the promotion of activity, the silencing of or even suppression of criticism. . . . Using and unifying the manifold interests of social groups and individuals calls for the elaboration and implementation of a new political system in our lives, a new model of socialist democracy." The vehicle for this was to be the National Front, "the political expression of the many-sided interests of the society,"[55] and its role is discussed at length in the program. The discussion of democratization included both democratization of the society and intraparty democracy: "The party realizes that a deeper democracy will not take hold in this society if democratic principles are not consistently applied in the internal life and work of the party and among communists."[56]

The "Action Program's" statement that "socialism . . . must provide for a greater degree of self-fulfillment" recalls Kosík's remarks of 1957 that socialism should give meaning to the everyday lives of people and enable them to realize their longings for a full life of feeling.[57] But the "Action Program" most clearly echoes the ideas of Kosík and Sviták in its discussion of culture. One whole section of the program is on the "Humanistic Mission of Culture." It explicitly renounced "administrative and bureaucratic methods of implementing cultural policy" and stressed that "it is necessary to overcome a narrow understanding of the social and human function of culture and art, overestimation of their ideological and political role and underestimation of their basic general cultural and aesthetic tasks in the transformation of man and his world."[58]

To be sure, the statement was qualified by a call for those active in art and culture to cooperate in the "formation and responsible, independent implementation of the policy of the Party," though the word "independent" leaves open some room for maneuver. This qualification is a good example of the tension inherent in the "Action Program" between efforts at reform and attempts to keep the pace of the reform under control. This same tension is evident in the discussion of the National Front, where it is not clear whether the "leading role of the party" was indeed to be changed. Still, "the phraseology of the program was perhaps less significant than the fact that a document existed to which party leaders at lower levels and reform spokesmen could refer in advocating innovative measures."[59] Both the fact and the phraseology owed much to the critical writings of Kosík and Sviták. Some of the ambiguities regarding the specifics of political reform that were evident in the "Action Program" were clarified and made policy in the Draft Statutes of the Party of 10 August 1968. In these statutes the rights of the minority within the party on any given issue were safeguarded and indeed extended far beyond the hitherto-existing "democratic centralism."[60]

These events prompted the Soviet Union to intervene to put an end to the process of reform in Czechoslovakia. Sviták was in Vienna on vacation at the time of the Soviet invasion and chose not to return to Czechoslovakia. He subsequently emigrated to the United States, where he now teaches philosophy at Chico State University in California. Kosík, on the other hand, took part in the extraordinary Fourteenth Congress of the Czechoslovak Communist Party, held secretly soon after the Soviet invasion. There he was elected to the Central Committee of the party. When he would not support the campaign for "normalization" (i.e., returning things to the way they had been before the Prague Spring, and even before the cultural revival of the 1960s), Kosík was expelled from the party and from all of his positions. He was not allowed to teach or to publish, and his writings were banned.[61] He spent some time under house arrest in 1969, during which time his research notes and manuscripts were confiscated, only to be returned later after an international outcry (the manuscripts were said to include a lengthy work on Heidegger). Although not active politically, he still came under official attack.[62] Kosík continues to live in Prague. A collection of his essays has been published in translation in Yugoslavia and is currently being prepared for publication in English in the United States. The fact that this is taking place now is testimony to the lasting impact Kosík has had and to the vital part he played in the Czechoslovak reform movement. Anyone who wishes to understand the dynamics of reform in postwar Eastern Europe must understand the role critical intellectuals such as Kosík and Sviták played in this process.

Critical Marxism, "Charter 77," and "Civic Forum"

Although most of what had been achieved was reversed in a formal sense after 1968, the ideas had become a part of Czechoslovak life. They were carried further by the Charter 77 movement. This movement was named after a declaration issued on 1 January 1977 which pointed out the discrepancies between the realities of life in Czechoslovakia and the provisions of the "Final Act" of the 1975 Helsinki Conference on Security and Cooperation in Europe dealing with "Respect for human rights and basic freedoms, including those of thought, conscience, religion and creed," which Czechoslovakia had signed and which formally became part of Czechoslovak law in 1976.[63] Though certain aspects of that movement remind one more of the period of the late 1950s, there is one crucial difference in terms of the practical issues addressed. In the late 1950s aspiring reformers had been struggling toward a new theoretical expression of hitherto inchoate ideas. In 1977 they had behind them years of gradual development of reformist ideas as well as the experience of the Prague Spring and the "normalization" that followed. Charter 77 reiterated some of the points made by the early proponents of "socialist legality," applying the lessons learned and moving beyond them in an innovative way.

One participant in that movement, Miroslav Kusý, has observed that the Charter movement "appeared on the political scene at a time of ideological resignation, political apathy and moral nihilism."[64] By 1976 the regime had succeeded in the program of political "normalization" and even seemed to be regaining some sort of international acceptance. "It was into this idyll that Charter 77 exploded like a bomb. It damaged the regime's new-found renown and knocked down the façade of socialist consolidation it had worked so hard to erect."[65] Although initially the populace reacted with some skepticism, the regime had no doubts that the Charter represented a threat. The Chartists wanted "*only* to call things by their real names," but "consistently calling things by their proper names means pulling away the entire ideological façade of real socialism, taking down the scenery and then removing the masks in this pantomime about the achievement of paradise on earth." [66] This is precisely what Kosík was talking about when he said that the role of art and philosophy was to "demystify, to cut through appearances to the essence of phenomena."

The second major demand of the Charter 77 movement, for the legal order under socialism to occupy the same place that it occupied in a pluralist democracy, harks back to the discussion of "socialist democracy" in Kosík's "Our Present Crisis" as well as in the "Action Program." The real issue was the destruction of the system of "real socialism." As Kusý characterizes it, "real socialism" was absurd, and Chartism was "a particular (and in its own way, an absurd) reaction to these conditions." [67]

> The absurdity of this reaction is distinguished by a certain degree of unalloyed Švejkism. The Good Soldier began to take the Dual Monarchy seriously at a time when that attitude had gone out of fashion once and for all. . . . But what is Švejkian about the Charter? The Charter takes the regime's declarations and proclamations seriously, something that neither the regime nor the nation does. [68]

This interpretation of the Charter movement by one of its participants recalls an earlier discussion of Švejk by Kosík, in an essay entitled "Hašek and Kafka." Here is what Kosík had to say about Švejk:

> If Švejk appears as an idiot at certain times and at other times shrewd, if he acts as a servant at times and at other times as a rebel (while always remaining what he is), his changeability, elusiveness and "mystery" are consequences of the fact that he is part of a system which is based on the general premise that people pretend that they are what they are not. . . . One of the characteristics of the system is regular and mutual mystification. . . . People in it who take things seriously and literally reveal the absurdity of the system and at the same time make themselves absurd and laughable.[69]

The resemblance is not accidental. Kusý, like Kosík, who had written twenty years before,was engaged in a critique of the world of "real socialism" in the name of an alternative vision of socialism. In Kusý's words, "the original moral appeal of the Charter had the potential of forcing the regime back on its own proclaimed principles." If this attempt did not succeed, then the Charter movement could always adopt "those principles itself by forming an alternative socialist program, an alternative socialist movement. . . . From its inception, socialism was accepted as a given framework for Charter activity, even though it was understood as a socialism deformed by real socialism; . . . the pseudo-socialism of the regime and an alternative socialist program that embodies the moral and political aims of the Charter."[70]

Although the signatories of Charter 77 were repressed by the Czechoslovak government, the movement did not die out.

> As the Prague Spring contributed to the treasure box of reformist experience in the entire Soviet bloc, so did the Charter take a little further the oppositional stream which had been evolving along similar lines in the Soviet Union and, after the 1976 price riots in Poland. . . . Charter 77 may yet come to be regarded as a

factor which set in motion the internationalization of opposition in Eastern Europe.[71]

The ideals of the Charter came to be associated particularly closely with the person of Václav Havel, playwright and chief spokesman for the movement. Havel's essays, like his plays (which were not allowed to be staged in Czechoslovakia), distilled the insights of the "dissidents" into a crystal-clear form. In this activity Havel was acting in accordance with the primary role of a "dissident" as described by Czech philosopher Martin Hybler in an essay entitled "Dissident Thinking," contained in a recent collection edited by Havel: "the absolutely most important task of dissident thought is to restore the word in its communicative and nominative functions, which in large part have been distorted or completely annulled." [72] Thus did the Czech writer Milan Kundera describe Havel's writing: "The real sense of Havel's plays from the 1960s was precisely the *radical demystification* of the vocabulary."[73] This was simultaneously a demystification of the social and political world as well.

Many of the ideas Havel developed in his essays are reminiscent of those expressed by Kosík and Sviták. Again, the similarity is not accidental. Although Havel was not writing from a self-consciously critical Marxist perspective, his agenda was the same: to create, through a process of demystification, a sphere free of distortion in which humans could live their lives. This kinship is particularly evident in the discussion of art in Havel's essay "Six Asides about Culture," written in 1984, but it permeates all of his writing. In this essay Havel writes:

> "If we start with the proposition that art constitutes a distinctive way of seeking truth—truth in the broadest sense of the word, that is, chiefly the truth of the artist's inner experience—then there is only one art, whose sole criterion is the power, the authenticity, the revelatory insight, the courage and suggestiveness with which it seeks its truth, or perhaps the urgency and profundity of this truth."[74]

Havel continues:

> the degree to which politics is present or absent has no connection with the power of artistic truth. . . . The essence of the conflict [between regime and artist], that is, is not a confrontation between two ideologies . . . but a clash between an anonymous, soulless, immobile and paralyzing ("entropic") power, and life, humanity, being and its mystery. The counterpart of power in this conflict is not an alternative political idea but the autonomous, free humanity of man and with it necessarily also art—precisely as art!—as one of the most important expressions of this autonomous humanity.[75]

The continuity with Kosík and Sviták is evident here, as it is in Havel's discussion of ideology in his most important and best-known essay, "The Power of the Powerless," which recalls Kosík's *Dialectics of the Concrete*. In the same essay Havel raises another theme central to all "dissident" thought—the creation of an "autonomous humanity," and with it, the nature of power. The two are intertwined in Havel's thinking, as signaled by the title of the essay. It is precisely those without political power who are able to create this sphere of autonomous life by setting up what Havel refers to as "parallel structures." These structures, he says, "represent the most articulated expressions so far of 'living within the truth.'. . . For what else are parallel structures than an area where a different life can be lived, a life that is in harmony with its own aims and which in turn structures itself in harmony with those aims?" [76] Later in the same essay he writes: "any existential revolution should provide hope of a moral reconstitution of society, which means a radical renewal of the relationship of human beings to what I have called the 'human order,' which no political order can replace." [77] Havel here explores many of the issues raised by Kosík in a round-table discussion on Machiavelli in 1969. [78]

Havel further explores this theme in his essay "Politics and Conscience." Here he takes on the wider issue of rationalism in the modern world and in modern politics—a preoccupation of Havel's to which Kundera alluded when he observed Havel's fascination with "the absurdity of the rational." [79] Havel wrote: "system, ideology and *apparat* have deprived humans—rulers as well as ruled—of their conscience, of their common sense and natural speech and thereby, of their actual humanity. States grow ever more machine-like, men are transformed into statistical choruses of voters, producers, consumers, patients, tourists or soldiers." [80]

Although the thrust of Havel's critique was aimed at the societies of Eastern Europe in general and Czechoslovakia specifically, he was also aware (as Kosík had been earlier) that this deformed rationality was the problem of modern society per se. In fact, Western Europe had "provided and frequently forced on the world all that today has become the basis of such power: natural science, rationalism, scientism, the industrial revolution, and also revolution as such, as a fanatical abstraction." [81] Western countries, he believed, should not make the error of failing to understand that "totalitarian systems" are ultimately "a convex mirror of all modern civilization and a harsh, perhaps final call for a global recasting of that civilization's self-understanding." [82] The same forces are at work in all modern societies, although in the West "people are manipulated in ways that are infinitely more subtle than the brutal methods used in the post-totalitarian societies." [83]

Through the efforts of Havel and others, the legacy of Charter 77 was incorporated into the new movement known as "Civic Forum," which in November and December of 1989 transformed the Czechoslovak political scene. Václav Havel is now president of the republic, and it appears that "real socialism" has been swept out. Havel presented his vision of what this society might look like in 1978, in the concluding sections of "The Power of the Powerless"; he now has the opportunity and the challenge of embodying this vision.

In Czechoslovakia today, Marxist discourse no longer serves directly as the currency for reform thought. For most people Marxism was discredited through its use as the official ideology. This does not mean, however, that the same concerns are not there or that the work that was done by the critical Marxist intellectuals of the 1960s has lost validity. If Czechoslovakia continues to move toward some kind of social democracy, as seems likely, then the legacy of the Prague Spring will retain its currency. In any case, the contributions of Marxist thinkers such as Kosík and Sviták remain part of the intellectual heritage of the country.

Notes

1. Party general secretary Rudolf Slánský and ten other party officials were hanged in 1952 after a show trial. See Vladimir V. Kusín, *The Intellectual Origins of the Prague Spring* (Cambridge: Cambridge University Press, 1971), 29.

2. Ibid., 28.

3. *Literární noviny*, 21 April, 17 November, 1 December, 29 December 1956; 9 March and 16 March 1957; 4 January 1958.

4. Kusín, 37.

5. J.M. Bocheński, "The Great Split," *Studies in Soviet Thought* 8, no. 1 (March 1968).

6. Ivan Sviták, *Lidský smysl kultury* [The Human Meaning of Culture] (Prague: Č.S. Spisovatel, 1968).

7. Sviták managed to contribute to a wide variety of conferences, including one in Dubrovnik, Yugoslavia, in 1963, on "Man Today." In the same year he participated in a conference at Liblice on the theory of literature and another devoted to the works of Franz Kafka. Kafka's work was extremely important to the Czech intellectuals because it raised the question of alienation and for its relevance to what Kosík called "the artistic destruction of pseudoconcreteness," or fetishized reality. See the collection of papers from the Kafka conference, Vědecká konference věnovana dilu Franze Kafky, *Franz Kafka* (Liblice, 27-28 May 1963). See also the chapter on "Alienation" in Kusín, *Intellectual Origins*, for a discussion of Kafka's significance to the reform movement.

8. It was subsequently published in the United States as *The Czechoslovak Experiment: 1968-69* (New York: Columbia University Press, 1971).

9. See Marx's preface to *A Contribution to the Critique of Political Economy*, in Robert C. Tucker, *The Marx-Engels Reader* (New York: Norton, 1972), 3.

10. V.I. Lenin, "The State and Revolution," *Collected Works*, 4th ed., trans. and ed. S. Spresyan and Jim Riordan, vol. 25 (Moscow: Progress Publishers, 1964), 404.

11. V.I. Lenin, *Materialism and Empirio-Criticism* (New York: International Publishers, 1927; New World Paperbacks, 1970), 128. "Matter is a philosophical category designating the objective reality which is given to man by his sensations, and which is copied, photographed and reflected by our sensations, while existing independently of them." See all the discussion under "Does Objective Truth Exist?" 120-29; also, the reader is referred to L. Kołakowski, "Karl Marx and the Classical Definition of Truth,"

Toward a Marxist Humanism (New York: Grove Press, 1968).
12. Karel Kosík, "Hegel a naše doba," *Literární noviny* 17 (November 1956).
13. Ibid.
14. Ivan Sviták, *Man and His World: A Marxian View* (New York: Dell, Delta, 1970), 6.
15. Ibid., 8-9.
16. Karel Kosík, *Dialektika konkrétního* [Dialectics of the Concrete] (Prague: ČSAV, 1966), 29.
17. Ibid., 17. Emphasis in original.
18. Ibid.
19. J. Sedlák discusses this point briefly in his essay, "Filosofie a dnešek," *Literární noviny*, 1 December 1956.
20. Kusín, 51.
21. Kosík, "Hegel a naše doba."
22. Karel Kosík, "Přeludy a socialismus," *Literární noviny*, 9 and 16 March 1957.
23. Kosík, *Dialektika konkrétního*, 69.
24. Ibid.
25. Ibid., 58.
26. Ibid., 60.
27. Ibid., 88.
28. Ibid., 91.
29. See Lenin, *Materialism and Empirio-Criticism*, 128. See also Kołakowski, "Karl Marx and the Classical Definition of Truth."
30. Kosík, *Dialektika konkrétního*, 91.
31. Ibid., 78.
32. Ibid., 79.
33. Ibid., 84.
34. Ibid., 87.
35. Ibid., 88.
36. Ibid., 87.
37. Ibid.
38. Kusín, 49.
39. Karel Kosík, "Naše nynější krize," *Literární listy* 7-12 (April-May 1968), as translated in A. Oxley et al., *Czechoslovakia: The Party and the People* (London: Penguin, 1973), 48, 110, 160.
40. In 1957 Kosík was quite bold for his time, but he was still calling for a return to the Leninist norms of "democratic centralism," although he stressed that a "return to Lenin" could not mean a return to the pre-Stalinist days. He saw Marxism as a "philosophy of everyday life and the everyday relations of people," in addition to being a "theory of historical growth or a strategy for class struggles." Therefore, if socialism did not give meaning to the everyday lives of people and enable them to realize their longings for a full life of feeling, something was wrong. See Kosík, "Přeludy a socialismus." See also idem, "Třídy a realná struktura společnosti," *Filosofický časopis* 5 (1968).
41. Oxley et al., 48.
42. Ibid., 112.
43. Ibid., 162.

44. See the debate on "The Role of the Party" in G. Golan, *The Czechoslovak Reform Movement* (Cambridge: Cambridge University Press, 1971), 163-176.

45. J. Liehm, *The Politics of Culture* (New York: Grove Press, 1967), 397.

46. Ibid., 398.

47. Ibid., 404.

48. Ibid.

49. Ibid., 405.

50. "Key cultural developments, such as the emergence of a 'new wave' in the Czechoslovak cinema, the dispute about the recognition and understanding of Franz Kafka, the emergence and flourishing of modern Czechoslovak drama and of a modern concept of the theatre, the renewed public and private debates about the 'Czech question,' the discussions about the essence of a Socialist "cultural policy," and eventually the Fourth Congress of the Writers' Union, were in direct or indirect relation to philosophy understood as Kosík's 'concrete totality.' " See Kusín, 53.

51. *Nová mysl* 5 (1968): 537, quoted in H. Gordon Skilling, *Czechoslovakia's Interrupted Revolution* (Princeton: Princeton University Press, 1976), 217-18.

52. Ivan Sviták, "Hlavou proti zdi" [Head against the Wall]; English version in *Winter in Prague*, ed. Robin Remington (Cambridge, MA: MIT Press, 1969), 73-80.

53. Kusín, 108, quoting Zdeněk Mlynář, *Stát a člověk* [State and Man] (Prague: Svobodné slovo, 1964), 18.

54. Kusín, 111-12, citing Mlynář, "K demokratické politické organizaci společnosti," *Nová mysl* 5 (1968). Kusín also cites Mlynář's article "Právo, právní věda a náš politický vývoj," *Právník* 5 (1968).

55. "The Action Program of the Communist Party of Czechoslovakia," published originally in *Rude pravo*, 10 April 1968, translation in Remington, *Winter in Prague*. Quotes from pp. 93, 97, and 99.

56. Ibid., 100.

57. "Action Program," 104; Kosík, "Přeludy a socialismus."

58. "Action Program," 131.

59. Skilling, 222.

60. Remington, 264.

61. Kosík, Jiří Lederer and Rudolf Slánský, Jr. filed suit at the end of 1972 against the police who searched their homes and confiscated books and manuscripts there. Kosík also wrote an open letter to Jean-Paul Sartre, and it was this letter and Sartre's reply in the same form that provoked the international outcry. Kusín, *From Dubček to Charter 77* (New York: St. Martin's Press, 1978), 283-84.

62. Lubomir Sochor, entry on Karel Kosík in Robert Gorman, *Biographical Dictionary of Neo-Marxism* (Westport, CT: Greenwood Press, 1986), 240.

63. The text of this part of the Helsinki "Final Act" is given in *Since the Prague Spring: The Continuing Struggle for Human Rights in Czechoslovakia*, ed. Hans-Peter Riese and trans. from the German by Eugen Loebl (New York: Random House, 1979), 9-10.

64. Miroslav Kusý, "Chartism and 'Real Socialism',," in Václav Havel, et al., *The Power of the Powerless: Citizens against the State in Central-Eastern Europe*, ed. John Keane (Armonk, NY: M.E. Sharpe, 1985), 166.

65. Ibid., 166-67.

66. Ibid., 170.

67. Ibid., 152.

68. Ibid., 171-72.

69. Karel Kosík, "Hašek and Kafka," in *Cross Currents* 2 (Ann Arbor, MI): 134 (translation of "Hašek a Kafka neboli groteskní svět," in *Plamen* 6 [1963]).

70. Kusý, 176-77.

71. Kusín, *From Dubček to Charter 77*, 321.

72. Martin Hybler, "Disidentní myšlení" [Dissident Thinking], in *Hostina*, ed. Václav Havel (Toronto: Sixty-Eight Publishers, 1989), 63.

73. Milan Kundera, "Candide Had to Be Destroyed," in *Václav Havel: Living in Truth*, ed. Jan Vladislav (London and Boston: Faber and Faber, 1986), 261.

74. Václav Havel, "Six Asides about Culture," in *Václav Havel: Living in Truth*, 131.

75. Ibid., 133.

76. Havel, "The Power of the Powerless," in Havel et al., *The Power of the Powerless*, 79.

77. Ibid., 92.

78. Karel Kosík, "Machiavelli a machiavellismus," *Plamen* 2, 3 (1969). Forthcoming in English translation in the collection of essays by Kosík edited by this author entitled *Dialectics of Crisis*, translated from the Serbo-Croatian edition by Julianne Clarke.

79. Kundera, "Candide Had to Be Destroyed," 260.

80. Havel, "Politics and Conscience," in *Václav Havel: Living in Truth*, 144.

81. Ibid., 145.

82. Ibid.

83. Havel, "The Power of the Powerless," 91.

7

From Arrogance to Irrelevance
Avatars of Marxism in Romania

Vladimir Tismaneanu

To say that in contemporary Romania Marxism is an obsolete, unappealing ideology is to state the obvious. Nicolae Ceauşescu's more than two decades of rule succeeded in compromising the very name of Marxist political and social doctrine. In true Stalinist style, Ceauşescu, the "Genius of the Carpathians," postured as an oracle of revolutionary theory, a new "coryphaeus of science," and his zealous court ideologues spared no praising epithet in their efforts to contribute to his ludicrous legend. The few serious Romanian Marxist (or neo-Marxist, i.e., anti-Stalinist) thinkers were forced to emigrate or to engage in research on topics tolerated by an increasingly idiosyncratic power.

A regime that trumpeted *urbi et orbi* its commitment to the values of "socialist humanism" ironically became, toward the end of its existence, totally hostile to any thoroughgoing Marxist analysis. In Romanian philosophical and sociological discussions of the ongoing search for a "socialism with a human face," there were none of the echoes that characterized the Soviet Union after Gorbachev's rise to power. On the contrary, the official propaganda went out of its way to deny the need to rethink Marxism's theoretical heritage. On the one hand, the Romanian Communist Party (RCP) championed a conservative, Honecker-style approach to attempts at regenerating or revising the revolutionary theory. On the other hand, through its unabashed support for the reemergence of rightist, ethnocentric groups and formations, Ceauşescu and his clique made a mockery of their own passionate plea for the preservation of the "sacred values" of historical materialism and internationalism. For example, in the early 1980s when philosopher Henri Wald tried to publish a Marxist Reader, which included young Marx's early philosophical inquiries, he encountered opposition from precisely those official "instructors" who were supposed to watch over the ideological purity of Romanian cultural life.

What, therefore, was the ideological nature of the Ceauşescu regime? Was it a left-of-center, Leninist political order, or was it a populist, authoritarian, neo-feudal organization in which Marxism was destined to become what it indeed became: an instrument for the legitimation of a power-thirsty, usurping clan whose only allegiance was to its privileges and power? In a study published several years ago, Romanian mathematician and dissident Mihai Botez identified the dramatic ambivalence of Marxist doctrine under the circumstances of a "National-Stalinist" regime. He pointed out that in the symbolic economy of Ceauşescuism, with its emphasis on national communitarian and solidarist values, "organic national cohesion," and crypto-Fascist xenophobia, Marxism could acquire a seditious value. According to Botez, this explained both the tolerance shown by the powers-that-be toward the metaphysical investigations of the circle surrounding Constantin Noica, the author of an ontology rooted in the Hegelian and Heideggerian traditions, and the irritation shown toward any attempt at an uninhibited development of the Marxist discourse.[1]

The *agitprop* experts feared that the negative, emancipatory dimension of Hegelian-Marxism would inspire a critique of the status quo in the name of its professed values. Romanian students and intellectuals would not have adopted necessarily the Marxian paradigm as an explanation for the systemic dysfunctions they were confronting; however, some of the Marxist concepts might have served a function in an oppositional approach in the same way they had been used in Yugoslavia with the *Praxis* group, in Hungary with the Budapest school, and in Poland with Leszek Kołakowski, Jacek Kuroń, and Karol Modzelewski.

In Romania, unfortunately, most undertakings aimed at revivifying Marxism did not transcend the limits of the merely academic exercise. The ruling power did its best to encourage and reward the most hackneyed, the most trite, and the most opportunistic exercises in vulgar interpretations of historical materialism. Conformity and voluntary mental emasculation were the premises for successful careers in the field of humanities. "Scientific socialism" limited itself to exalting the tremendous victories of Romanian communists and to echoing Ceauşescu's primitive, extremely anachronistic sermons on revolution, party, nation, and state. However, there was real drama, or even tragedy, for Marxism in Romania.

The fate of revolutionary thought paralleled the general degradation and decay of the pseudorevolutionary praxis. As Matei Calinescu has observed, many cultural phenomena in Romania have evolved under the sign of pseudo, and Marxism, especially in its last avatars, made no exceptions.[2] It is, therefore, important to examine the premises of this dereliction, the main causes and circumstances that made the described phenomenon possible.

After all, some of the most prominent Marxist thinkers of this century (Lucien Goldmann, Georges Haupt) started their intellectual curricula in Romania; and since Romania embarked between 1965 and 1970 on a peculiar version of

Eurocommunism *avant la lettre*, an exercise in intellectual history is both fascinating and justified.

The Traditions of Romanian Marxism

First and foremost, there have been impressive theoretical contributions by the patriarch of Romanian socialism, Constantin Dobrogeanu-Gherea (Solomon Katz). The author of a number of sociological studies and books, the Russian-Jewish-born Gherea played an immense role in the modernization of Romanian social thought.[3] He provided an articulate body of ideas to the still embryonic Romanian socialist movement. An exponent of a positivistic version of Marxism, which resembled the ideas advocated by Karl Kautsky and the German Social Democracy, Gherea came to oppose the Bolshevik revolution and its insurrectionary–terrorist logic. He resented violence and advocated a gradualist, evolutionary transition to socialism. Romanian communists would later brand his ideas as "Menshevik," and Gherea would became the nemesis of the hotheaded, sectarian Romanian supporters of the Comintern. Among those supporters was Dobrogeanu-Gherea's son, Alexandru, a founding member of the Romanian Communist Party who was executed during the Great Purge in the Soviet Union. Nevertheless, evolutionary Marxism found a remarkable development in a different direction in the works of Serban Voinea, one of Gherea's most gifted disciples.

The creation of the RCP in 1921 ushered in a new stage of Romanian Marxism. For the communists, Marxist theory was simply an instrument in the hands of the history-designated elite. Like their peers in Czechoslovakia, Hungary, and Poland, Romanian communists did nothing to advance their understanding of historical and economic situations beyond the Comintern-revealed dogma. The party propaganda blindly parroted the Stalinist theses. The RCP doctrinaires failed to offer any original reflection on the country's social and ethnic tensions, let alone an analysis of the growing popular and rabidly racist far-right radicalism symbolized by the Iron Guard.

The RCP, an ecstatic community of zealots whose unique purpose was to promote Moscow-dictated decisions, including the suicidal (for the Romanian communists) thesis regarding the "imperialist" character of post-Trianon Romania, vegetated at the periphery of Romanian political life. At a historical juncture when nationalism was increasingly contagious and when the revisionist powers (including the Soviet Union) were questioning Romania's borders, the communists advocated the country's dismemberment and the cession of the provinces of Bessarabia and Bukovina to the USSR. It is, therefore, no wonder that the party could never become part of, or at least influence, mainstream political and cultural debates during its clandestine period. With its fewer than one thousand members paralyzed in millennial fixations and alienated from both the intelligentsia and the working class, the RCP engaged in the self-defeating strategy of unlimited and unconditional support for any Soviet initiative and claim, including the territorial ones.

A strong sense of discipline combined with fear of excommunication prevented even those communist intellectuals who might have realized the scope of the Stalinist disaster to raise their voices against the Moscow show trials and the Comintern's absurd strategy in the 1930s. The obsessional hostility to Social Democracy further aggravated the RCP's political and cultural isolation.

The political culture of Romanian communism was thus marked from its very outset by fanaticism, sectarianism, and an eternal, pervasive inferiority complex.[4] Although dominated by intellectuals, the party elite displayed unbounded contempt for theoretical creativity and originality. Instead of trying to connect itself to the domestic socialist tradition, the RCP made breaking any continuity almost a title of honor, defining itself as "a new type of party," the history-appointed avant-garde of a mythological Romanian proletariat. Later, Ceauşescu would deplore this narcissistic self-centeredness, but he never admitted that the source, the ultimate cause of the RCP's marginality lay in its militaristic, inherently antidemocratic structure as well as in its fateful subordination to the Leninist tenets—the precondition for its slavish subservience to the Moscow center.[5]

Generations of Romanian communists, like their peers in other East and Central European countries, found consolation for their estrangement from the national communities in their belonging to a supranational army of crusaders for the "glowing tomorrows." As long as they felt that they were acting in accordance with the "objective laws of history," it mattered little to them that their party was widely seen as a Trojan horse.

For understanding the characteristics of this political culture, with its neuroses, excruciating factious strifes, and unreconstructed illusions, it is useful to examine the biographies of Lucreţiu Pătrăşcanu and Miron Constantinescu, two of the very few true Marxist intellectuals who played important roles in the history of Romanian communism. Awareness of these individuals' personal histories is even more important now that Romanian intellectuals, still traumatized by the incredible hardships and humiliations imposed by the Ceauşescu regime, seem unwilling to engage in dispassionate discussion of the fate of Marxism in their country. By simply discarding left-wing radicalism as a mental and political aberration, they cannot exorcise the demons they so colorfully denounce in staunch anticommunist pamphlets. For in Romania, as has been the case in Germany, assuming the past, in all its gravity and complexity, is the only path toward a much-desired national reconciliation.

The Quest for a Romanian Marxism

Lucreţiu Pătrăşcanu was born in 1900 to a respected intellectual family. He joined leftist circles as a teenager, was expelled from high school for subversive activities, and went to Germany (Leipzig) where he earned degrees in both law and economy. From the very beginning, he was under the spell of Marcel Pauker (Luximin), a young revolutionary well known both for his theory of the hunger strike and for his marriage to Ana Pauker, a major personality of the tiny Romanian communist enclave. While in Germany, Pătrășcanu became acquainted with the feverish polemics between Trotskyists and Stalinists and decided to join the Stalinist faction. Once back in Romania, equipped with an unusual political and economic culture, the young lawyer soon became one of the most prominent figures within the minuscule RCP.

In a political collectivity plagued with endemic sectarianism, unable to transcend its peripheral status and establish its credentials as a representative of the social group whose interests it claimed to defend, Pătrășcanu was definitely a *rara avis*. Under less abnormal conditions, he undoubtedly would have been destined to a brilliant career. Known within the party under the *nom de guerre* Andrei, Pătrășcanu was soon elected a Central Committee member. After 1936, he served as a liaison between the home leadership and the exiled Moscow center. When the Stalinist purge of the Comintern reached its murderous apogee, in 1937–38, Pătrășcanu was the RCP delegate to the International's Executive Committee. Simultaneously, under the pseudonym Ion C. Ion, he published a number of historical and sociological articles in *Viata Romanească* (Romanian Life), one of the most respected democratic magazines in interwar Romania.

Pătrășcanu was one of the very few RCP militants knowledgeable of the Trotskyist opposition's publications, able to grasp the reasoning of Nikolai Bukharin's contributions to the development of Marxist sociology, and interested in the dialectical subtleties of such works as György Lukács's *History and Class Consciousness* and Karl Korsch's *Marxism and Philosophy*. In a way, he is almost a Romanian counterpart to Gramsci, whose doubts about the Stalinist charges against the Bolshevik "Old Guard" led to a silent, albeit unambiguous, break with his fellow communists. But from the very beginning, unlike Gramsci, Pătrășcanu had been educated in the cult of the party, completely internalized the Leninist logic of who–whom (*kto–kogo*), and could not pass the threshold between the realm of faith and that of doubt. He did not afford himself the luxury of questioning the official Stalinist demonology and frantically endorsed the frozen certainties of what Kostas Papaioannou once called *l'idéologie froide*. Marxism functioned for him as a moral drug, a balm supposed to cure all mental torments. It offered the ultimate answers to any metaphysical anguish. Attached to Marcel Pauker, a close friend of Elena Filipovici, the RCP secretary executed in 1937, and of militants like Imre Aladar, David Fabian, and Eugen Rozvany (all exterminated in the Soviet Union), Pătrășcanu closed his eyes to the appalling evidence of Stalinist repressions. For him, as for Lukács or Ernst Bloch, the assassination of his political and ideological comrades was a personal tragedy, not an invitation to a drastic reassessment of an increasingly enslaving creed.

Although a first-rate intellectual, a thinker often able to recognize nuances and avoid catechistic simplifications, Pătrăşcanu was incapable of assuming the uncomfortable truths about the movement he so selflessly served. Even more disturbing, at the moment when others (Arthur Koestler, Anton Ciliga, Boris Souvarine, Panait Istrati, Manes Sperber, and André Gide) were exposing the moral decay of the Bolshevik revolution and the transformation of the Comintern into an appendage of Stalin's policy of terror, Pătrăşcanu remained mute and continued to worship a political system in which he saw the triumph of historical rationality. To the extent that he surrendered his personal freedom to the benefit of an allegedly universal idea, Pătrăşcanu was a Hegelian. He refused to admit there was a risk that this sacrosanct value could be perverted and its fanatics could be cynically manipulated for the most inhuman purposes.[6]

Although intellectually prepared to take measure of the catastrophic events in which he was involved, Pătrăşcanu behaved like so many other sleepwalkers who refused to admit the criminal nature of Stalinism. In the aftermath of the Soviet occupation of Romania in 1944, he supported, in full awareness, the implementation of the communist system in that country. As a minister of justice he played an important (and nefarious) role in the destruction of the legal system and the establishment of a "class-based," actually communist controlled, justice. Until the very end of his life, when he was executed as a foreign agent in April 1954, Pătrăşcanu nourished illusions regarding the humanist potential of "genuine Marxism." It was precisely this nostalgia for the generous promise of an original, unadulterated, and pristine Marxism that motivated an intellectual of Pătrăşcanu's caliber to continue as a member of a political group dominated by ideological illiterates and hypocritical timeservers. He may well have despised them—and it is likely that he did indeed hold people like Gheorghe Gheorghiu-Dej and his associates in deep contempt—but he never publicized his feelings.

For a true communist, and especially for an intellectual, any attack on the party's monolithic unity was a mortal sin. According to people who knew him well, Pătrăşcanu was an irresistible partner in conversation, a strange blend of innocence and vanity, a doctrinaire magnetized by politics, an academic Marxist mesmerized by mass movements and revolutionary rhetoric. His book *Curente si tendinţe in filosofia romanească* (Currents and Trends in Romanian Philosophy) was written in 1945 and published in three successive editions that same year. The book, one of his notable theoretical accomplishments, paradoxically combines the Leninist reductionist criterion of *partiinost'* (party-mindedness) with a genuine respect for the facts of culture and for philosophical currents as legitimate undertakings of the human mind.[7] Philosophical idealism was for him a gnoseological error, not a criminal offense. Compared to the obscurantist schemes of Zhdanovism, imported and codified in Romania by the ruling tandem Iosif Chişinevschi–Leonte Răutu, Pătrăşcanu's works were a monument of objectivity and fair-mindedness. To be sure, his writings were often incisive, opaque to the metaphorical suggestions and symbols in the works of philosophers like Nae Ionescu, Lucian Blaga, Mircea Vulcănescu, or Constantin Noica, but his discourse was still within the parameters of the civilized polemic and mutual tolerance. In this respect, *Curente* perfectly epitomized Pătrăşcanu's mind set, the frontiers of his theoretical imagination, and a cultural-polemical behavior that was far from that which his party comrades approved.

Nevertheless, Pătrăşcanu became one of the principal actors in the historical drama of the communist takeover in Romania. A full Politburo member and the first communist member of the democratic cabinets under generals Sănătescu and Rădescu, he maintained decent relations with the leaders of the traditional parties and the monarchist circles. Continuously making the front page, representing Romania in the armistice negotiations with the Soviet Union, being one of the few RCP luminaries to enjoy nationwide prestige and intellectual authority, Pătrăşcanu may have thought that he was entitled to become the number one in his party. Possibly, it was precisely this miscalculation of the real balance of power at the RCP's top and the underestimation of Soviet apprehensions regarding his intellectual background and philosophical interests that led to his isolation and eventual political defeat.

Convinced that no one in the party ideological apparatus could better formulate the communist strategy during the 1944-45 period, when the RCP was pledging its infinite commitment to pluralist values, Pătrăşcanu went so far as to author an original blueprint for the country's evolution into a modern industrial society. His book *Problemele de baza ale României* (Romania's Basic Problems) was in many respects suggestive of a personal search for an original Romanian road to socialism. There was no talk in it about the need to establish the dictatorship of the proletariat or the "universal significance of the Soviet model." On the other hand, with his hesitation to carry the logic of his approach to a fully elaborated platform, Pătrăşcanu's vision promised, rather than embodied, an alternative to the hard-line communist strategy spelled out by Gheorghiu-Dej at the October 1945 RCP National Conference.[8] Pătrăşcanu failed to understand, or if he understood, he failed to accept, that a "program" for Romania's future had already been devised in Moscow and that the strategy of building "people's democracies" in East-Central Europe was a major priority for the Kremlin.

As a Romanian Marxist thinker, he fooled himself with the illusion that he could play an historical role in Bucharest. Stalin, Zhdanov, and Molotov needed only obedient mouthpieces, perfect instruments for the satellization of Eastern Europe. Yet, there is not enough substantiated evidence to support the hypothesis that Pătrăşcanu consciously articulated a Romanian challenge to Soviet political and theoretical hegemonism. Unlike his sociological and historical essays, his political texts were conceived in the same wooden language as the ones produced or performed by other party stalwarts in the same epoch (Gheorghiu-Dej, Ana Pauker, Miron Constantinescu). The most controversial piece, used by his enemies in the RCP Politburo, was Pătrăşcanu's speech in Cluj in November 1946, when he made clear his attachment to Romanian national values. Immediately after that discourse, Pătrăşcanu lost his Politburo seat and was viciously attacked by Gheorghiu-Dej for catering to Romanian nationalism and jeopardizing the good relations with the Hungarian ethnic minority. Needless to say, there was nothing in Pătrăşcanu's speech that would have justified these charges. But Dej and his associates took advantage of some ambiguous formulations to construct a whole "Pătrăşcanu case" in order to get rid of a dangerous rival in what eventually evolved into a fratricidal struggle for power.

The Cluj speech indeed was an appeal to national reconciliation, but only Pătrăşcanu's sworn adversaries could misconstrue it as proof of chauvinism and nationalism. Thus, it is difficult to detect in his writings of that period indications of an emerging alternative strategy rooted in national values and potentially conducive to a full-fledged "national-communist" platform similar to Gomułka's or Tito's efforts anathematized by the Cominform. It was symptomatic, however, that in spite of the absurdity of these accusations, in his notorious 1949 anti-Tito Cominform speech Gheorghiu-Dej listed Pătrăşcanu together with Rajk, Kostov, and Gomułka among the Titoist "archtraitors" infiltrated in the communist parties and planning "to sell out to the bourgeoisie the heroic conquests of the revolutionary proletariat."[9]

Pătrăşcanu's defeat in the struggle for power was directly linked to his intellectual stature: for the RCP elite nothing looked more suspicious and presumably threatening than efforts to offer personal interpretations of the country's political past and future. By writing theoretical analyses, Pătrăşcanu ignored the party's pretense to universal and unquestionable knowledge. His political, and eventually physical, liquidation was a warning addressed to all those who might have imagined that the Stalinist dogmas needed any revision or completion. Pătrăşcanu's political crushing served as a form of mental domestication and moral emasculation. For decades after his purge, Romanian Marxism did not recover and survived mostly in the degenerated form of party documents.

It was not only Pătrăşcanu's theoretical superiority that bothered Gheorghiu-Dej and Ana Pauker but also his close contacts with the national intelligentsia. For Dej, the issue was to proceed as fast and as ruthlessly as possible toward the Sovietization of Romanian culture. To implement this design, he appointed to the head of the RCP Propaganda Department the Moscow-formed, Bessarabian-born activists Iosif Chişinevschi (Roitman) and Leonte Răutu (Oigenstein). Whether it was intended or not, the years that followed were perceived by the Romanian intelligentsia as a period of cultural colonization by the Russian empire through its local agents, many but not all of whom belonged to ethnic minorities. The relationship between Dej and Pătrăşcanu summed up the basic complex of Romanian communism, i.e., the hostility and even phobia toward intellectuals, the horror of theory, and the anguish experienced in the face of any form of spontaneous cultural development. Meanwhile, the RCP ruling elite suffered from a chronic deficit of political legitimacy that was characteristic not only of Ana Pauker and Gheorghiu-Dej but also of Nicolae Ceauşescu.

As for Pătrăşcanu, his fate was sealed at the moment the Stalinist witch-hunts were set in high gear. Kept under house arrest for several years, then imprisoned and tortured, he faced the most grotesque charges. To his credit, he refused to confess, and instead of cooperating with his tormentors and engaging in self-deprecating rituals, he proudly denied all the accusations proffered against him by the Securitate-manipulated "witnesses." Pătrăşcanu was executed as a traitor and spy in April 1954. The sentence had been anticipated by a Politburo resolution adopted several days earlier. Changes were happening in the whole Soviet bloc, and the terrorist edifice bequeathed by Stalin to his successors was beginning to totter. Gheorghiu-Dej was conscious of the Moscow meetings with the leadership of the Hungarian Communist Party and the Soviet Politburo's scathing criticism of Mátyás Rákosi as well as the imposition by Moscow of Imre Nagy as Hungary's prime minister (1953-55). He realized that Pătrăşcanu could have been used by the new Soviet leadership as a candidate to replace him at the helm of the RCP. Precisely because he wanted to prevent such a denouement of the ''New Course'' in Romania, Dej preferred to act without delay and physically suppress his nemesis.

In April 1968, eager to establish his credentials as an anti-Stalinist reformer, Ceauşescu would launch a public attack against Dej's political crimes and announce Pătrăşcanu's rehabilitation. Ironically, the earthly remains of the most prominent communist victim of Romanian Stalinism were transported to the ''Monument of the Heroes of Socialism'' in the Liberty Park in Bucharest, where Gheorghiu-Dej and Ana Pauker are buried as well. Pătrăşcanu's rehabilitation was, however, only a deceptive beginning of de-Stalinization. Instead of inaugurating a soul-searching revision of the party history and dogmas, it only served to consolidate Ceauşescu's legend as an adamant opponent of Stalinist atrocities and restorer of socialist justice.

The Romanian break with Stalinism did not take place until the December 1989 revolution—then the whole institutional and symbolic infrastructure of the regime fell apart almost overnight. The anemia of the Romanian Marxist resistance to totalitarianism—in conspicuous contrast to other East European countries, with their sagas of revisionism and apostasy—resulted in the almost complete discredit of any socialist or even left-of-center ideas and programs. A religious, nationalist, and even ethnocentric revival tended to compensate for the long intellectual and moral lethargy of the previous decades. In a country where the civil society has been systematically mauled and mutilated, the new democratic, Western-oriented groups and publications now appear increasingly beleaguered.

Ideological Apparatus and Stalinist Orthodoxy

Immediately after the communist takeover, the RCP embarked on an overall Sovietization of Romanian cultural and scientific life. Russian contributions were emphatically proclaimed the most advanced in world history, Romania's past was rewritten to fit this new mythology, and the old intelligentsia was literally decimated. Many of the most important writers, philosophers, sociologists, historians, and economists were either deported to the infamous Danube–Black Sea Canal, jailed, or, in luckier cases, simply denied the right to practice their profession. A desolating and apparently inexorable anticultural tornado swept through Romanian intellectual life. As in Poland, Hungary, and Czechoslovakia, several attitudes were possible. There was, to be sure, the option of direct resistance and challenge to the cultural colonizers, but such an attitude was almost a suicidal option. There was also the possibility of simulating support for the new regime without engaging in direct collaboration. Such "simulation" could not last long, and those who favored it ended up by joining the arduous collaborationists. As for the true believers, their number in Romania was extremely small. This is why the process of converting the intelligentsia to the "New Faith," to use Czesław Miłosz's metaphor, was particularly radical and uncompromising.[10]

The two most instrumental party leaders engaged in this operation were the aforementioned Iosif Chişinevschi and Leonte Răutu. While the former was actually a professional apparatchik with a rudimentary Marxist background, the latter has been widely described as a sophisticated dialectician, a sort of Romanian version of Zhdanov or Revai (the Soviet and Hungarian cultural dictators). In fact, Răutu cynically and efficiently presided over the Zhdanovization of Romanian culture and the complete eradication of any critical temptation among Romanian intellectuals. For instance, in 1949 he instituted a real pogrom in the country's cultural institutions under the banner of the struggle against "objectivism and cosmopolitanism in social sciences." Several years later, when other communist regimes accepted a minimal ideological relaxation, Răutu further tightened the grip of the party's ideological control. Between 1956 and 1958 the fledgling attempts to launch a debate about the leadership's responsibility for the Stalinist crimes was nipped in the bud. The effects of the 1949-53 purges were felt during the so-called "thaw" period, when the Romanian intelligentsia, with very few exceptions, refrained from directly questioning the party's ideological monopoly. One should not think, however, that the shock waves of Khrushchevism did not affect the RCP and its political outlook.

The Dej team, and its principal doctrinaire Răutu, engineered a number of frame-ups whose "pedagogical" value was to deter critical intellectuals and students from engaging in free debates similar to those in Poland and Hungary. The specter of revisionism and "anarchic liberalism" was brandished, and those few who dared to open their mouths and advocate reform were expelled from the party. The most interesting case of such an attempt to launch a Romanian version of "national communism" inspired by the anti-Stalinist philosophy of the CPSU Twentieth Congress was that of Miron Constantinescu (1917-1974). His political defeat under Dej as well as his short-lived resurrection under Ceauşescu are noteworthy.

Constantinescu's involvement in the leading nucleus of Romanian communism engendered painful distortions of his creative personality. It is not idealizing his intellectual stature or his moral commitment to say that Constantinescu never abjured his Leninist credo. His career as a Marxist militant—whose background and attitudes would seem to indicate that he was, especially after 1956, a possible alternative to the ossified Stalinists headed by Gheorghiu-Dej—was filled with political torments and personal tragedies.[11]

As in Pătrăşcanu's case, Constantinescu's continual humiliation—first under Dej's rule, then after 1965 during the period of his revival—clearly expressed the permanent anti-intellectual bias of the RCP elite. No expression of doubt was permitted by the Romanian hard-liners, no hesitation was forgiven, no spark of critical interrogation was tolerated. A former student of Dimitrie Gusti, the founder of the ''Bucharest sociological school,'' Constantinescu was an avid reader of historical and economic literature. Especially after 1960, he focused on the Marxian category of Asiatic despotism and tried to use it for the interpretation of Romanian medieval history. In his research on Oriental despotism, Constantinescu was profoundly indebted to Henri H. Stahl, one of the most original Romanian thinkers and author of several path-breaking studies on the ''tributary social formation.''[12]

Through his mounting political influence, Constantinescu contributed to the renaissance of the sociological discipline after 1965, restored Stahl's professorship at the University of Bucharest, and encouraged young researchers to rethink such traditional Marxist categories as social structure (Mihail Cernea) and political praxis (Nicolae S. Dumitru). His own investigations on the sociology of alienation were strongly influenced by revisionist endeavors opposing young Marx to the prevailing *diamat* dogmas. Brought up as a Stalinist but disappointed by the ethical collapse of the Soviet system, he began to reexamine the metaphysical origins of Marxism.

Constantinescu's reading of the *Economic and Philosophical Manuscripts of 1844* and particularly the *Grundrisse* led him to reassess the contemporary, antidogmatic message of Marxist anthropology. Although he certainly remained far removed from the unsparing critique of ''real socialism'' undertaken by Leszek Kołakowski and Milovan Djilas, he was one of the very few Romanian intellectuals who broached the potentially explosive topic of ''alienation under socialism.'' His cordial polemic with Adam Schaff, the Polish philosopher, was proof of his desire to go beyond the petrified tenets of Soviet Marxism and invoke young Marx as an ally in the struggle for the renewal of socialism.

Constantinescu's thorough knowledge of the history of socialism—he had been a close friend of Georges Haupt—did not prevent him from maintaining an optimistic perspective on the future of this movement. Like Lukács, he used Émile Zola's phrase: ''L'avenir est en marche et finalement rien ne pourra l'arrêter." He obstinately refused to see the transformation of communism into what Ferenc Fehér called a modern bestiarium[13] and persevered using an abstract, unconvincing doctrinairism. Unable to envision the redemptive value of heresy, he was forced to comply with the rules of a system that, had Constantinescu abided by his own professed intellectual and ethical standards, he should have execrated.

While Ceaușescu promised a new approach to history and culture, some intellectuals, including Alexandru Ivasiuc, Nicolae Tertulian, and Ion Ianosi, tried to move away from the party orthodoxy and restore the intellectual dignity of Marxism. Ivasiuc, a writer and a former philosophy student jailed during the 1956 events, emerged after 1965 as one of the most outspoken proponents of Marxist humanism. His essays published in the pages of *România Literara* and *Contemporanul* focused on the meaning of political and philosophical radicalism and on the pressing need to recapture the emancipatory dimension of early Marxism by breaking the dogmatic constraints on the autonomy of mind. Ivasiuc used Marx to protest the reductionist and simplistic theses upholding the party's right to curb aesthetic experimentation. He died during the earthquake in March 1977 before completing a book on Marx.[14]

Nicolae Tertulian, a literary theorist and philosopher of culture, was well versed in German modern and contemporary thought. After 1965 he published illuminating essays on anti-Stalinist and even anti-Leninist Marxists. His restless writings provided young Romanians access to works by Lukács, Rosa Luxemburg, Ernst Bloch, Karl Korsch, Walter Benjamin, and the Frankfurt school. In the 1970s Tertulian was instrumental in the Romanian publication of Lukács's late philosophical works, including the *Ontology of Social Existence* and his monumental *Aesthetics*. The party, certainly irritated by Tertulian's refusal to celebrate the official dogmas, eventually forced him to emigrate to France where he teaches at the École de Hautes Études en Sciences Sociales in Paris.[15]

Less controversial than Ivasiuc and Tertulian, Ion Ianosi managed to remain a professor at the University of Bucharest and to publish an impressive number of studies on Marx, Hegel, Dostoevsky, and Thomas Mann. As the political and cultural situation in Romania worsened during the 1970s and 1980s, Ianosi took great pride in emphasizing his conviction that humanist Marxism represented the opposite of the egregious nationalist pageants engineered by the ideological apparatus.[16] Trying to survive those dark times honorably, he avoided any public denunciation of the immense imposture represented by Ceaușescu's impersonation of a "creative Marxist." On several occasions he gave in to official pressure and wrote paeans for the "great socialist achievements" and the "visionary" policy of the RCP.

Two "free-floating" Marxist thinkers who did publish their works outside Romania and who became politically and culturally prominent after the December 1989 revolution are Silviu Brucan and Pavel Campeanu. Both started their careers in the underground RCP, worked in the party and state apparatus during the first Stalinist stage, were eventually marginalized, and engaged in independent theoretical research. Neither Campeanu nor Brucan engaged in any form of apologetic celebration of Ceauşescu's alleged contributions to Marxism. In this respect they are vivid proof that one could be a Marxist in Romania without accepting full co-optation in the system. On the other hand, the fact that in their works they stopped short of an overall critical diagnosis of the Stalino-Fascism practiced by Ceauşescu indicated the limits of this autonomy.

Silviu Brucan's major interest lies in the political reforms in Soviet-style regimes. Brucan's thought evolved from a monistic, party-centered sociology of change to a more flexible interpretation of the transition to postcommmunism and the need to abandon the rusty Leninist schemes.[17] Especially after 1987, Brucan showed personal courage in criticizing Ceauşescu's disastrous course and calling for the democratization of Romania's political system.[18] After the December revolution, he was first a member of, then an adviser to the new leadership. He was forced to resign as a result of some controversial statements regarding the pace of the country's democratic opening. Although on various occasions Brucan denied the relevance of old-fashioned ideological blueprints, his mental framework is still indebted to the Marxist obsession with the dialectic of productive forces and relations.

Like Brucan's work, Pavel Campeanu's books on state socialism were published in the United States. Campeanu proposed a deterministic analysis of Stalinism as a political formation rooted in historical and economic backwardness. He implicitly considered Stalinism as a distortion of Leninism, let alone of Marxism. Unlike Brucan, Campeanu avoided any public criticism of the Ceauşescu regime and limited his "dissent" to a highly speculative version of structuralist Marxism with very little, if any, direct relevance for Romania's dismal situation.[19] After the December revolution, Campeanu joined the independent Group for Social Dialogue in Bucharest and began to publish his essays in the group's weekly, 22. But even within this group, his ideas sounded vaguely obsolete, and Campeanu has not found much of an audience for his objectivist axioms.

Less respectable and less respected than Ianosi, Brucan, or Campeanu is Radu Florian, a professor of scientific socialism at the University of Bucharest. The postrevolutionary government appointed him head of the new Institute of Political Science. In the early 1980s Florian championed the values of Eurocommunism and published a monograph on Antonio Gramsci.[20] His works, imbued with a sense of historical providentialism, offered a theoretical justification to Ceauşescu's claims about the superiority of socialism over any other political system. Florian's diatribes against Hannah Arendt, Raymond Aron, Zbigniew Brzezinski, Karl R. Popper, and other critics of Leninism were well remembered by students who boycotted his courses and asked for his resignation.

Conclusion: The Breakdown of Marxism in Romania

Marxism in Romania, as in other East European countries, died many years before the official collapse of the communist regime. For the older generations, communism represented the grammar of the country's political enslavement, a technique used by amoral cliques to establish and perpetuate their unchecked monopoly on power. For younger Romanians, Marxism was synonymous with the ludicrous showmanship and extravaganzas of the Ceaușescu era. "Scientific socialism" was enshrined as the ultimate peak of human knowledge.

For all practical purposes, the appeals of Marxism, even in its humanist version, are extinguished. Instead, there is a widespread disgust for any philosophy pledging mandatory collective happiness. Like their peers in the other East-Central European countries, Romanians look for political doctrines that protect rather than subvert the value of the individual.

Whether this twilight of Marxism is a temporary setback or irrevocable remains to be seen. At this moment, with the exception of a few nostalgics of the "Old Church," Marxist utopian radicalism is seen as inseparable from, if not directly responsible for, the calamities of the communist dictatorship. The absence of a Marxist critique of the existing conditions in Romania and the brazen appropriation of Marxist phrases by a gang of profiteers headed by a paranoid despot have resulted in the emergence of solid, and in all likelihood enduring, anti-Marxist consensus among the Romanian intelligentsia. In Romania at this moment the name of Karl Marx is a subject of irreverent derision or bitter memory.

Notes

1. See Mihai Botez, "Declinul marxismului și criza comunismului," in *AGORA* (Philadelphia) 2, no. 2 (July 1990): 77-100. For a general discussion of the tribulations of Marxism in Stalinist and post-Stalinist East European regimes, see Vladimir Tismaneanu, *The Crisis of Marxist Ideology in Eastern Europe: The Poverty of Utopia* (London and New York: Routledge, 1988). The absence of a home-grown, left-wing critique of the communist experience in Romania is correctly seen by Michael Shafir as one of the sources of the political stagnation in that country, particularly in the 1980s. See Michael Shafir, "Political Stagnation and Marxist Critique: 1968 and Beyond in Comparative East European Perspective," *British Journal of Political Science* 14, no. 4 (1984): 435-59.

2. See Matei Călinescu's intervention in the colloquium *Romania: A Case of "Dynastic" Communism* (New York: Freedom House, 1989), 73-75; for ideological decay in Ceaușescu's Romania, see Michael Shafir, "L'involution idéologique du parti communiste roumain," *Les Temps Modernes*, no. 522 (January 1990): 2-24.

3. For Gherea's paramount role in the development of the Romanian left, see Michael Shafir's illuminating analysis "'Romania's Marx' and the National Question: Constantin Dobrogeanu-Gherea," *History of Political Thought* 5, no. 2 (Summer 1984): 295-314.

4. See Vladimir Tismaneanu, "The Ambiguity of Romanian National Communism,"

Telos, no. 60 (Summer 1984): 65-79. For a comprehensive interpretation of the relationship between ideology and power in communist Romania, see Michael Shafir, *Romania: Politics, Economy and Society. Political Stagnation and Simulated Change* (Boulder, CO: Lynne Rienner, 1985), 1-106.

5. See Kenneth Jowitt's essay "Moscow 'Centre,' " *East European Politics and Societies* 1, no. 3 (Fall 1987): 296-348.

6. For the leftist fascination with Hegel and the Marxist "esoteric doctrine of wickedness," see Franz Borkenau, *World Communism: A History of the Communist International* (Ann Arbor: The University of Michigan Press, 1971), 172-75.

7. See Lucrețiu Pătrășcanu, *Curente și tendințe în filosofia românească* (Bucharest: Editura politică, 1971).

8. See Ghița Ionescu, *Communism in Romania 1944-1962* (London and New York: Oxford University Press, 1964), 151-56; Vladimir Tismaneanu, "The Tragicomedy of Romanian Communism," *East European Politics and Societies* 3, no. 2 (Spring 1989): 329-76.

9. Ionescu, *Communism in Romania*, 152.

10. See Dorin Tudoran, *Frost or Fear: Reflections on the Condition of the Romanian Intellectual* (Daphne, AL: Europa Media, 1988).

11. See Vladimir Tismaneanu, "Miron Constantinescu or the Impossible Heresy," *Survey* 28, no. 4 (Winter 1984): 175-87.

12. See Henri H. Stahl's books *Eseuri critice despre cultura populară românească* (Bucharest: Editura Minerva, 1983); *Controverse de istorie socială românească* (Bucharest: Editura științifică, 1969); *Studii de sociologie istorică* (Bucharest: Editura științifică, 1972). For the Western impact of Stahl's ideas, see Daniel Chirot, *Social Change in a Peripheral Society: The Creation of a Balkan Colony* (New York: Academic Press, 1976).

13. See Ferenc Fehér, "In the Bestiarium—A Contribution to the Cultural Anthropology of 'Real Socialism,' " in Ferenc Fehér and Agnes Heller, *Eastern Left, Western Left: Totalitarianism, Freedom and Democracy* (Atlantic Highlands, NJ: Humanities Press International, 1987), 261-78.

14. See Alexandru Ivasiuc, *Radicalitate și valoare* (Bucharest: Editura Eminescu, 1972).

15. See N. Tertulian, *Experiență, artă, gîndire* (Bucharest: Editura Cartea Românească, 1977), especially the chapters on György Lukács, Theodor W. Adorno, and Herbert Marcuse. For the interest shown by young Romanian intellectuals in "critical theory" as an alternative to the petrified version of official Marxism, see Vladimir Tismaneanu, *Noua Stingâ și Școala de la Frankfurt* (Bucharest: Editura politică, 1976) and Andrei Marga, *Herbert Marcuse: studiu critic* (Cluj: Editura Dacia, 1980).

16. See Ion Ianosi's attempt to defend the philosophical dignity of Marxism in Gabriel Liiceanu, *Epistolar* (Bucharest: Editura cartea Românească, 1987), 253-99.

17. See Silviu Brucan, *World Socialism at the Crossroads: An Insider's View* (New York: Praeger, 1987).

18. See Vladimir Tismaneanu, "La révolte de la vieille garde," *Les Temps Modernes*, no. 522 (January 1990): 25-41.

19. See Felipe Garcia Casals (Campeanu's pseudonym), *The Syncretic Society* (Armonk, NY: M.E. Sharpe, 1980) and Pavel Campeanu, *The Origins of Stalinism: From Leninist Revolution to Stalinist Society* (Armonk, NY: M.E. Sharpe, 1986). For insight on

Campeanu's theoretical effort, see Steve Sampson's review of his book on the origins of Stalinism in *Telos*, no. 70 (Winter 1986-87): 193-201.

20. See Radu Florian, *Antonio Gramsci: Un marxist contemporan* (Bucharest: Editura politică, 1982). In 1968, when Marxist revisionist philosophers in East-Central Europe were trying to "resubjectivize" Marxism and assert the centrality of human freedom in all political actions and situations, Florian advocated a strictly deterministic and ultimately dogmatic vision of "historical progress." See Radu Florian, *Sensul istoriei* (Bucharest: Editura politică, 1968). As the official line hardened after 1971, Florian conveniently renounced any critical stance and offered theoretical support to Ceaușescu's rudimentary outlook. See his book *Întroducere în teoria marxistă a determinismului social* (Bucharest: Editura științifică și enciclopedică, 1979).

8

Bulgaria

From Critique to Civil Society?

Mark Baskin

Throughout the summer of 1990, in front of the tomb of Georgi Dmitrov in downtown Sofia stood a broken-down old Moskvich dubbed the "dustbin of history." On it were pasted pictures of the great Marxists, Joseph Stalin, Viacheslav Molotov, and Georgi Dmitrov, smiling as they signed an agreement. Strewn over, under, and around the car were books, magazines, and journals, old and new, some of which were the classics of Marxism-Leninism and others, the official Bulgarian interpretations of this noble corpus. And as often as these texts were carted off in the middle of the night, new ones appeared to take their place. This popular political tourist attraction, located halfway between Sofia's "City of Truth" and its more radical, less well-behaved tent city of "civil disobedience," was frequently the scene of creative political theater. Once at the beginning of August, for example, five youths ceremonially undressed there to demand that the socialist leaders of Bulgaria reveal the "naked truth" and "come clean" about the sins of the Zhivkov regime now blessedly past. Having already shamed one political patron of Bulgaria's critical Marxists, President Petar Mladenov, to resign, these denizens of the "dustbin of history" were seeking a far higher truth—that of political salvation—and would settle for nothing less.

In late summer 1990, in short, Sofia had little place for critical Marxists. This chapter explores why a genuine critical Marxism standing in opposition to an official Marxist order has played a relatively minor and contingent role in Bulgarian politics. It represents less an exhaustive investigation than an impressionistic and critical interpretation that focuses on the chronic inability of a genuine critical Marxism to find a political patron in socialist and postsocialist Bulgaria. It suggests that official Bulgarian Marxism incorporated the rhetoric of reformist and critical Marxism without ever embodying its oppositional spirit.

And only in officially sponsored nationalism did the country's leadership patronize a critique of mainstream Leninism by encouraging Bulgarian humanists to explore the deep and unique roots of Bulgarian history and culture.[1] But as Todor Zhivkov's ancien régime began to decay, a genuine Bulgarian critical Marxism emerged as an effort to revive a spirit of opposition and mass movement within the Bulgarian Socialist Party (BSP)—formerly the Bulgarian Communist Party (BCP). It has not become a dominant, or even terribly prominent, strain of political thinking or activity in Bulgaria's postproletarian era. In early 1991, the BSP, which was narrowly victorious in national elections, has closed its ranks to its reformers and seemingly rejected the path of critique.

The Incorporative Tradition of Official Bulgarian Marxism

Few observers have doubted the significance of Soviet Marxism for postwar Bulgarian political thought.[2] For example, *Nauchen komuniz"m* (Scientific Communism), a standard university text used in humanities and social sciences curricula, was a joint project of Soviet and Bulgarian scholars.[3] As might be expected, this text celebrates the ideological and organizational basis of the Marxist-Leninist party's leading role in society and criticizes "revisionists" for disputing the "objective necessity" of BCP leadership and for supporting some sort of pluralist political organization.[4] The text rejects a "national path" to socialism in view of the "huge international significance" of the USSR's experience in socialist construction.[5] Indeed, even as the "proletarian internationalist" order began to crumble, the latest Soviet edition of *Political Economy* was dutifully and quickly translated into Bulgarian as if to suggest that Soviet Marxism stood virtually unchallenged to the end in its authority in official Bulgarian thought.[6]

The prominence of Soviet Marxism excluded other variants of the corpus. Those schools of Marxist thought inspired by Gramsci, Lukács, or the Frankfurt school, for example, have found little resonance in Bulgarian intellectual life. Curiously, very few humanists and social scientists even seemed aware of neighboring Yugoslavia's *Praxis* group, and no one was familiar with its work.[7] Both in social science and in *agitprop* literature, citations from Lenin, Zhivkov, and Gorbachev far outnumber any from the critical tradition.[8] Bulgarians even followed the Soviet lead in proclaiming reforms. So in Sofia the sacred tradition of Soviet Marxism-Leninism was to be ritually invoked, repeated, and emulated—but never openly challenged.[9]

To be sure, official Bulgarian social science was "modernized" to become policy relevant by examining the "socio-class structure, urban and rural development, the socialist way of life, industrial organization, family, youth, the role of women in society, ideology, religion."[10] In addressing these issues, however, it was to retain its "Marxist militancy."

Our sociology is the party's science, and it cannot make any concessions to efforts to "refute" Marxism, to utilize bourgeois and generally un-Marxist perspectives to interpret problems, phenomena, and processes *to which Marxist sociology long ago gave a scientific answer*. This problem is no less critical and necessary in relation to un-Marxist interpretations and explanations of philosophy as it is to sociology.[11]

So all interpretation of issues—including those from a critical Marxist perspective—that fell outside of the officially sanctioned "line" could be labeled as "un-Marxist" or "revisionist" and arbitrarily rejected. This unity of views should not imply the complete absence of alternative perspectives in Bulgarian Marxism. A critique of the existing order was articulated by "in-house dissidents" co-opted within officially sanctioned organizations, such as the League of Dmitrov Communist Youth, the Sociology Section of the Academy of Sciences, and similar organizations. Bulgarian academics recently suggested that efforts were made to include "critical thinkers," such as Chavdar Kiuranov, Mincho Semov, Goran Goranov, Petar-Emil Mitev, and Liuben Nikolov into the decision-making halls of the hierarchy of official institutions.[12]

These claims raise an untrivial methodological issue of how to recognize "critical Marxism" in socialist Bulgaria. Through the beginning of 1988, for example, it was difficult to find more than the slightest trace of an autonomous critical Marxism in Bulgarian public life—either in the published record or in the activity of unofficial groups—because a general fear of official reprisal stifled Bulgarian intellectual and political life. And the tales of problems, harassments, and assassinations that existed before 10 November 1989 are legion. Although very little critical discourse ever found its way into print, informants suggest that the memos and papers of the in-house critics provided the proper internal intellectual climate for a variety of political and economic reforms.

By the mid-1980s a political climate in support of reform had emerged across a broad spectrum of socialist countries. The reforms launched by governments of Poland, Hungary, the USSR, and the People's Republic of China in the latter half of the decade provided a political setting in which Bulgaria's official critical Marxists could develop their vision of reform socialism. The Zhivkov leadership depended heavily on the critical vision of these in-house dissidents to construct its vision of an unalienated, developed socialist system in a series of economic and political "reforms."[13] In this vision, "ministries" were to be replaced by "associations" and linked to newly established "commercial banks." Much was said about economic decentralization. Firms were encouraged to enter into "dialogues" with central planners over compulsory norms and indicators. A variety of different types of state firms, associations, trusts, private firms, and brigades began to litter the economic organizational landscape. Firms were to be allowed to issue bonds and interest-bearing notes. The Bulgarians borrowed the idea of commercial banks from the Hungarian reformers and took from the

Yugoslav reform agenda the symbol of "self-managing . . . enterprises [as] the key economic organization and producer of goods."[14]

This reform of existing socialism extended to political life as well.[15] Borrowing from Budapest, Moscow, and Belgrade, the Zhivkov critique ordered dramatic changes in the source of political initiative and authority. It called for "democratization" as well as for open and frank political discussion and a restructuring of the mass media: "It is of paramount importance to make socialist democracy a powerful lever of restructuring and at the same time, through restructuring itself, to establish a new type of socialist democracy in our country."[16] It set the *"historical task to create all the conditions so that our socialist society can function and develop as a self-managed system"* in economic *and* political decision making.[17] In order to overcome the dominance of "bureaucratism" and "statism" in political life, Bulgaria's political institutions were supposed to be organized "from below" rather than imposed "from above."[18]

This critique also had its pragmatic side in its reflection of official reforms elsewhere in the socialist world. We find the usual invocations that multi-candidate elections are "rapidly becoming the essential feature of restructuring in socialism."[19] We find the typical commitment to the inexorable construction of a "constitutional socialist state" in which "it is necessary to strictly abide by the rule not to allow the decisions of party, state, and economic bodies at any level to be in contradiction with the country's laws."[20]

Changes in the party itself also became a standard refrain in the reform chorus. The party would no longer be "a tier in the hierarchy of state management" or a "subject of state power." Instead, it would create the proper political, moral, and ideological climate; it would *"renounce . . . administrative methods"*; it would concern itself with "its links with the masses" through surveys of attitudes and opinions of the Bulgarian citizens; and leaders at all levels of the party apparatus would be accountable to the constituencies that elected them.[21] Thus, the Bulgarian critique echoed reforms implemented elsewhere since the Yugoslav Sixth Party Congress in 1952.[22]

Inasmuch as the man who publicly constructed this critique—Todor Zhivkov—was the dominant political figure in the existing order, it seems fair to say that the party's direct control over political life was never seriously in question before 10 November 1989. Indeed, Zhivkov's political reforms never went terribly far in practice—or in theory, for that matter. For example, the party did not retreat from its frequent affirmation of its leading role. The BCP was to remain "at the helm of the processes of renewal underway in this country" and as the "strike force of restructuring."[23] It retained the right to "define the general course . . . [and] the basic directions of social and economic development" and control of cadre policy.[24] Indeed, in the July 1988 political housecleaning which saw the fall of Politburo member Chudomir Aleksandrov, critical thinkers, such as sociologist Petar-Emil Mitev, were also cut out of Bulgarian high politics. At the end of Bulgaria's socialist old regime, in short, officially supported "critical Marxism" had become part of an official dogma whose chief function was to legitimate the existing system.[25] It represented neither a serious critique nor a genuine project of reform.

"Critical Nationalism" in Bulgaria

A serious critique of Leninist socialism was supported by Bulgaria's political leadership in the late 1970s. The study of Bulgarian history led to the emergence of a "critical nationalism," which utilized official Leninist rhetoric to challenge some fundamental assumptions of the existing Leninist order. This exploration into Bulgarian roots extended far beyond the initial goals of exposing the Bulgarian national past to the light of day. For many intellectuals, Bulgarian "critical nationalism" provided a rich, nuanced, and divine escape from the dreary and oppressive rhythms of official intellectual and political life. Unfortunately, others desperately (or cynically) exploited this "critical nationalism" to legitimate the Zhivkov regime's policy of ethnic discrimination against Bulgarian Turks as it preempted more "liberal" or critical forms of discourse.[26] Both forms of "critical nationalism" remain more prominent in postsocialist Bulgaria than are liberalism or critical Marxism.

In the late 1970s Liudmila Zhivkova, the daughter of the Bulgarian general secretary and chairman of the Committee for Art and Culture, enthusiastically took up the search for Bulgaria's national past.[27] Most significantly, she directed the lavish observance of the thirteen-hundredth anniversary of the Bulgarian state, when Bulgarians would "acquire the historical privilege of getting a glimpse into the depths of their evolutionary past, of the difficult . . . path of the Bulgarian nation's evolution passing once again through the consciousness of each Bulgarian."[28] This holiday was to be less a weekend at the dacha than the "coming-out party" for a Bulgarian nation prepared for full membership in the international community. It was supposed to celebrate Bulgaria's ascent to its "greatest cultural and spiritual maturity" from "those pages in the historical destiny . . . filled with despair, ignorance and suffering."[29] This tale, of course, was the stuff that (national) dreams are made of, for it is "only in this unity and mutual conditioning of the developing evolutionary process which is accompanied by constant struggle that, to our eyes [and] those of contemporaries, will be revealed the true image of our country and our people, showing their real value and their place in the spiritual and historical development of mankind."[30] In short, Zhivkova clearly used this festival of Bulgarian statehood—as she used numerous gallery openings, book publications, political meetings, and academic conferences—as an occasion at which the Bulgarian people could "tell itself a story about itself."[31] And as in the *negara* in Clifford Geertz's account of nineteenth-century Bali, "the extravagance of state rituals was not just the measure of the king's divinity, which we have already seen it to be; it was also the measure of the realm's well-being. More important, it was a demonstration that they were the same thing."[32] Here the message was loud and clear: the Bulgarian state had arrived.

But the emperor needed new clothes. This celebration allowed Bulgarian scholars to develop a nationalist[33] critique of the existing order by reinterpreting its past. It was an opportunity to move beyond the quaint but vulgar official folk tales that had been passed off as the truth since World War II. It gave historians the task of investigating the economic, social, cultural, and political history of the Bulgarian nation.[34] And who better to outline this critique and new interpretation of Bulgarian history than Liudmila Zhivkova herself? She had legitimate scientific credentials in her candidate degree in history—the equivalent of an American Ph.D.—and frequently discussed the unique character and contributions of the Bulgarian people. In her hands the history of the Bulgarian people acquired an autonomy quite removed from the sum total of its parts; it gained a deep and almost organic significance.

> The Bulgarian national cultural tradition is closely related to the particular spiritual features of the Bulgarian people—direct successors to the ancient traditions of the Thracian and Proto-Bulgarian civilizations, welded together and enriched by the vivid spirit of the Slavonic tradition. Having originated and developed in close contact with and under the immediate impact of the Byzantine Empire, medieval Bulgarian culture followed a complex and *sui generis* path of evolution.[35]

We learn that an acquaintance with medieval Bulgaria's rich and varied culture will lead Bulgarians to become better citizens in a socialist society. The study *and* methods of study from Bulgaria's past were essential in building an enlightened future.

> The safeguarding and preservation of the Bulgarian cultural heritage is not an end in itself. The age-old cultural traditions of Bulgarian scholarship, the rich and varied spiritual heritage, are made use of under the conditions of the socialist society as a powerful factor in forming the new socialist consciousness. In enriching and further developing these traditions, in building a new socialist culture, there is pursued the noble goal of molding highly cultured and spiritually rich personalities with their eyes courageously and daringly fixed on the supreme ideals of our communism. [36]

In the new history of socialist Bulgaria, we find less emphasis on the historic links between the Bulgarian and Russian peoples than on the Bulgarian contributions to Slavic culture; less attention to the special relationship between the Soviet Union and Bulgaria than to the significant role in the history of socialism played by Blagoev and Dmitrov; and less recognition of the importance of socialist internationalism in the development of the Bulgarian state than of how the socialist Bulgarian state is the culmination of thirteen hundred years of continuity and struggle of the Bulgarian people.

> The Bulgarian people have had a hard historical fate. At certain . . . moments, Bulgaria has been called on by history to take a place at the head of great historical and cultural processes. Our people have passed through the melting pot of historical trials, through the fire of the national liberating and revolutionary movement, along the hard path of class struggle, but Bulgaria has preserved her revolutionary spirit, her will for free creative development.[37]

Here we find more than a small nation coming of age, but one that travels with the march of history: tempered in fire, the heroic Bulgarian nation is moving ever forward toward communism! Zhivkova used the language of Leninism in an increasingly bold critique of the Leninist definition of the international order. This search for national roots served the Bulgarian regime in many ways. It helped establish socialist Bulgaria's moral-historical—if not immediate political—claim to all Bulgarian land (including that in Macedonia) and was a way of asserting its identity as one of the legitimate historical nations in the Balkans.

Bulgarian critical nationalism also helped to redefine Bulgaria's relationship with the family of socialist countries led by the Soviet Union. Indeed, Bulgarian historiography's coming of age, its new self-awareness, and its distinct schools of thought all helped to legitimate Bulgaria's claim to its place in the family of world cultures as a small nation that is a rich source of Slavic cultural tradition. In sum, Zhivkova's critical nationalism helped to redefine Bulgaria from an inconsequential Soviet client to a country that could, in principle, act autonomously and identify with a variety of external identity references. This could not please Soviet elites accustomed to the docile fealty of its little Bulgarian brothers.[38]

To the extent that critical nationalism brought Bulgarian culture into direct conflict with official Soviet conceptions of relations among socialist regimes, it became all the more attractive to individuals opposed to the existing system. Critical nationalism offered one acceptable way to oppose the dominant socialist order defined by proletarian internationalism. In it, a humanist intellectual could separate himself from the inherited Marxist dogma while remaining a Bulgarian patriot. He could push out the envelope of politically acceptable discourse and pursue previously taboo themes of research. He could relive the conflicts of yesteryear between Hristo Botev and Liuben Karavelov. He could explore the medieval sources of contemporary Bulgarian culture. He could defend with relish the Bulgarian position on the Macedonian question at international conferences. In short, an officially patronized critical nationalism gave to humanists a sense of political autonomy, an escape into history, an opportunity for intellectual discovery, and most importantly, the ability to live as if free.

Zhivkova's death in 1981 at the age of thirty-nine cut short the full flowering of her authoritative vision of Bulgarian critical nationalism, while it allowed her father's regime to adopt a contemporary, secular saint.[39] After her death, this critical discourse split into a romantic academic nationalism on the one hand and a radical, integral nationalism on the other.

In the first of these, Bulgarian humanists found their personal, cultural, and political autonomy in their research into Bulgarian history. Nikolai Genchev is one of the leading historians now of the older generation—an accomplished scholar who is sufficiently authoritative to have trained an entire generation of younger historians while developing good relations with the critical movement that emerged in the late 1980s (this will be discussed in the next section).

Genchev starts from the assumption that nations are irreducible social and political categories; they provide the basic building blocks that make up the natural division of humanity. Thus, history necessarily becomes the telling of a variety of many-volumed stories of national development. In this context, Genchev shares Zhivkova's enthusiasm for the animate and spiritual character of the Bulgarian nation. He holds, moreover, that some nations are more legitimately preordained than others. The Bulgarian nation's inability to consolidate completely its "national consciousness" was not unusual during the "complex historical circumstances" of Ottoman rule, for example.[40] Genchev explains that one part of the Bulgarian "flesh and blood" began to call itself Macedonian instead of Bulgarian because of "the explosion" of national consciousness that more generally emerged out of the slow and delayed formation of nations.[41] Indeed, this proliferation of different types of national consciousnesses is responsible for "the Bulgarian nation's incomplete consolidation."[42] To Genchev, of course, these arrested processes did not alter in the slightest the moral right of the Bulgarian national consciousness to consolidate all people within its historical compass.

But it was not always so simple. He rues the unscientific efforts, in the late 1940s, of Bulgarian historians to "prove" that the Bulgarian land and nationality (*narodnost*) formed two nationalities (*narodnosti*)—Bulgarians and Macedonians—and drew an "artificial boundary" between these two nationalities that follows the state boundaries—all because of the political demands of the moment.[43] Indeed, the "misfortune is that, for a long time, [Bulgarian historians] did not argue, i.e., they were inclined to remain silent when they could not speak the truth and when they were unable to staunchly hold to the [nation's] true and complete historic legacy."[44]

Genchev does not apologize for an official socialist historiography that lacked a scientific methodology or discourse: "Every half-baked idea, scribbling, and plagiarism could . . . freely flourish because no effective scientific public opinion could be undertaken."[45] He called, therefore, for an open and critical discussion of the past. He confidently sought to end confusion about historical details "which often do not speak favorably of our forebears. We are not a new nation, we have a mature spiritual force and need to confront colleagues who hold unfavorable views of the Bulgarian past more frequently. There is nothing terrible in this. We know that each epoch, each generation has its pluses and minuses."[46]

Genchev, needless to say, has preferred to focus on the pluses: on the formation of the Bulgarian state in the seventh century in particular, when Bulgarians became a mainstay in Slavic culture; on the nation's adoption of Christianity; on its role in developing a Slavonic literary language; and on its struggle against the Ottomans, when it and other Balkan nations "risked their skins against the Ottoman conquerors [and], in essence, saved the renaissance blossoming in Europe."[47] He did not view the "tragedy of the Ottoman domination" in the "pogroms and murders" emphasized by many people. Rather, "it was tragic because Bulgarian society was forced . . . into a socioeconomic system that for several centuries was unable to modernize. So, as in eleven other nationalities in the Ottoman Empire, Bulgarian society was for centuries separated from those centers that were building modern societies and creating a new world."[48] In the end, of course, the sacrifice paid off:

> Bulgarian society nonetheless accomplished a historic feat with its national awakening during this period. In less than two centuries—the eighteenth and nineteenth—Bulgaria succeeded in compensating to a significant degree for its historical backwardness and established a major, biologically vital, and spiritually vigorous nation. It succeeded in creating . . . a culture that is deeply linked with its tradition [and] that reflects the great achievements of the contemporary world.[49]

For Zhivkova, naturally, all was well because the socialist Bulgarian state "is the legitimate heir . . . of everything progressive and democratic in the thirteen centuries' history of Bulgaria . . . a type of state new in principle, one which expresses the interests not of the exploiters but of the working class, of all working people, *irrespective of their ethnical origin and affiliation*, strong because of their moral-political unity, real masters and creators of the destiny of man and people."[50] This line of reasoning foreshadowed an integrally nationalist discourse that had, by the early 1980s, redefined the character of the Bulgarian nation to include all ethnic groups living in the historic lands of Bulgaria. This redefinition may have flowed from a recognition of a very low birth rate among ethnic Bulgarians. Genchev himself noted, "the question of biological vitality of the nation is . . . very important [and] now presents a real danger for Bulgarian survival: the absence of a normal national growth rate."[51] Others were prepared to go much further. They openly proclaimed a new "Ottoman" threat under which the Bulgarian nation had fallen and proposed measures that would resolve the problem.

In a spirit of integral, exclusive nationalism, the Bulgarian government articulated an authoritative interpretation and solution to the Bulgarian nation's problem of "biological vitality in the mid-1980s." The interpretation was the culmination of trends in place since the April 1956 Plenum of the Bulgarian Communist Party.[52] In this forced assimilation—or "renaissance process," as it was officially called—Bulgarian leaders denied the existence of Turks or Pomaks on Bulgarian soil: all were actually Bulgarians who had been "forcibly Islamicized" by Bulgaria's "Ottoman conquerors" during the long and dark Turkish yoke.[53] Turkish-language schools were closed. Broadcasts and publishing in the Turkish language ceased. Islamic religious customs, such as circumcision and ritual washing of the dead before burial, were outlawed. And in the official formulations Bulgarian Turks "made their historical choice wisely and with foresight. They reverted to their Bulgarian names."[54] Still, the effort to convince the Turkish Moslems that they are really Bulgarians proved both more difficult and fraught with greater risk than the Zhivkov leadership had bargained for.

The logic and evidence of the change was promptly provided by some hired guns in the Bulgarian Academy of Sciences, who produced several interdisciplinary collections speciously proving that all Bulgarian Moslems were forcibly converted by the Ottomans. They marshaled evidence to highlight the surviving glimmers of Bulgarian national consciousness through the centuries. Only under socialism, these accounts naturally hold, have Bulgarian Moslems been able to express their true national identity.

> It would be insufficiently one-sided to explain the heightened national consciousness among the descendants of the forcibly Islamicized Bulgarians only with the historical truth that they are ethnic Bulgarians. Of course this is very important. . . . *But decisive, in the final analysis, are the real changes of people's material circumstances, their vigorous participation in the construction of socialist society, . . . and their [integration into] the framework of the territorial, socioeconomic, political, and cultural community of the Bulgarian socialist nation.*[55]

The press was also mobilized in the campaign for "patriotic education" to portray Turkey as a hostile and primitive country. It routinely depicted the Turks as aggressive, uncivilized, delusional, and just plain dumb.[56] Reviews praised the American film *Midnight Express* for portraying "the tragic fate of the hero, who falls into the endless labyrinths of violence and cruelty that are modern-day Turkish prisons" because "we Bulgarians rode for five centuries on this express."[57] The two-part film *Vreme razdelno* (A Time of Division), directed by the chairman of the Film Artists' Union and based on the popular novel by Anton Donchev, focuses on the Islamization of the Pomaks in the Rhodopes in the seventeenth century—a period little studied by historians. The film, which inaccurately portrays a massive Islamization as an experience of unrestrained violence, may well have strengthened the popular view that violence and repression against the Turks was simply justifiable revenge for Turkish crimes of the past.

And there was no little repression. Amnesty International reported that in the initial stages, from December 1984 through March 1985, 100 Turks were killed and more than 250 Turks were arrested by the Bulgarian security forces for demonstrating against the campaign, for refusing to take new (Bulgarian) names, or in clashes with authorities.[58] Only people who accepted new names were released from jail. Amnesty International also reported a variety of other incidents: that mosques had been destroyed; that Turks who did not change their name were not allowed to work in state enterprises; that people received fines for speaking Turkish in public; and that people were harassed when wearing traditional Turkish clothing in public.[59]

The implementation of the "renaissance process" led to the severe deterioration in Bulgarian–Turkish relations; to the hasty exodus of over 300,000 Bulgarian Turks to Turkey in 1989; and to serious labor shortages in heavily Turkish regions. Most ominously, perhaps, the violence and dislocation that stemmed from the "renaissance process" led to a loss of faith in the Zhivkov leadership among the attentive public and critical thinkers. The summer of 1989 provided the final straw: even a coterie of "nomenklatura liberals," including Foreign Minister Petar Mladenov and Defense Minister Dobri Dzhurov, turned against Zhivkov's continued leadership. And for a brief time at the end of Zhivkov's reign and at the outset of the postsocialist era, critical nationalists, official dissidents, and critical thinkers rubbed shoulders and shared their visions for the future.

Critical Marxism in Bulgaria

Independent groups had begun to organize outside of the inner sanctum of the party by the beginning of 1988.[60] They promoted a range of interests, including human rights, religious freedom, historical preservation, environmental protection, and working class concerns. Some groups, such as "Eco-Glasnost' " or the "Discussion Club for Glasnost' and Pereustroistvo," boasted as members influential intellectuals who were well connected in official circles.[61] And an increasingly repressive regime rendered an increasingly large number of formerly prominent individuals available for political mobilization in one of the informal groups. As they grew progressively more horrified at the consequences of the "renaissance process," many intellectuals with links to the nomenklatura joined one of the groups.[62] These groups gained still more strength as members noted the success of such groups elsewhere in Eastern Europe and in the USSR. By the fall of 1989, in short, the informal groups had moved far beyond their natural constituencies among the congenital malcontents and political outsiders to include the best sons and daughters of the system itself, many of whom had became "critical Marxists" by the force of circumstances. In the end, of course, Zhivkov and his closest allies fell in the fall of 1989 less as a result of direct pressure from without than in an internal party coup that reflected the regime's

increasing disarray and incompetence. Over the next several months an atmosphere of political openness gave critical Marxists the opportunity to act and
freely disseminate analyses critical of the existing order. Two book-length
studies in the critical tradition were quickly published.

The first one was written by the current president of Bulgaria, Dr. Zheliu
Zhelev. By training a philosopher, Zhelev was elected the president of the Union
of Democratic Forces (UDF), which quickly became the chief oppositional
coalition to the Bulgarian Communist Party after 10 November 1989. Zhelev's
credentials as a dissident and critical Marxist were impeccable. As a graduate
student he was forbidden from defending his candidate's dissertation in philosophy because he criticized Lenin's definition of materialism. Instead, he was
kicked out of the BCP and exiled to his wife's village from 1965 until 1972.[63]
He wrote a text entitled "The Totalitarian State" in 1967, which was published
in 1982 under the title *Fascism* by the Narodna Mladezh publishing house in a
press run of 10,000.[64] It was banned and pulled from the stores three weeks later
because officials were made uncomfortable by the text's implicit comparison between German fascism and Bulgarian socialism. Many individuals involved in
its publication were subjected to disciplinary action. Because of his warmly positive review of the book, for example, Nikolai Genchev (see above) was forced
to resign as dean of the Faculty of History and his programs on Bulgarian history were taken off television for several years.[65] The book only appeared again
in Bulgaria after Zhivkov's fall. Zhelev headed up the UDF at round-table talks
in February 1990, in the election campaign in the spring of 1990, and within the
Grand National Assembly until his election by that body as president of Bulgaria
in August 1990. The book, with a new introduction and postscript, has become
his political testament and an act of faith in the UDF.[66]

If Blagovest Georgiev's study *Power and Inequality in Socialism* had a far
shorter and less difficult road to publication, its appearance has not been a public
event, nor has its critical analysis become an object of faith.[67] Georgiev is a
young sociologist in the Department of Contemporary Sociopolitical Systems of
the Philosophy Faculty at Sofia University. He completed his study in 1987 and
it was only published in the immediate aftermath of Zhivkov's fall. Georgiev
was and remains a member of the BCP (now BSP) in good standing. He has
been active in the reformist "Bulgarian Path to Europe" faction of the party,
which formed after Zhivkov's fall during and after the election campaign in the
spring of 1990.

Both texts represent critiques of state socialism that stand apart from those of
the official dissidents and from those of the critical nationalists because they
focus on the institutions of authority. They avoid Maoist, New Left critiques that
stress that the problems in socialism derive from the party's loss of revolutionary élan; from its lack of a specific revolutionary "task" that would fill the
moral and practical worlds of loyal members of the regime; or from the regime's
inability to create a genuine commune state in which the social, political, and

economic position of the "direct producers" is made equal to that of the political class.[68] Indeed, they ignore the substantive, normative goals of achieving social or political equality and focus instead on the manner in which state socialism malfunctions as it attempts to maintain itself.

The different metaphors employed by Georgiev and Zhelev to reveal the essence of "real socialism" lead to different images of how the system changes. Zhelev's detailed analysis of German fascism implies that the logic of totalitarianism—the absence of civil liberties, state ownership of production, and the like—flows from a single party's "absolute monopoly" of power. In the introduction written in 1989, he points to "the complete coincidence of the two types of totalitarian regime—the fascist and our communist. Although an analogy was not explicitly made [in the book], the reader can learn the horrifying truth from the manner in which documentary material is organized, that the few differences between the nazi and communist political systems do not serve the interests of communism."[69] Zhelev suggests that communism is a more perfect form of totalitarianism and borrows a bon mot from his good friend Genchev: "Fascism is an early, unsystematic, bon-vivant variation of communism," while Hitler was a "pitiful imitation and a blowhard compared to Stalin."[70] Indeed, "we Marxists were the first in history to create a totalitarian regime, a totalitarian state" that forcibly eliminated or degraded other parties into transmission belts of the Communist Party. The party has wielded an "absolute monopoly of political power" and gave to its members at each level of the state "uncontrolled and unlimited power" over every aspect of economic life.[71] Even the most developed fascist party, the Nazi Party, did not control society as completely as has "the most perfect and complete model of a totalitarian regime in history," the communist regime. Because it does not control the economy, a fascist regime "is less perfect and less stable" than its well-endowed communist relative.[72]

How does a system as stable as communism democratize? Although Zhelev does not specify clearly what forces a totalitarian regime to change, he has much to say about the transition itself. He argues that as the level of official repression decreases, a regime could progress along a line from a totalitarian system through a phase of military dictatorship before it discovers the joys and wonders of a multiparty democracy. In this context, perestroika represents a superior "alternative to military dictatorship" because it is "more humane, cultured, and democratic, i.e., a civilized transition from totalitarianism to democracy."[73] Nonetheless, such a system is likely to travel through a period of instability such as that characteristic of a fascist regime—as in the "perestroika from above" in the Soviet Union or in the repression of youth and intellectuals in China in 1989.[74] A totalitarian regime will attempt to preserve its power against that class of people made increasingly conscious and autonomous by the regime's economic reforms. Thus, "if perestroika is accomplished as the nomenklatura has conceived it—starting first in the economy and then in the political system—it will end in the Chinese variant of the dismantling, and its 'fascicization' will be completely and clearly expressed.''[75] According to Zhelev, then, ''there is no way of moving from totalitarianism to democracy except to destroy its political system''—or by implication, the power of the Communist Party, which controls the political system.[76]

By the winter of 1989-90 he had cause for hope. Zhelev saw the eclipse of real socialism in the weakening of the worst forms of repression, in the ''collapse of the party's ideological monopoly in society,'' and in the appearance of independent political parties and mass organizations.[77] He saw the reemergence of a civil society that sought to create a constitutional state: ''The final phase of the disintegration is emerging, when the Communist Party [will be] forced to separate its financial, personnel, and structural relationships, in which the backbone of the totalitarian system—the organic link between the party and the state—is being destroyed.''[78]

He also found some reason to pause, particularly in the relative weakness and inexperience of Bulgaria's civil society. Indeed, he notes that Bulgaria was the only Warsaw Pact country (sic) in which a significant challenge to the totalitarian system had not taken place:

> We have not had a dress rehearsal. . . . This is why our new and young political opposition is forced to struggle with every accessible legal means for the complete and effective destruction of the totalitarian structures, for their complete dismantling, so that the democratic process will become irreversible . . . so that . . . the possibility of a violent transition will be excluded.[79]

On one level, Zhelev's analysis remains strangely Leninist. He does not really account, for example, for the mellowing of the system except as a result of the potentially voluntarist ''political energy'' of the opposition's mass movement. In February 1990 he complained that democratization in Bulgaria was proceeding ''slowly and sluggishly'' because of the absence of ''mass pressure from below.''[80] Thus, although the intelligentsia had been active a year earlier, he despaired that the ''broader masses of our nation'' have not achieved ''the necessary political activity and political energy that would destroy the structures and institutions condemned by history, to remove them from sociopolitical life and to open the path to the quick construction of truly democratic institutions, democratic constitutions and laws.''[81] This is Leninist pessimism at its finest. With terms such as ''dress rehearsal'' for democratization, the ''complete destruction'' of the ''organic link'' between the state and the party, and ''irreversibility of democratization,'' moreover, Zhelev also employs the Leninist rhetoric of struggle in which he was raised. It must be difficult to leave behind.

On another level, his analysis is oddly ahistorical: he describes an impressively broad array of nondemocratic countries as ''totalitarian''—those in Eastern Europe, the Soviet Union, nazi Germany, fascist Italy, Franco's Spain,

Pinochet's Chile, etc. Thus, the logic of his analysis cannot really account for the varying social and cultural contexts of specific authoritarian and totalitarian regimes, although such an accounting would lead us to see more clearly the sources of support for such regimes and the processes by which they lose their legitimacy. Taken in *its historical context*, then, *Fascism* remains a bravely conceived and pioneering study in Bulgarian critical Marxist thought that remains most important for its political role and that of Zhelev himself as Bulgaria "transits" the path from Leninist state socialism.

The strength of Georgiev's study lies precisely in its identification of a cultural context for the "acute social crisis" taking place in European socialist countries: "No serious analysis can attribute everything to the incompetence of the subjective factor, to a lack of political will, or to the low morality of administrative culture."[82] To understand the logic underlying the stagnation in which no socialist leader can "be interested," he addresses the "historical and cultural traditions . . . that affect socialist development of all countries."[83] He specifically cites the extremely low degree of adaptability and innovation in the Stalinist version of "the Asiatic mode of production," which is "the most important methodological principle for understanding the past, present, and future of real socialist societies."[84] This tradition links different models of socialism "as cultural facts with thousands of cultural currents from the East . . . [which are] much different from the classical cultural, political, and economic traditions of Western Europe."[85]

Georgiev finds that the basis of authoritarian bureaucratic rule in the Asiatic mode of production lies in a state-monopoly economy that is simply another hierarchy of state power rather than a product of civil society. "Since the ownership function of property is not differentiated and all administrative functions are centralized in the state," the state becomes the only institution that legitimately organizes economic activity.[86] "Consequently, economic relations of social inequality are politicized . . . [and] beget a bureaucratic command system of totalitarian control. And it could be no other way since the state possesses a monopoly over the legal use of political force and is . . . unified through a system of bureaucratic regulation."[87] This political, administrative, and economic unity leads to inflexibility and ultimately stagnation in social systems characterized by the Asiatic mode of production.

Socialist societies follow similar principles. The basis of the division of labor is not economic achievement but political status in which the bureaucratic political class is established on the basis of its functional importance in society. Its monopoly of legitimate social activity leads it, by necessity, "to assume all economic initiative, political activity, as well as the ideological diversity that should fall naturally to civil society."[88] And a society in which the bureaucracy has expropriated all these important functions is divided into "two unequal forces: the organized bureaucrats . . . and a huge, differentiated, but economically and politically amorphous mass" that constitutes a potential civil society.[89]

The problem, once again, is stagnation. We find little innovation in such societies because changes would "come into conflict with the law of the bureaucracy and consequently . . . with interest groups in the bureaucracy from top to bottom. The problem is that the monopoly bureaucracy has been transformed from an administration into political power itself. Herein lies the 'deepest secret' of all existing models of real socialism."[90] With this transformation the absence of autonomous centers of economic power leaves civil society even more weak and dependent upon the unified political class for patronage.

Georgiev laments the broader sociopolitical outcome: "Despite its unarguable achievements in industrialization and in [creating] the conditions for . . . the scientific-technological revolution, our society is constructed on 'Asian' principles . . . in other words, its rationality is expressed in maintaining the goals of stagnation and of stability . . . and not the goal of change and adaptation."[91]

Such societies, characterized by "asocial rationality," are not only "condemned to stagnation, but . . . [also] to the disintegration of social relationships and to the inability of the only social actors who could possibly act as agents of change in the system to liberate themselves."[92] Instead, the "principle of socialist statehood differs from that of the great Eastern despots" in the monopoly of power held by a "single party."[93] In the Stalinist version of real socialism, moreover, this ruling "party-class . . . not only usurps the power of the civil society and the state, but . . . imposes [its] values onto the entire society."[94] Nor is the project of reform planned by the "in-house dissidents" discussed above likely to succeed: "The problem of socialist perestroika lies not only in the absence of a civil society but also in the political powerlessness of state institutions. Without a strong state as a center of political power, a strong and autonomous civil society as a center of economic and social power makes no sense."[95] This may not be old hat to Western students of comparative communism, but when this appears in a BSP edition, heads do turn.

Georgiev breaks little new ground in his prescriptions for a solution to the problem of socialist stagnation. He proposes what seems to be the standard critical program: the emergence of a genuine, autonomous civil society; the separation of political power from economic control; a division of labor based on market relationships rather than on a system of bureaucratic ranks; innovative initiatives in social, economic, and political life from autonomous individuals; an economic reform stressing markets, new forms of ownership, and individual entrepreneurial initiatives; and the emergence of a genuine political pluralism based not merely on a multiparty system but on the existence of a genuine opposition based on differing economic interests.[96]

How can this be achieved? Like Zhelev, Georgiev implies that a civil society will emerge when the totalitarian state is eliminated. Like Zhelev, too, he offered no precise blueprint for change. Unlike Zhelev, however, he suggests that the source of change is not necessarily found in the oppositional movements that arise in an "amorphous civil society" but could emerge within the "political elite" itself.[97] A close reading of his text suggests that the emergence of a civil society could be engineered by some sort of consensus on the basic rules of the game among elites who have emerged in the wake of Zhivkov's fall from power on 10 November 1989. Georgiev's text thus calls generously for a society marked by tolerance and a genuine opposition. It is no surprise that a radical reformer within a terribly compromised ruling party will be far more magnanimous in his approach to an opposition long cut out of power than that opposition is likely to be to the radical reformers themselves.

From Critique to Civil Society?

At the end of the Zhivkov era the various critical schools shared a minimalist consensus. Critical Marxists, critical nationalists, and official dissidents found themselves agreed on several things: on their opposition to the further rule of Todor Zhivkov; on the vague desire to transform the Bulgarian government into some sort of a "political democracy"; and on the equally vague desire to replace the command economy with some sort of market economy. These groups were not just cut out of the loop of policy making, they had all concluded that the Zhivkov regime had lost touch with the demands of history. They rejected the air of unreality surrounding its policies, e.g., its flair for ritualistic innovation in the absence of genuine efforts at political-economic transformation. And even critical nationalists opposed the renaissance process as badly implemented and crude.[98]

The critics also shared some positive symbols. A "political democracy" could link the nation to more successful governments the world over, governments more resilient than those socialist governments that were crumbling all around Bulgaria. Similarly, the ideas of "markets" and "competition" seemed to provide a means by which the country could generate the wealth and abundance on which Marx predicated the Marxist idea in the first place. Nonetheless, the consensus so important in November 1989—that some sort of change was necessary—was not matched by a consensus on what exactly to change, i.e., on who should rule or on the type of program that would most effectively democratize Bulgaria in its postproletarian phase.

In the year following Zhivkov's political demise, this "critical" consensus may have been transformed into the seeds of a genuine Bulgarian civil society, i.e., a broad and dense network of autonomous associations and institutions of which government is but one. A civil society would free individuals to pursue their interests as they themselves define them. In their articulation of a critique of the existing order, the presence of critical Marxists would be one sign of a healthy civil society. To be sure, we might characterize the breakdown of consensus as the creation of a permanent stalemate, and we might portray the nascent civil society as a highly volatile and polarized set of movements engaged in the politics of moral absolutism. The initial enthusiasm surrounding the hyper-production of meetings, declarations, and demonstrations soon turned into inevitable disputes among different groups over specific political differences.

The critical nationalists were the first to fall away from the consensus after a decision of the BCP Central Committee plenum on 29 December 1989 that condemned the policy of assimilation and allowed Turks in Bulgaria to practice their religion, speak Turkish in everyday life, and assume their old names if they so desired.[99] Demonstrations on the weekend of 5-7 January 1990 against the Turks and the ''traitors'' to the Bulgarian nation led to an immediate compromise solution but foreshadowed deeper divisions on a range of issues among Bulgarian Turks and ethnic Bulgarians.

The frailty of the consensus between the Bulgarian Socialist Party and the Union of Democratic Forces was revealed during a hard-fought election campaign in the spring of 1990. The UDF complained about the reformist BSP's unfair campaign tactics throughout Bulgaria.[100] The most radical adherents of the opposition even rejected the moral right of the BSP to join any post-proletarian government and established a ''City of Truth'' in the center of Sofia during the summer of 1990. It arose spontaneously after the UDF broadcast a videotape of President Mladenov at a demonstration in December 1989, at which he said that it would be best to bring in the tanks to disperse the demonstrators. Residents of each large Bulgarian city's ''City of Truth'' —composed of tents and placards covered with political slogans—articulated a radical critique of all mainstream Bulgarian political parties. And during most of 1990 the cities of truth provided a far more vital political life than that offered by a Grand National Assembly, which debated more than a month to elect Zhelev as president; it then debated for several more months before it selected, then rejected, a socialist government and approved of the current coalition government. Nor do we find consensus on procedure in the circumstances surrounding the fire at the BSP headquarters on the evening of 26 August 1990—an event suggesting less the emergence of a civil society than a Hobbesean world in which political trust is a precious commodity.[101]

Nonetheless, a civil society may still be slowly forming. The crucial question is not whether the disparate groupings of Bulgarian society can sustain a consensus on substantive matters but whether they can regain their consensus on procedural issues. And here there is good news. First, a coalition government composed of the BSP, the UDF, and the Agrarians and headed by a nonparty personality was finally installed and has begun to adopt the economic and political reforms under discussion since November 1989. This would suggest a minimal consensus on some basic rules of the game. Interviews with BSP reformers in June and August 1990 suggest clearly that they are a voice of moderation and tolerance in a difficult political universe. The years 1990-91 have certainly not been a time for reflection, analysis, and critique of the injustices of the existing order, a role usually performed with such aplomb by critical thinkers. It has been, rather, a time of deeds. And critical Marxists have remained active within the Alternative Socialist party (ASP) and within one of several reformist wings of the BSP.[102] In addition, Aleksand"r Tomov, the leader of the reformist DEMOS faction within the party, has entered the coalition government as a vice-premier. Thus it seems fair to say that to the extent that the BSP remains an important political force within Bulgarian society and its reformers remain within the party, critical Marxists will retain access to organizational resources in Bulgaria's postproletarian era. Indeed, if the neoliberal economic reforms actually work, they will lead to a situation congenial to a vital critical Marxism: increasing wealth, increasing social inequality, and heightened social tensions. In an emergent civil society, in short, Bulgarian critical Marxism may come to resemble that in the West—a critique of the existing order.

Notes

1. Liudmila Zhivkova, *Liudmila Zhivkova, Her Many Worlds, New Culture and Beauty Concepts and Action* (New York and Oxford: Pergamon Press, 1982).

2. Indeed, the topic is rarely discussed in the Western literature on Bulgaria.

3. *Nauchen komuniz"m* (Sofia: Nauka i izkustvo, 1979). Among the Soviet authors were E. Anufriev, A. Koval'ev, A. Lashin, and E. Tadevoskii.

4. Ibid., 64-71.

5. Ibid., 184.

6. *Political Economy* (Sofia: Nauka i izkustvo, 1989). The authors' collective included Vadim Medvedev, Leonid Abalkin, and A.G. Aganbegian.

7. Interviews with Aleksand"r Mirchev and Petar-Emil Mitev in June 1990.

8. For example, see Niko Iakhiel, "Sociologiia pred novite zadachi," in *Sotsiologiia i sotsialna promiana* (Sofia: Nauka i izkustvo, 1988), 407.

9. See the manner in which Kenneth Jowitt has developed this line of thinking in the following works: *The Leninist Response to Dependency* (Berkeley: Institute of International Studies, 1978); "Soviet Neotraditionalism: the Political Corruption of a Leninist Regime," *Soviet Studies* 35, no. 3 (July 1983): 275-97; "Moscow Centre," *East European Politics and Societies* 1, no. 3 (Autumn 1987): 296-348; and "Gorbachev: Bolshevik or Menshevik?" in *Development in Soviet Politics*, ed. Stephen White, Alex Pravda, and Zvi Gitelman (Durham: Duke University Press, 1990), 270-91.

10. Niko Iakhiel, "Sotsiologicheski izmereniia na Aprilskata Liniia," in *Sotsiologiia i sotsialna promiana* (Sofia: Nauka i izkustvo, 1988), 347.

11. Iakhiel, "Sotsiologiia pred novite zadachi," 407-8. Emphasis added. The essay was first published in 1986.

12. Interviews conducted in Sofia with Petar-Emil Mitev and Aleksand"r Mirchev in June 1990. Not everyone on this list is viewed as a critical Marxist in Bulgaria.

13. These were only the latest in a long series of reforms that had been promulgated in the Bulgarian economy since the early 1960s—in 1963, 1965, 1968, 1970-72, 1978-79, 1982, 1985-87, and 1989. See John Lampe, *The Bulgarian Economy in the Twentieth Century* (London: Croon Helm, 1986), for a good history of economic reform in Bulgaria; also see Richard Crampton, " 'Stumbling and Dusting Off,' or an Attempt to Pick a Path through the Thicket of Bulgaria's New Economic Mechanism," *East European*

Politics and Societies 2, no. 2 (Spring 1988): 333-95.

14. Prime Minister Georgi Atanasov, cited in Rada Nikolaev, "BCP Plenum on Economic Reform," RFE/RL 12, SR/1, 13 February 1987.

15. See, for example, Todor Zhivkov, "Osnovni polozheniia na kontseptsiiata za ponat"shnoto izgrazhdane na sotsializma v NR B"lgariia," *Ikonomicheska mis"l* 32, no. 10 (1987): 3-44; idem, "Vst"pitelno slovo pred plenuma na TsK na BKP 28 iuli 1987 g.," *Ikonomicheska mis"l* 33, no. 10 (1987): 45-56; idem, "Restructuring: A Cause of the Party, A Cause of the People" (Sofia: Sofia Press, n.d.).

16. Zhivkov, "Restructuring," 36.

17. Zhivkov, "Osnovni polozheniia," 16. Emphasis in original.

18. Ibid., 13.

19. Zhivkov, "Restructuring," 86; Crampton, " 'Stumbling and Dusting Off,' " 387.

20. Zhivkov, "Restructuring," 39, 41-42.

21. Ibid., 58; Decision of the National Conference of the Bulgarian Communist Party "On Restructuring and the Further Construction of Socialism in the People's Republic of Bulgaria," 28-29 January 1988 (Sofia, n.d.), 107.

22. On Yugoslav reforms, see Dennison Rusinow, *The Yugoslav Experiment* (Berkeley: University of California Press, 1977).

23. Zhivkov, "Restructuring," 56.

24. Zhivkov, "Osnovni polozheniia," 42.

25. The same could be said for the many and varied official Yugoslav (i.e., Kardelj's) efforts to institutionalize self-management, the delegate system, and the like. At the same time, genuinely critical Marxists—such as those in the Praxis group—were limited in their expression.

26. See Michael Shafir, "Xenophobic Communism—the Case of Bulgaria and Romania," *The World Today* 45, no. 12 (December 1989): 208-12.

27. In many respects, her actions only strengthened trends that had been under way among Bulgarian historians for some time. With her untimely death at the age of thirty-nine in 1982, she was elevated into secular sainthood. For a marvelous example of contemporary hagiography, see the two editions of her book, *Liudmila Zhivkova* (1982 and 1986).

28. Zhivkova, "Unity of the Past, the Present and the Future," *Liudmila Zhivkova* (1982), 42.

29. Ibid.

30. Ibid.

31. Clifford Geertz, "Deep Play: Notes on a Balinese Cockfight," *Interpretations of Cultures* (New York: Basic Books, 1973), 412-53. See Zhivkova, "Unity of the Past," 46, for the explicitly public-relations dimension of the celebration.

32. Clifford Geertz, *Negara, The Theatre State in Nineteenth Century Bali* (Princeton: Princeton University Press, 1980), 129.

33. I am *not* using this term as it has been commonly used in Eastern Europe—as a synonym for chauvinism, intolerance, bigotry, prejudice, irredentism, and the like. As used here, it poses the nation as the natural unit of accounting in world history and pursues the investigation of its traditions and cultures as the most meaningful of all intellectual activities.

34. Zhikova, "Unity of the Past," 43

35. "Introduction to the monograph 'The Tetraevangelia of Tsar Ivan Alexander,'" in

Liudmila Zhivkova (1986), 122.

36. "The Feat of the Old Literati," *Liudmila Zhivkova* (1982), 17.

37. Zhikova, "Unity of the Past," 46.

38. See Jowitt, "Moscow Centre," for the logic of this analysis, although he develops it with references to China's challenge to Soviet hegemony.

39. We can appreciate the malleability of this sainthood when we observe that her name was removed from most public places soon after her father's fall from power.

40. Vera Staefanova, *S"dbata na B"lgariia prez pogleda na ucheniia* (Sofia: Otechestveniia Front, 1980), 152.

41. Ibid.

42. Ibid.

43. Ibid., 158-59.

44. Ibid., 159.

45. Ibid.

46. Ibid., 151.

47. Ibid., 155.

48. Ibid., 153.

49. Ibid., 153-54.

50. "A Remarkable Jubilee," *Liudmila Zhivkova* (1982), 51. Emphasis added.

51. Staefanova, *S"dbata na B"lgariia*, 153.

52. John Bell, *The Bulgarian Communist Party* (Stanford: Hoover, 1986), 114-18. By the 1960s the official Bulgarian policy had changed once more and stressed the development of a unified Bulgarian nation. The Bulgarian government refused to recognize previously recognized minorities, such as the Macedonians—still a bone of contention between Bulgaria and Yugoslavia. From 1972 to 1974, the government implemented a campaign to "Bulgarize" the names of Pomaks and Bulgarian Gypsies. By 1975 neither the census nor identification cards recorded nationality other than Bulgarian. The Turkish department at the University of Sofia was transformed into one on general Arabic studies and Turkish was no longer offered as a language of instruction.

By 1971 an assimilationist party program asserted that "the citizens of our country of different national origins will come ever closer together." By the mid-1970s one could find references to the "unified Bulgarian socialist nation." G.S., "Officials Say There Are No Turks in Bulgaria," RFE/RL 10, SR/5, 28 March 1985.

53. Pomaks are Bulgarian speakers of the Islamic faith. See Girgin Girginov, "Za sotsialisticheskoto natsionalno s"znanie," *Probleme na razvitieto na B"lgarskata narodnost i natsiia* (Sofia: Izdatelstvo na B"lgarskata Akademiia na Naukite, 1988), 200. Also see Stanko Todorov, "Name Changes in Bulgaria," in *From Stalinism to Pluralism*, ed. Gale Stokes (New York: Oxford University Press, 1991), 232-34.

54. Girginov, "Za sotsialisticheskoto natsionalno s"znanie"; also see Stephen Ashley, "The Islamic Minorities and Perestroika," RFE/RL 13, SR/4, 8 April 1988.

55. Girginov, "Za sotsialisticheskoto natsionalno s"znanie," 200.

56. See, for example, Dobromir Zadgorski, "Imperial Ambitions and Medieval Mentality," *Rabotnichesko delo*, 3 July 1989, in FBIS EEU, 5 July 1989.

57. *Rabotnichesko delo*, 8 June 1986 and *Literaturen front*, 19 June 1986, cited in RFER SR/8, 9 September 1986.

58. Amnesty International, "Bulgaria, Imprisonment of Ethnic Turks, Human Rights Abuses during the Forced Assimilation of the Ethnic Turkish Minority" (London, April

1986); Amnesty International, "Bulgaria, Imprisonment of Ethnic Turks and Human Rights Activists" (London, February 1989).

59. Amnesty International (April 1986 and February 1989).

60. Jiri Pehe, "An Annotated Survey of Independent Movements in Eastern Europe," RFER RAD, *Background Report 100 (Eastern Europe)*, 13 June 1989.

61. Among the prominent individuals who joined these groups were the sociologist Chavdar Kiuranov, the writer Blaga Dmitrova, the philosopher and current president Zheliu Zhelev, and others.

62. Interviews conducted in January, May, and June 1990.

63. In 1974 he defended his dissertation on "Possibility, Reality, and Necessity" and in 1987 he received a doctorate for his thesis called "Relational Theory of the Personality." See Duncan Perry, "Dissident Becomes New President," *Report on Eastern Europe*, 17 August 1990, pp. 3-6 for details on Zhelev.

64. Zheliu Zhelev, "Bmesto Predgovor 'Fashizm"t' ili politicheskata biografiia na edna kniga," *Fashizm"t* (Sofia: BZNS, 1990), 6.

65. Ibid., 18. Between 1982 and 1989, book publishers from a variety of socialist countries—China, Hungary, Poland, Czechoslovakia, and the USSR—all expressed interest in various parts of the text; see pp. 6-7.

66. Editions sold in Sofia in the summer of 1990 at 4 leva 60 stotinki included an additional 5 leva contribution to the SDS.

67. Blagovest Georgiev, *Vlast i neravenstvo pri socializma* (Sofia: Otdel "Mezhdunarodno rabotnichesko i komunisticheso dvizhenie" na Instituta po istoriia na BKP, 1989).

68. Zhelev suggests that "he who promises to create democracy by perfecting the totalitarian system engages in the most despicable demagogy." *Fashizm"t* (Sofia: BZNS, 1990), 10.

69. Ibid., 8.

70. Ibid., 11.

71. Ibid., 10.

72. Ibid., 11.

73. Ibid., 8, 16.

74. Ibid., 14-15.

75. Ibid., 15.

76. Ibid., 10.

77. Ibid., 355

78. Ibid., 356.

79. Ibid., 357.

80. Ibid., 356.

81. Ibid.

82. Georgiev, *Vlast i neravenstvo*, 2.

83. Ibid., 2, 3.

84. Ibid., 199.

85. Ibid., 200.

86. Ibid., 64.

87. Ibid.

88. Ibid., 196.

89. Ibid.

90. Ibid.

91. Ibid., 201.

92. Ibid., 201-2.

93. Ibid., p. 203.

94. Ibid.

95. Ibid.

96. Ibid., 205-17.

97. Ibid., 196.

98. Interviews conducted with Mincho Minchev and Dimit"r Arnaudov of the Obshtenarodniia komitet za zashtita na natsionalnite interesi in August 1990.

99. For a detailed account of these events, see Stephen Ashley, "Ethnic Unrest During January," *Report on Eastern Europe*, 9 February 1990, pp. 4-11.

100. Interviews conducted in May, June, and August 1990 in Sofia, Sliven, Nova Zagora, Kardzhali, Lovech, and Veliko Tarnovo.

101. See Mark Baskin, "The Politics of the Attack on the BSP Headquarters," *Report on Eastern Europe*, no. 39, 28 September 1990, pp. 8-12.

102. See Duncan M. Perry, "The Bulgarian Socialist Party Congress: Conservatism Preserved," *Report on Eastern Europe*, no. 43, 26 October 1990, pp. 4-9.

9

Praxis and Democratization in Yugoslavia
From Critical Marxism to Democratic Socialism?

Oskar Gruenwald

Yugoslavia at the Crossroads

A specter is haunting Yugoslavia—the specter of totalitarian democracy, moral, economic, and political bankruptcy, national separatism, civil war, and possible dissolution as a state. Providentially, the seeds of a democratic, pluralist Third Yugoslavia, which would inaugurate the rule of law and constitutional guarantees of basic human rights and freedoms, have also sprouted throughout the country in the form of institutionalized dissent, alternative movements and associations, and even opposition parties that by the end of 1990 toppled the Communist Party's monopoly of power in four of the six constituent republics.[1] It is the thesis of this chapter that Yugoslavia's critical Marxists or Marxist humanist theorists of the *Praxis* school have contributed substantially, though not exclusively or unequivocally, to the rebirth of an autonomous civic culture and civil society, along with such individual dissenters as Milovan Djilas, Mihajlo Mihajlov, and the "Belgrade Six," as well as numerous groups and associations, culminating in the reexamination of Tito's legacy in camp literature and the formation of independent movements and opposition parties by the end of the 1980s.[2]

In the spring of 1991, Yugoslavia found itself on the brink of civil war. In the first arguably free elections since Tito's communists rose to power in Yugoslavia in 1945, nationalist parties took over republic governments in Slovenia, Croatia, Bosnia-Hercegovina, and Macedonia in 1990. According to Peter Palmer, the press was "the first casualty."[3] There were already eight presses in Yugoslavia, apart from unofficial and samizdat publications: one for each of the six republics and two autonomous provinces (the latter two severely curtailed following the Serbian leadership's revocation of provincial autonomy by 1990).

Slovenia, and then Croatia, declared their sovereignty and determination to restructure Yugoslavia into a genuine confederation. Both also established the primacy of republic over federal laws, raised interrepublic tariffs (as did Serbia), and undertook to build up their own armed forces based on republic police and militia. Ominously, by May 1991, nineteen people had died in interethnic conflicts in Yugoslavia, not counting Kosovo, where martial law has been in force since the army quashed mass demonstrations in 1981.[4]

On 15 May 1991, the Serbian communist leader Slobodan Milošević, riding the wave of resurgent Serbian nationalism, upped the ante in the interrepublic nationalist struggle for power by blocking Croatia's Stipe Mešić from rotating into the post of president of the collective state presidency. Along with the 1974 Constitution, which created a de facto confederation under the tutelage of the League of Communists of Yugoslavia, Tito also bequeathed to his heirs a cumbersome mechanism of succession in the form of a rotating state presidency, which was to insure that no single Communist Party leader could ever dispose of Tito's unlimited personal mandate.[5] Mešić, a former political prisoner and ex-communist, was thus prevented by a 5–3 vote of the state presidency from becoming the new head of state and commander of the armed forces. Mešić warned that if the veto was not reversed, allowing him to assume the rotating leadership, Croatia would secede from Yugoslavia.[6]

The unknown factor in this crisis was the Yugoslav Army, whose predominantly Serbian and Montenegrin high command and officer corps, with a 95 percent Communist Party membership, had issued warnings on previous occasions that it would not allow the break-up of Yugoslavia or the endangerment of the achievements of the socialist revolution.[7] Yet 70 percent of the Yugoslav Army are one-year conscripts drawn proportionately from all the republics. At the outbreak of World War II in Yugoslavia, the Armed Forces of the First Yugoslavia (1918-45) disintegrated along national/ethnic and even regional lines. Tito's Yugoslav Army officer corps contains probably the largest contingent of hardline, dogmatic Marxist-Leninists groomed and pampered by Tito and his heirs and dedicated to the preservation of their power and privileges and, implicitly, Tito's heritage.

But nationalism has corroded communism throughout Eastern Europe and the Soviet Union. In Yugoslavia itself, communists won in the 1990 elections in Serbia and Montenegro due to their exploitation of Serbian nationalist sentiment concerning Albanian atrocities against the Serbian minority in Kosovo and the alleged inequality of the Serbian position in the federation under the 1974 Constitution, which in effect granted republic status to Serbia's two autonomous provinces, Kosovo and Vojvodina, but without corresponding political responsibility.[8] Thus, it was not unlikely that in the event of a civil war, the Yugoslav Army—far from being able to act as arbiter and a peace-keeping force—would itself become Balkanized and disintegrate along national/ethnic lines. The old Titoist Bolshevik officer corps would be forced to choose between the Scylla of remaining true to Tito and his socialist legacy, which has become discredited even among party members, and the Charybdis of declaring itself as belonging to particular national groupings and thus automatically assigned to a faction in the civil war.

The most pertinent question today, however, is not whether Yugoslavia may or may not survive as a multinational state. Rather, it is whether postcommunist Yugoslavia will be a democracy or a dictatorship. Would Yugoslavia as a unified state or as six, seven, or more separate successor states guarantee basic human rights and freedoms? Could it protect all its minorities dispersed widely over its territory? Would there be the rule of law or the rule of men? Could the press(es) become truly autonomous, professional, objective, pluralistic, and tolerant? In brief, can Yugoslavia, unified or separate, overcome the heavy hand of the past, crystallized in the Titoist legacy of moral, economic, and political mendacity and bankruptcy?[9]

If freedom is to have a new lease on life in postcommunist Yugoslavia, it will be only via the development of a democratic political culture that emphasizes the freedom and dignity of each individual, regardless of nationality, race, sex, religion, or political persuasion. In sum, only the rebirth of a genuine public opinion and a tolerant, pluralistic civic culture characteristic of a civil society autonomous from any state—communist, nationalist, or democratic—can offer all nations and nationalities in Yugoslavia the possibility of charting a more humane future.[10]

Has the *Praxis* school of thought contributed to this vital process of democratization of Yugoslavia's prevailing political culture and societal institutions? What, indeed, are the chief theoretical foundations of this school of critical Marxism?

The *Praxis* School: A Summary

The *Praxis* school of Marxist humanist thought in Yugoslavia (1963-75) achieved international recognition for its creative, nondogmatic, open-ended, humanistic reconceptualization of Marxist-Leninist theory and critique of socialist practice.[11] While the 1960 Bled Symposium rejected the Engels-Lenin theory of reflection and the concomitant dogmatic conception of dialectical materialism as antithetical to creative Marxism, it was the Korčula Summer School (1963-74) and the Yugoslav (1964-74) and international (1965-74) editions of *Praxis* that became the primary forums for the development of this new school.[12] Among the most frequent Yugoslav contributors to *Praxis* were Branko Bošnjak, Mihajlo Djurić, Danko Grlić, Milan Kangrga, Veljko Korać,

Andrija Krešić, Ivan Kuvačić, Mihailo Marković, Zagorka (Pešić-) Golubović, Gajo Petrović, Svetozar Stojanović, Rudi Supek, Ljubomir Tadić, Predrag Vranicki, and Miladin Životić. There were also less frequent, yet important, contributions to *Praxis* by Dobrica Ćosić, Branko Horvat, Božidar Jakšić, Vojin Milić, Veljko Rus, Josip Županov, and many others.[13]

Praxis theorists became anathema to the late Tito by 1968, when they were accused of corrupting the youth and encouraging student demonstrations. Following the ill-fated Croatian national renaissance in 1971 and the crackdown on both national and liberal intellectuals and party leaders, *Praxis* theorists found themselves increasingly isolated and harassed. Eight *Praxis* theorists— Golubović, Trivo Indjić (who later recanted and left the "Belgrade Eight"), Marković, Dragoljub Mićunović, Nebojša Popov, Stojanović, Tadić, and Životić—were suspended from teaching in 1975 and dismissed from the University of Belgrade by the end of 1980.

But the regime's campaign against independent Marxist thinkers was much broader and affected at least thirty scholars, resulting in blacklists covering radio, television, and public appearances and publishing in general. In 1975, *Praxis* and *Filozofija*, two leading journals for neo-Marxist thought, were forced to close. The 1975 and 1976 Korčula Summer Schools with the theme "Socialism and Human Rights" were banned, as was the 1975 Meeting of the Yugoslav Sociological Association. Following vigorous protest by the international academic community, the "Belgrade Seven" were reinstated in a new Center for Philosophy and Social Theory at Belgrade University's Institute of Social Sciences in July 1981. Marković and Richard J. Bernstein began editing *Praxis International* (Oxford), while Golubović, Rus, Stojanović, Supek, and Tadić joined its editorial board. By 1990, five of the "Belgrade Eight" were reportedly restored to their teaching positions at Belgrade University, along with Djurić who was fired from his job in 1972 and sentenced to two years (commuted to nine months) for criticizing the proposed 1974 Constitution.[14]

The scholarly output of *Praxis* theorists in terms of books, journal articles, and symposia has been prodigious, though relatively little has been translated thus far. The theoretical contributions of the *Praxis* school to Marxism lie primarily in philosophical anthropology, political sociology, epistemology, and ethics. Drawing on the writings of the young Marx and the Western intellectual heritage, *Praxis* theorists advanced one of the most far-reaching theoretical critiques of Stalinism as "state capitalism" (later modified to "state socialism"). Their critique of Stalinism and dogmatic Marxism focused on the conception of the state as the instrument of change in society from capitalism to socialism. Stalinism was a system designed to utilize the state as a "dictatorship of the proletariat" in order to abolish private property, collectivize agriculture, and eradicate the remnants of "bourgeois" mentality, class relationships, exploitation, and conflict in society. In practice, the Yugoslavs point out, the Stalinist version of Marxism resulted in a counterrevolution, that is, in the domination of totalitarian forms of the state machinery and bureaucracy *over* the proletariat. While private property was abolished as the primary exploitative agency in society, its role was assumed by state ownership and control of nationalized property. This, in effect, meant control by a huge governmental, party, and state bureaucracy. Clearly, there was no room in such a system for either creative Marxist thought or the simultaneous liberation of the individual and society.

Dogmatic Marxism and Stalinism eschewed Marx's concept of alienation and the dynamic conception of man as an active agent in history—a being of praxis, a free, creative, and self-creative (self-actualizing) being. The idea of praxis—of man's potential to transform both himself and the world—thus became the distinguishing hallmark and the fundamental conceptual framework of the *Praxis* school of thought. This radicalization of Marxist thought shifts the balance of Marx's economic and historical determinism from the determinist toward the voluntarist or action-oriented end of the scale. *Praxis* theorists emphasize that while consciousness is determined by life and men are prisoners of their circumstances, men can also change these circumstances.

Influenced by existentialism and personalism, *Praxis* theorists developed a perspective that centers on the liberation and all-round development of the human individual. This amounts to a Copernican revolution in Marxism—a modern odyssey explored in this author's interdisciplinary study, *The Yugoslav Search for Man*. Combining elements of socialist personalism with existentialism and a noneschatological vision of communism as a continuous open-ended process, *Praxis* theorists came close to formulating a Yugoslav Marxism-existentialism. Unlike orthodox Marxists, *Praxis* theorists elaborated a vision of the classless society that is not devoid of all conflict and in which individuals may continue to be alienated. Hence the Western impression of Petrović's Heideggerian Marxism. The Yugoslav conception of man as a being of praxis—a being of freedom—led spontaneously to the question of responsibility and ethics. Yet on this epochal issue—as on many others—*Praxis* thinking diverges. Thus, Kangrga argues for Marx's "permanent revolution," understood as the continuous revolutionizing of underlying social conditions that give rise to the question of ethics.[15] Stojanović and Supek, on the other hand, erect new ethical rules to govern the relationship between the individual revolutionary and the revolutionary movement and its avant-garde, the party.[16] In contrast to Marx's, Engels's, and especially Lenin's moral-ethical relativism, Yugoslav theorists posit the need for a socialist "ethical imperative" as an essential constitutive element of man as a free being.

Inspired by Marx's concept of a "free association of producers," conceived as a dealienated community (*Gemeinschaft*) of liberated personalities, *Praxis* theorists engendered a radicalization of the Yugoslav theoretical innovation in self-management. Holding up a theoretical mirror to everyday practice, they offered one of the most trenchant critiques of the shortfalls of actual self-management practice, which they saw impaired by the triumvirate of party organs and bureaucracy in the political sphere, hierarchical power structures in the sphere of industrial relations, and anarchy, selfishness, and embourgeoisement buttressed by "market socialism" in the economic sphere.[17]

While the *Praxis* school of thought has contributed to a greater understanding of the mutual interrelationship of the individual and society, it has failed to deal with the question of power, preferring to follow Marx's quest for the abolition of power instead of its institutionalization, division, and limitation. Second, while *Praxis* theorists have begun to connect Stalinism with Lenin's organizational dilemmas, they still insist on separating Stalin from Lenin and Lenin from Marx and Engels. Thus, Golubović in her controversial 1982 *Sociologija* article expressed the *Praxis* consensus on the need for socialism to integrate bourgeois freedoms and basic human rights and took issue with the "metaphysical" conception of the party as the infallible representative of "historical truth."[18] Yet Marx and Engels clearly rejected any and all "bourgeois" notions of rights, freedoms, and morality as so much hypocrisy and "false consciousness" bolstering exploitation and alienation in a class society.[19] In spite of Tadić's insight that "from absolute knowledge to absolute power is but one step,"[20] *Praxis* theorists have yet to discover the Stalinist epistemological roots of party monopoly in Marx's and Engels's claim in the *Communist Manifesto* that communists see further and understand better the nature and goals of the revolutionary workers' movement.[21]

Third, *Praxis* theorists urge the democratization of the party and blame the monopoly of social, economic, and political power on bureaucracy and the Stalinized conception of the party, as if the *Communist* Party could consider itself Bolshevik yet act as a Menshevik, that is, a social-democratic, party. What is unusual is that Stojanović's call for the democratization of the Yugoslav League of Communists at the 1983 meeting of the Yugoslav Sociological Association in Portorož reflected a consensus among both the Yugoslav intelligentsia (including *Praxis* theorists) *and* liberal party members themselves.

The greatest contribution of the *Praxis* school to neo-Marxism as well as to the liberalization, democratization, and humanization of Yugoslavia's sociopolitical system has been its insistence upon freedom of inquiry and communications, critical thought, and an open society. Marx's "ruthless critique of everything existing" was applied consistently not only to capitalism but also to state socialism (Stalinism) and party-guided self-management socialism as well. This critical methodology opened up many new fields of inquiry, but it also raised doubts concerning the adequacy of Marxist analytical tools for conceptualizing twentieth-century phenomena in capitalism or socialism.

Theoretically, the 1980s appear as a lost decade for the *Praxis* school of thought. It is not because *Praxis* theorists were inactive or stopped creating and thinking.[22] Rather, their theoretical models in the 1980s have lagged considerably behind the innovative works this author has characterized elsewhere as "camp literature" as well as social developments highlighted by the rebirth of civic culture and civil society. Works by the younger generation of Yugoslav scholars, such as Kosta Čavoški and Vojislav Koštunica's *Party Pluralism or Monism*, exposing the true nature of the party's monopoly of power, projected a much larger trajectory.[23] Whereas in the 1960s and 1970s the *Praxis* theorists represented the intellectual avant-garde—indeed, a sort of loyal opposition—in the 1980s this role was assumed by a much broader array of intellectuals, writers, students, and citizens engaged in reclaiming both personal autonomy and historical truth.[24]

Some *Praxis* theorists admit that much. Thus, Stojanović writes in his *Perestroika* that "critics of existing communism who rely on Marx's communism are threatened with a new, now deadly, danger: that of becoming conservative."[25] Furthermore, during a round-table discussion of her 1988 book *The Identity Crisis of Contemporary Yugoslav Society*, organized by the journal *Sociologija*, Golubović agreed with her critic that "it is necessary to reexamine also Marxist concepts and their content as well as the entire conceptual apparatus and their enrichment by new achievements in the knowledge process."[26] A reexamination of the *Praxis* school of thought has already begun among Yugoslav philosophers themselves. For example, *Theoria*, the journal of the Serbian Philosophical Association, devoted a double issue in 1988 to the theme "*Praxis* Marxism and Yugoslav Philosophy." The most compelling critique concerns the very concept of praxis itself. Dragan Mistrić claims that praxis lacks a normative foundation, which can only be established via dialogue and consensus. Hence, concludes Mistrić, political pluralism and a multiparty system are the necessary preconditions for a truly emancipatory social practice.[27] While the *Praxis* school of thought lagged behind reality in the 1980s, its practitioners more than made up for the continuing theoretical gap by actively contributing to the emergence of an autonomous civic culture and civil society in post-Tito Yugoslavia.

Praxis and the Rebirth of Civil Society

Adam Michnik concludes in his "New Evolutionism" that the source of fundamental change in the Soviet bloc is "an unceasing struggle for reform and evolution that seeks an expansion of civil liberties and human rights."[28] Yugoslavia in the post-Tito era has seen a remarkable rebirth of civic culture and civil society. The 1980s witnessed a society-wide search for the historical truth and the expansion of autonomous space. This multifaceted dissent could be examined in terms of the three tiers of "camp literature," namely, controversial biographies of Tito, novels regarding the incarceration of the "Cominformists" on Goli Otok (a prison camp on the Naked Island), and testimonies and memoirs of former political prisoners published abroad but proscribed in Yugoslavia.[29]

Even more important in terms of the rebirth of a civil society are the hundreds of petitions signed by thousands of intellectuals, students, professionals, workers, and citizens during the 1980s, culminating in the institutionalization of dissent in various committees in defense of basic human rights and freedoms, alternative movements, and, finally, political parties. *Praxis* Marxists actively contributed to this society-wide renaissance.

The fearless Montenegrin Partisan, Professor Ljubomir Tadić, was the first among the "Belgrade Eight" to sign a petition in the post-Tito era calling for an amnesty of political prisoners on 6 June 1980.[30] Six of the "Belgrade Eight"—Golubović, Mićunović, Popov, Stojanović, Tadić, and Životić—signed the petition to delete the category "hostile propaganda" from the Socialist Federal Republic of Yugoslavia (SFRY) Criminal Code on 3 November 1980.[31] Even Indjić found the courage by 21 June 1983 to sign a petition to amend Article 154 of the Constitution concerning political beliefs.[32]

But it is only following the death of Radomir Radović that Mihailo Marković ignored his own advice concerning permissible "limits" for a critically minded intellectual and signed the first petition ever in postwar Yugoslavia calling on the interior minister to account for an unexplained death or accept responsibility for it and resign from office.[33] Marković's change of heart was all the more significant since it occurred during the post-Tito era of uncertainty and increasing repression. Not only were critical issues of *Theoria* and other journals banned, along with such books as Nebojša Popov's *Social Conflicts*, but the regime's prosecution of intellectuals following the 20 April 1984 arrest of twenty-eight participants in a "flying university" and the death of one of them (Radović) appeared to be the least opportune moment for any expression of dissent or criticism.[34]

The trial of the "Belgrade Six" in 1984 had the opposite effect of that intended by the post-Tito collective leadership seeking to intimidate the Yugoslav intelligentsia.[35] Instead, the show trial galvanized the Yugoslav intelligentsia and produced not only more petitions from all over the country but resulted also in the founding of the Committee for the Defense of Freedom of Thought and Expression (CDFTE) on 10 November 1984, which Marković calls "the first successful breakthrough of civil society in Yugoslavia since the war."[36]

Apart from the *Praxis* group's Open Letter to the Serbian Assembly of 28 August 1984 protesting renewed political trials and demanding democratic reforms,[37] the CDFTE was the boldest civil-rights initiative of the decade. The Committee for the Defense of Freedom of Thought and Expression was founded by nineteen intellectuals in Belgrade, including two *Praxis* Marxists—Marković and Tadić—later joined by Golubović.[38] Among the founders were no fewer than twelve members of the prestigious Serbian Academy of Arts and Sciences. CDFTE is sometimes referred to informally as "Ćosić's Committee," after Dobrica Ćosić, perhaps the best-known living Serbian writer in Yugoslavia today. Due to regime pressure, harassment, and persecution, the CDFTE membership has changed over the years, with some members forced to drop out and others replacing them, yet the committee has stuck unflinchingly to its original mission. In its Founding Statement, addressed to the assemblies of the Socialist

Republic (SR) of Serbia and the SFRY and to the Yugoslav public, the CDFTE reaffirmed the inalienable human right of freedom of thought and expression and pledged that ''the Committee will support citizens who are persecuted for expressing their opinions.''[39]

But the CDFTE went further than just the issue of free speech, calling by 1986 for political democracy. In its ''Proposal for Establishing the Rule of Law,'' addressed to the Federal Assembly and the Yugoslav public on 4 October 1986, the CDFTE demanded the abolition of single-party monopoly of power through free and direct elections; restoration of uniform legal and political equality of citizens; democratic control of power and officials by free public opinion; actual independence of courts from the executive and legislative branches; abolition of the authorities' discretionary privileges to curb rights and freedoms; deletion of constitutional provisions that limit or revoke rights and freedoms; abolition of preventive arrest and confinement without a time limit; abolition of the crime of thought; inviolability of private life, the right to privacy, and the secrecy of mails and other means of communication; the right to peaceful assembly and association; and the right to strike.[40] The 1986 CDFTE proposal was an unprecedented development for a Communist Party state, even ''liberal'' Yugoslavia, and reflected the timeless aspirations of countless others throughout the communist world, realized, at least in part, in the peaceful revolutions that swept Eastern Europe in 1989.

By 1988, the committee sought a public reappraisal of Tito's role in the country's worsening economic and political crisis. By 1-2 December 1989, even Djilas signed a statement expressing concern regarding the party's continuing monopoly of power as the main barrier to solving the national and all other Yugoslav problems.[41] The committee's petitions appeared in the Yugoslav media for the first time on 22 June 1989, in the Belgrade daily *Borba*, which printed CDFTE's Open Letter calling for the abolition of preventive detention in reference to the political trials of Albanians in Kosovo.[42] The CDFTE remains one of the few instances in Yugoslavia where a group of human-rights activists or anyone else defends the civil liberties and rights of *all* people, regardless of nationality. Already on 15 June 1987, the CDFTE directed an Appeal to the Presidencies of the SFRY and the SR Bosnia-Hercegovina, asking for the reversal of the ban on the book *Islam Between East and West* by Alija Izetbegović, a respected Islamic scholar who served half of his nine-year term in prison only to be elected president of Bosnia-Hercegovina in 1990.[43] Thus far, the press in Bosnia-Hercegovina is the least encumbered in postcommunist Yugoslavia.

Popov reflects in an 1989 interview that ''without a well-developed culture, even an 'underground one,' it is difficult to imagine, and even less to begin, practical changes of the existing state of affairs.''[44] As indicated above, individual *Praxis* Marxists were actively engaged in contributing to the institutionalization of dissent. It can, of course, be argued that their contributions have been uneven, and, more plausibly, that they are still haunted by Marx's, if not Stalin's, ghost.[45] But no one can deny *Praxis* and other Yugoslav activists their civic courage.

The independent, all-Yugoslav orientation of the CDFTE, for example, is affirmed by Marković:

> All other similar initiatives in the past have taken place within officially recognized and approved organizational forms: journals (*Pogledi, Perspektive, Praxis, Filozofija, Nova Revija*), newspapers (*Student, Studentski list, Mladina*), societies (Philosophical Society, Sociological Society, Writers' Union), scholarly institutions (Center for Philosophy and Social Theory in Belgrade, Faculty of Philosophy in Belgrade, Serbian Academy of Sciences and Arts). All of those are controlled by some political authority. According to Yugoslav laws, no group is permitted to meet, no journal or newspaper is allowed to exist and function, unless they are properly registered and approved by the corresponding authority.[46]

Marković contends that in contrast to other initiatives, the CDFTE "never asked to be recognized and officially approved."

In fairness, though, one should recognize all the manifold groups and committees in Yugoslavia that sought to expand the space for independent thought and action during the 1980s. Most of these groups chose the "Mihajlov strategy" of working for the transformation of the one-party dictatorship using the existing laws and the constitution as guides and demanding that the authorities respect their own laws. Among many such human-rights groups, notable are the Yugoslav Chapter of the International Helsinki Federation, the efforts to publish an independent paper, *Self-Management* (which finally succeeded in February 1990 after a five-year legal struggle), and the quest by the Action Against Abuses of Psychiatry and Medicine to stop the medical criminalization of dissent.[47] By 23 April 1989, more than thirty human-rights organizations from all over the country met in Sarajevo and elected a three-member commission to investigate all political trials in Yugoslavia since 1945.[48]

Praxis and Nationalism

While the CDFTE represented the institutionalization of *dissent* along an all-Yugoslav orientation in 1984, the first all-Yugoslav opposition *movement*—the Association for Yugoslav Democratic Initiative (AYDI)—was founded by *Praxis* Marxists and their sympathizers in February 1989. True to *Praxis* philosophy, the AYDI was conceived as a movement rather than a political party, and, hence, AYDI did not field candidates for office in the 1990 elections. In spite of its self-limitation, the AYDI has been harassed by both communists and nationalists, many of whom switched allegiances but kept their dogmatic, totalitarian ways of thinking and acting in the postcommunist era.

The Association for Yugoslav Democratic Initiative, headed by the Croatian economist Branko Horvat, held its initial meeting in Zagreb on 10 January 1989, announcing its aim as the "democratic integration of Yugoslavia with full respect for civil rights and freedoms, national identities and choices."[49] AYDI's formal organizing meeting took place in Zagreb on 2 February 1989. Among the members of AYDI's executive and advisory committees are such noted *Praxis* scholars as Milan Kangrga, Andrija Krešić, Ivan Kuvačić, Milan Mirić, Nebojša Popov, Rudi Supek, Ljubomir Tadić, Predrag Vranicki, and Srdjan Vrcan. By the end of 1989, AYDI expanded to some sixteen branches and 1,500 members, even though only the Titograd branch was officially registered. As Popov explains, AYDI sees as its major goal "a reform of the Yugoslav constitution that would guarantee individual rights and freedoms and not merely collective rights and freedoms, in the first place national rights."[50]

One might recall that the *Praxis* theorists have consistently advocated the principle of national/ethnic tolerance in Yugoslavia. Prevailing *Praxis* thought, adumbrated by Popov, Tadić, and Golubović, has also consistently advocated democratization and a truly federal parliamentary system for Yugoslavia with constitutional guarantees of *individual* rights and freedoms. Yet *Praxis* theorists are also aware of the "Catch 22" dilemma when it comes to democracy and nationalism in Yugoslavia, since the solution of the national question presupposes a democratic political framework, whereas a democratic political framework presupposes a strong democratic political culture that emphasizes individual rather than group or national rights. Thus, Tadić perceives the national and nationalistic excesses in Yugoslavia as a substitute for democracy.[51] Golubović is careful to distinguish between national identity and culture on the one hand, and nationalism as ideology or a negative attitude toward other nationalities on the other. For Golubović, the problem of nationalism in contemporary Yugoslavia is "predominantly a question of eradicating republican-cum-national statism and bureaucracy, which inevitably incites nationalism."[52] Yet the dilemma of nationalism as an ideology that incites hatred of other nationalities and embroils Yugoslavia in a no-win civil war goes much deeper—to the lack of a developed democratic political culture. In Popov's summary:

> Without a strong enough democratic tradition . . . the knowledge that the threat to human rights and freedoms affects primarily individuals and not only ethnic groups or nations, is slow in growing and spreading. The UJDI [Udruženje za Jugoslovensku Demokratsku Inicijativu—AYDI] advocates precisely such a broader comprehension of human rights and freedoms as well as their institutionalized protection and development.[53]

The AYDI's all-Yugoslav orientation is reflected in its three-point program:

1. We are not an alternative movement. For every alternative there is a need for at least two options. For Yugoslavia there is no alternative to radical democratization.

2. We are not a new party similar to those organized in Slovenia. Every party is an organization of like-minded people who struggle to gain power. We are not interested in power and like-minded we are not. . . . We do not want to be a party because we advocate something more fundamental: a formation of a movement for the democratic transformation of Yugoslavia. Therefore, we are not interested in power but in creating conditions that would facilitate this transformation.

3. We are not a militant, revolutionary organization. We do not intend to destroy the regime by creating unrest or organizing street demonstrations of solidarity or protests. We oppose destruction and anarchy and favor transformation and construction by democratic methods.[54]

While neither a political party nor a revolutionary organization, and largely ignored by the Yugoslav public, the Association for Yugoslav Democratic Initiative received the same treatment by the authorities as the other fledgling organizations and political parties in post-Tito Yugoslavia—obstruction and harassment. At first, the Ministry of Internal Affairs of the SR Croatia refused to grant a registration permit for AYDI in an attempt to force AYDI to join the Socialist Alliance, the main transmission belt of the League of Communists. This the AYDI would not do, since it would then become part of a republic organization directly under the control of the local Communist Party. Undaunted, the AYDI opened a branch in Ljubljana, Slovenia, on 9 April 1989. In Belgrade, the AYDI branch applied for registration on 18 April 1989 but was denied registration by the Security Service on 13 September 1989. On 27 May 1989, AYDI's Mostar branch opened in Bosnia-Hercegovina with forty-one members. In March and May 1989, the AYDI published the first two issues of its independent paper, *Republika*. But AYDI's confrontation with the powers that be was only beginning. By the end of 1989, Popov and Rade Radovanović, leaders of AYDI's Belgrade branch, were charged with a misdemeanor for organizing AYDI meetings on 19 October and 2 November 1989. The CDFTE lodged a protest with the presidency of the SR Serbia on 11 December 1989, complaining that the ''state power in Serbia is not acting as it preaches and promises, and that its commission's recommendations for the reform of the social and political system are empty promises and a deception.''[55]

Even more ominous is the discrimination against AYDI by the post-1990 election nationalist regimes. Thus, on 30 May 1990, AYDI's Split branch protested the Croatian Democratic Alliance's methods in the elections to the city council, recalling that the communists used basically the same, undemocratic methods while they were in power. On 10 June 1990, AYDI's headquarters in Titograd, Montenegro, sent the following cable to the new Croatian president, Dr. Franjo Tudjman: ''We were informed that prominent members of our organization (in Zagreb), Prof. Dr. Branko Horvat and Prof. Dr. Žarko Puhovski, must appear in court because of their public activities at YDI conferences. We hope that one of the first acts of the new administration in the SR Croatia will not be the punishment of citizens for political activities."[56]

The most disturbing development of all, however, has been the growing polarization among dissenting groups and even *Praxis* Marxists themselves along nationalist lines. For example, Golubović entered into polemics with Tomaž Mastnak, criticizing his presumption that "anything that comes out of Serbia is not only anti-democratic but even fascist," and charged that Slovenia missed its chance at democracy in the early 1980s since "national feelings prevailed over democratic trends in both official and unofficial circles."[57] Even more divisive is the issue of Kosovo. Participants in a round-table discussion examining the 1990 Report on Kosovo by an independent commission, established by AYDI and the Yugoslav Forum for Human Rights and Legal Security of Citizens, concluded that

> Kosovo is only the most extreme case of that which is characteristic in the entire country: an unsatisfactory state of human rights and the absence of a dialogue. In part, this is due to the pre-eminence given to the national at the expense of civil rights, due to which the people and nationalities in Yugoslavia, including the members of various groups in Kosovo, gravitate towards ghettoization, instead of seeking solutions for living together.[58]

The 159-page preliminary report *The Kosovo Knot: Unravel or Cut?* brought praise as well as condemnation. In Ljubljana, Professor Rastko Močnik praised the report for its "factual analysis, aided by the latest scientific models and providing intelligent arguments."[59] In Belgrade, on the other hand, Tadić took AYDI's Belgrade branch to task for its efforts to establish a dialogue with Kosovo Albanians in order to arrive at solutions. In Tadić's purported view, "They are Serbian liberals who underwent surgery for the removal of every and all national feeling. They side with other nationalities when they claim that Serbia is threatening them. They are completely blind to the problems of Serbia."[60]

If true, Tadić's imputed critique of Serbian liberals would only confirm the almost total triumph of nationalist passions among Yugoslav leaders and intellectuals as well as the masses. It would also signify the reversal of Tadić's long-standing philosophical stance of personal autonomy and the centrality of a democratic political culture based on tolerance. It was Tadić, after all, who in his 1986 samizdat *Is Nationalism Our Destiny?* aptly summed up the essential element in a liberating political culture: "After the failures of socialist experiments in our century, which easily transformed liberating forces into repressive tyranny, we need to consciously nurture the *spirit of tolerance* in order to break the genealogy of tyranny and its easy propagation in world history, and thus conquer want in all its manifestations."[61]

As the situation has deteriorated, AYDI members have come under great pressure to proclaim unequivocally their allegiance to a particular national identity. Kangrga, for one, reportedly declared that he considers himself a Croatian nationalist and not a Yugoslav internationalist. By 1991, not only the AYDI but human rights activists, journalists, and dissidents throughout the country seemed anguished, if not demoralized, by the continuous stifling of independent thought and action by both the old, communist and the new, nationalist regimes in Yugoslavia. By January 1991, Ivan Zvonimir Čičak resigned from the Croatian Society for the Protection of Human Rights, followed by Dr. Žarko Puhovski, a prominent Zagreb sociologist, and for the same reasons. Čičak claimed in *Vjesnik* (29 January 1991) that under the present government it was "useless to strive to protect the human rights of others when one is unable to protect one's own rights." And Puhovski deplored in *Vreme* (18 February 1991) the "renewed emphasis on a totalitarian political atmosphere in Croatia," where "any attempt to seek justice for whatever minority group elicits a charge of antistate activity." Bucking the nationalist trend, *Vreme* (Time), an independent weekly founded in November 1990 by the Belgrade civil rights attorney Srdja Popović, emerged as a leading democratic, all-Yugoslav periodical.

Praxis and Democratic Socialism

There is a growing realization, East and West, that the key to the democratic evolution of postcommunist Yugoslavia is the democratic transformation of its most populous republic—Serbia. It is, therefore, all the more significant that by 1990 Serbia witnessed the revival of the Democratic Party (DP), led by none other than Dragoljub Mićunović, one of the "Belgrade Eight," with Tadić also joining the DP. The formation of the Democratic Party was announced at a press conference in Belgrade on 12 December 1989, and its founding congress was held on 3 March 1990. Mićunović was elected president, while Čavoški headed the executive committee. The Democratic Party's basic principles emphasize fundamental freedoms and human rights, the rule of law, parliamentarism, a multiparty system with an opposition, democratic federalism, and a market economy.[62] The Democratic Party thus represents a *tertium quid* between the left-wing nationalism of Milošević's communists (renamed the Serbian Socialist Party in 1990) and the right-wing nationalism of the Serbian Renewal Movement, led by the writer Vuk Drašković.

What is the relationship of the Democratic Party to the ruling party and the *Praxis* school of Marxism? In contrast to the *Praxis*-sponsored Association for Yugoslav Democratic Initiative, the Democratic Party is not simply an association, alliance, or movement but a full-fledged political party. This, in itself, represents a clear break with the prevailing *Praxis* tenet advocating not a multiparty system but a system without parties.[63] The Democratic Party fielded candidates for office in the 1990 republic elections in Serbia but lost to the ruling Serbian Socialist Party, which won 48 percent of the vote and 78 percent of the seats in the 9 December elections and the 23 December runoffs, while Milošević was elected to the presidency directly with 65 percent of the vote.

Just like the AYDI and other independent groups, associations, and political parties, the Democratic Party was obstructed and harassed from its inception.

Thus, the Democratic Party's attempts to register as a political party were repeatedly rebuffed; a private ad to be aired on Belgrade television for its independent paper, *Demokratija*, was banned on 15 May 1990; and police also banned DP's proposed meetings in such cities as Užice (29 May) and Titov Drvar (3 July). Not only did Milošević effectively control the media, the police, the Socialist Alliance, the veterans' organization, and other state and party networks throughout Serbia, but he also refused to legalize opposition parties until 27 July 1990. The Democratic Party organized mass rallies of 30,000-80,000 people during June and September 1990, which were dispersed by the police.[64] On 22 November 1990, the communist-run Serbian Assembly rejected opposition demands to participate in supervising the elections and counting of the votes. On 23 November 1990, twelve major opposition parties announced their boycott of the upcoming elections. Two days later, the Serbian Assembly reversed itself and granted the opposition demands.

In retrospect, the democratic opposition in Serbia had barely one month to campaign before the elections took place. The opposition also committed a tactical error by failing to unite until 12 December 1990, when twenty parties formed a coalition—the United Opposition of Serbia. There was also widespread apathy among the population. With Milošević's almost total control of the political and economic levers of power as well as the mass media, the outcome of the first semi-free elections in Serbia since World War II was a foregone conclusion.

Nevertheless, it is the Democratic Party, with its middle-of-the-road program of pluralistic democracy, market economy, and the rule of law, that lends hope for a democratic transformation of both Serbia and Yugoslavia. Clearly, the Democratic Party program transcends the utopian elements in *Praxis* philosophy, since it strives to institutionalize and limit, rather than abolish, political power. Ironically, the Democratic Party continues to encounter opposition not only in Milošević's Serbia but also in Tudjman's Croatia. Thus on 10 February 1991, M. Vujnović, president of the Zagreb branch of the Democratic Party, was detained for interrogation for alleged criminal acts of "provoking national, racial and religious hatred."[65]

Throughout Yugoslavia, the old, communist and the new, nationalist regimes are equally dedicated to muzzling the mass media. Independent-minded writers and journalists continue to be harassed, fired, or prosecuted in Slovenia, Croatia, Vojvodina, Serbia, and Montenegro.[66] Milošević's control of the mass media in Serbia led by March 1991 to massive demonstrations by Serbian students and oppositionists led by Vuk Drašković and his Serbian Renewal Movement. Their demand for the resignation of the communist media authorities was met with police and army using tanks to quell the four-day demonstrations, which left two dead and hundreds of demonstrators injured, followed by several hundred arrests, including that of Drašković. This only infuriated the protesters who then escalated their demands calling for the resignation of the government and for new elections.

Milošević made concessions as his popularity began to ebb. Drašković was released. The army withdrew. In a game of musical chairs, some media bosses were "rotated" once again. In the aftermath of the "Four Days in March," which shook the capital of Serbia and Yugoslavia, an atmosphere, if not the reality, of martial law prevailed. Yet Milošević's days seemed to be numbered. Whereas in 1988 Milošević and his supporters successfully manipulated mass nationalist demonstrations that brought down the governments in Vojvodina and Montenegro, the independent mass demonstrations in March 1991 came close to toppling Milošević himself.[67] By the spring of 1991, it became clear to both Serbian students and intellectuals that Milošević's promises of meaningful reform were just that—promises. Federal elections slated for the spring of 1991 were also postponed indefinitely, while republic leaderships continued their confrontational talks with Belgrade.

In another bizarre twist in Balkan politics and a desperate, last attempt to preserve its power and privileges, the ruling party took a page from the *Praxis* manual concerning political parties. Thus, a party-sponsored commission charged with drafting new proposals for socioeconomic and political reform in 1989 put forward recommendations including the need to go beyond the concept and the practice of a party-state. The commission proposed that workers and citizens should have the right to organize freely into alliances and associations under the aegis of the Socialist Alliance, with direct elections and an independent judiciary. However, the League of Communists would retain its "important" and "inevitable" integrative role.

Milošević spelled out the new party line in an interview with the Paris-based *Le Monde* in mid-July 1989. After paying lip service to the need for rehabilitating the market mechanism in Yugoslavia and defending Tito, Milošević admitted that the system of rotation destroyed the sense of responsibility and that the economic crisis could not be solved without changes in the political system. Significantly, Milošević was opposed to a multiparty system, since "the existence of more parties would not solve anything."[68]

There is, hence, an ominous theoretical convergence between Milošević's ruling party and the *Praxis* utopia concerning a system without parties. Among *Praxis* theorists, Marković has consistently championed this concept. It is, therefore, not altogether surprising that by 1990 Mihailo Marković was elected vice-president of the Serbian League of Communists—renamed the Socialist Party of Serbia. Of course, the basic theoretical and practical contradiction engendered by *Praxis*'s utopia remains: power is not abolished—it merely becomes camouflaged behind the wand of ideology. We thus "arrive finally at a socialist Camelot with all the earmarks of the totalitarian state."[69]

In conclusion, serious theoretical and practical challenges remain for Yugoslav intellectuals and policy makers alike on the road to a democratic future. These challenges encompass the democratic transformation of the entire society; the development of a civic culture and civil society that transcend national and group rights toward *universal human rights*; and a total social, economic, and political reconstruction of the country (or its successor states) that would recreate incentives and competition and reward competence in the economy and society and that would transcend radically *Praxis*'s socialist paradigm focusing on distribution and develop a new theoretical framework of wealth creation.

As Elie Abel and Milan Nikolić aver, Yugoslavia is a "graveyard of reforms," where all past economic and political perestroikas have come to naught.[70] At the beginning of 1991 an estimated one-third of Yugoslav enterprises were insolvent. Another third missed paying their employees regularly. Due to falling living standards, strikes proliferated throughout the 1980s. A year after dinar convertibility (Prime Minister Ante Marković's major achievement), there was still 60 percent inflation, 15 percent unemployment (in addition to a million Yugoslav "guest workers" in Western Europe), and a $22 billion foreign debt. The dire economic circumstances only sharpened ethnic conflicts and intensified the search for scapegoats. Corruption, bureaucracy, apathy, and disillusionment held sway at all levels of Yugoslav society, from top to bottom.

Ćosić himself realizes that "we tried reform long before the others, but we failed to produce a fundamental change."[71] As to marketizing socialism— anathema to *Praxis* Marxists but ubiquitous as a slogan in contemporary Yugoslavia—it is not only a contradiction in terms but also impossible in practice since the present economic system in Yugoslavia is incompatible with basic economic laws of market competition.[72] Given the historical legacy of forty-five years of communist rule that has brought the country to moral, economic, and political bankruptcy and civil war, a moral and spiritual renewal appear as a necessary precondition for social, economic, and political reconstruction and a more humane future for postcommunist Yugoslavia.[73]

Notes

1. On the downfall of communist Yugoslavia via the ballot box, see Mihajlo Mihajlov, "Can Yugoslavia Survive?" *Journal of Democracy* 2, no. 2 (Spring 1991): 79-91. On the rebirth of civil society, see "Yugoslavia's Permanent Crisis," *East European Reporter* 2, no. 2 (1986): 46-50.

2. On human rights and dissent in Yugoslavia, consult Oskar Gruenwald, *The Yugoslav Search for Man: Marxist Humanism in Contemporary Yugoslavia* (South Hadley, MA: J.F. Bergin, 1983), esp. chap. 11, "Tito's Legacy and Human Rights," pp. 268-87; idem, "Yugoslav Camp Literature: Rediscovering the Ghost of a Nation's Past-Present-Future," *Slavic Review* 46, no. 3-4 (Fall-Winter 1987): 513-28; and O. Gruenwald and Karen Rosenblum-Cale, eds., *Human Rights in Yugoslavia* (New York: Irvington Publishers, 1986).

3. Peter Palmer, "Truth the First Casualty in Yugoslavia," *East European Reporter* 4, no. 3 (Autumn-Winter 1990): 71-72; see also Slavenka Drakulić, "Letter From Yugoslavia: Living in a Le Carré Novel," *Nation*, 4 March 1991, pp. 261-64.

4. For background, see Sami Repishti, "Human Rights and the Albanian Nationality in Yugoslavia," in *Human Rights in Yugoslavia*, 227-81; Helsinki Watch, "Human

Rights in a Dissolving Yugoslavia," 9 January 1991, pp. 1-12; and the authoritative report of an independent commission set up by the Association for Yugoslav Democratic Initiative and edited by civil-rights lawyers and activists, *Kosovski čvor: Drešiti ili seći?* [The Kosovo Knot: Unravel or Cut?], ed. Srdja Popović, Dejan Janča, and Tanja Petovar (Belgrade: Chronos, 1990).

5. On the concept of totalitarian democracy and Tito's legacy, see Gruenwald, *The Yugoslav Search for Man*, 146-94 and 268-319, respectively.

6. "Serbs Block Croatian's Turn at Yugoslav Helm," *Los Angeles Times*, 16 May 1991, p. A1.

7. Marko Milivojević, "The Yugoslav People's Army: Another Jaruzelski on the Way?" *South Slav Journal* (London), no. 40-41 (Summer-Autumn 1988): 1-18; Milan Vego, "Yugoslavia in Crisis: The Army's Role" (Meeting Report, Wilson Center, East European Studies, Washington, DC, May-June 1991), 3. According to Vego, a group of retired generals has formed the League of Communists' Movement for Yugoslavia dedicated to the preservation of Tito's one-party system.

8. On Slobodan Milošević's manipulation of Serbian national sentiment concerning Kosovo, see Peter Ferdinand, "Yugoslavia—Beyond the Beginning of the End?" *Journal of Communist Studies* 6, no. 3 (September 1990): 99-104.

9. On the pitfalls of Titoism, see Marko Milivojević, "Descent Into Chaos: Yugoslavia's Worsening Crisis," *South Slav Journal*, no. 43-44 (Spring-Summer 1989): 2-38.

10. On democratic prospects for postcommunist Yugoslavia, see Michael Scammell, "The New Yugoslavia," *The New York Review of Books*, 19 July 1990, pp. 37-42; and idem, *Yugoslavia: The Failure of "Democratic" Communism* (New York: Freedom House, 1987).

11. This section updates my sketch of the *Praxis* school in *Biographical Dictionary of Neo-Marxism*, ed. Robert A. Gorman (Westport, CT: Greenwood Press, 1985), 349-53. For more comprehensive treatment, see Gruenwald, *The Yugoslav Search for Man*, and Gerson S. Sher, *Praxis: Marxist Criticism and Dissent in Socialist Yugoslavia* (Bloomington: Indiana University Press, 1977).

12. Rudi Supek, "Dix ans de l'école d'été de Korčula (1963-1973)," *Praxis International* 10, no. 1-2 (1974): 3-15 (International edition, henceforth cited as *Praxis* [I]).

13. On Marković and Stojanović, see David A Crocker, *Praxis and Democratic Socialism: The Critical Social Theory of Marković and Stojanović* (Atlantic Highlands, NJ: Humanities Press, 1983); on Grlić, Kangrga, Milić, Pešić-Golubović, Supek, Tadić, and Županov, see my biographical sketches in *Biographical Dictionary of Neo-Marxism*.

14. *CADDY Bulletin*, no. 53-54 (July 1989): 12 and no. 57 (January 1990): 8, respectively. (The *CADDY Bulletin* is put out by the Democracy International Committee to Aid Democratic Dissidents in Yugoslavia, founded in 1980 by Mihajlo Mihajlov.) While some *Praxis* scholars were reappointed to the Belgrade University faculty, Dr. Drago Roksandić was fired in December 1989 for his nineteenth-century historical research, which contradicts official historiography. See *CADDY Bulletin*, no. 58 (March 1990): 19.

15. Milan Kangrga, *Razmišljanja o etici* [Thoughts on Ethics] (Zagreb: *Praxis* Pocketbook Ed. No. 6, 1970), 38.

16. Svetozar Stojanović, "Stalinist 'Partiinost' and Communist Dignity," *Praxis* (I) 10, no. 1-2 (1974): 137; Rudi Supek, *Humanistička inteligencija i politika* [The Humanist Intelligentsia and Politics] (Zagreb: Studentski centar sveučilišta, 1971), 120.

17. For a dissenting view, see Josip Županov, "Egalitarizam i industrijalizam"

[Egalitarianism and Industrialism], *Sociologija* (Belgrade) 12, no. 1 (1970): 5-45, and *Samoupravljanje i društvena moć* [Self-Management and Social Power] (Zagreb: Naše teme, 1969).

18. Zagorka Golubović, "Kriza jugoslovenskog društva: Priroda krize i njeni koreni" [The Crisis of Yugoslav Society: Nature and Roots of the Crisis], *Sociologija* 24, no. 2-3 (1982): 323-31.

19. Karl Marx and Friedrich Engels, "Manifesto of the Communist Party," in *Marx and Engels: Basic Writings on Politics and Philosophy*, ed. Lewis S. Feuer (Garden City, NY: Doubleday, 1959), 22-27.

20. Ljubomir Tadić, "L'Intelligentsia dans le socialisme," *Praxis* (I) 5, no. 3-4 (1969): 407.

21. Marx and Engels, "Communist Manifesto," 20.

22. See, for example, Zagorka Golubović, "Mogućnosti za reforme u socijalističkim državama" [Possibilities for Reform in Socialist States], *Sociologija* 29, no. 4 (December 1987): 491-506; Svetozar Stojanović, "Sadašnja jugoslovenska kriza i perspektive" [The Contemporary Yugoslav Crisis and Perspectives], *Sociologija* 31, no. 2-3 (June-October 1989): 485-99.

23. Vojislav Koštunica and Kosta Čavoški, *Stranački pluralizam ili monizam: Društveni pokreti i politički sistem u Jugoslaviji, 1944-1949* (Belgrade: Center for Philosophy and Social Theory, 1983). Plates for the book were confiscated during a police raid of private printing shops in 1985. English translation by Columbia University Press, East European Monographs (1985).

24. Gruenwald, "Yugoslav Camp Literature."

25. Svetozar Stojanović, *Perestroika: From Marxism and Bolshevism to Gorbachev* (Buffalo, NY: Prometheus Books, 1988), 156.

26. Zagorka Golubović, in "Okrugli sto časopisa 'Sociologija': Razgovor o knjizi Zagorke Golubović *Kriza identiteta savremenog jugoslovenskog društva*," *Sociologija* 31, no. 1 (January 1989): 266.

27. Dragan Mistrić, "Jugoslovenska filozofija prakse i njene granice" [The Yugoslav Philosophy of *Praxis* and Its Limits], *Theoria* (Belgrade) 31, no. 1-2 (1988): 39, 49. For my critique of praxis from the normative standpoint, see "The Watershed: Kant's Categorical Imperative" and "The Principle of Love," in Gruenwald, *The Yugoslav Search for Man*, 76-78 and 106-8, respectively.

28. Adam Michnik, cited approvingly by Jeffrey C. Goldfarb, *Beyond Glasnost: The Post-Totalitarian Mind* (Chicago: University of Chicago Press, 1989), 195. On the distinction between civil society and the state, see, for example, John Keane, ed., *Civil Society and the State* (London: Verso, 1988).

29. Gruenwald, "Yugoslav Camp Literature."

30. "Petitions for Amnesty of Political Prisoners, 1980," in *Human Rights in Yugoslavia*, 561-563.

31. "Petition to Delete 'Hostile Propaganda' From the SFRY Criminal Code, 1980," in *Human Rights in Yugoslavia*, 567-80.

32. "Petition to Amend Article 154 of the Constitution Concerning Political Persuasion, 1983," in *Human Rights in Yugoslavia*, 604-10.

33. "Petition to the Interior Minister Concerning the Death of Radomir Radović, 1984," in *Human Rights in Yugoslavia*, 617-21. Golubović and Životić, inter alia, also signed this petition.

34. Nebojša Popov, *Društveni sukobi—Izazov sociologiji* (Belgrade: Center for Philosophy and Social Theory, 1983). Deals with 1968 student demonstrations. Banned.

35. O. Gruenwald, "Response: Camp Literature: Archetype for Dissent," *Slavic Review* 48, no. 2 (Summer 1989): 280-83.

36. See Toma Ognjanović's interview with Professor Mihailo Marković in *South Slav Journal*, no. 42 (Winter 1988-89): 38.

37. "Open Letter to the Serbian Assembly, 1984," in *Human Rights in Yugoslavia*, 639-43.

38. "Committee for the Defense of Freedom of Thought and Expression, 1984," in *Human Rights in Yugoslavia*, 644-48; nominated by the author for the 1988 American Association for the Advancement of Science "Scientific Freedom and Responsibility Award." The nomination summary stated: "The CDFTE has consistently upheld human rights and freedoms in post-Tito Yugoslavia. It has defended people, regardless of nationality, religion or political persuasion, persecuted for thinking independently and speaking freely. Its 'Proposal for Establishing the Rule of Law,' unprecedented in Communist Party states, called for democratic reforms and constitutional guarantees of rights and freedoms. Since there can be no scientific freedom or responsibility without freedom of thought and expression, the CDFTE, at great risk to its members, has contributed to the development of a more open society and the enhancement of the values of free inquiry essential for the advancement of science and human dignity."

39. Ibid., 647.

40. *CADDY Bulletin*, no. 38 (1986): 1-2.

41. "Proposal for a Free and Critical Re-Examination of Josip Broz Tito's Historical Role," *South Slav Journal*, no. 40-41 (Summer-Autumn 1988): 68-71; "Saopštenje Javnosti," *Naša reč* (Harrow, UK), no. 411 (January 1990): 3.

42. "Otvoreno pismo Odbora za odbranu slobode misli i izražavanja: Preventivno hapšenje uskraćuje slobodu," *Borba*, 22 June 1989, reproduced in *Naša reč*, no. 408 (September-October 1989): 21.

43. Alija Izetbegović, the seventy-five-year-old Islamic scholar, lawyer, and former political prisoner (1983 Sarajevo trial), was elected president of Bosnia-Hercegovina on 20 December 1990. Cf. *CADDY Bulletin*, no. 61-62 (December 1990): 2-3.

44. See Toma Ognjanović's interview with sociologist Nebojša Popov in *South Slav Journal*, no. 43-44 (Spring-Summer 1989): 74.

45. For *Praxis*'s contradictory theoretical legacy, see Gruenwald, *The Yugoslav Search for Man*.

46. Ognjanović's interview with Mihailo Marković, 38.

47. "Action Against Abuses of Psychiatry and Medicine, 1981," in *Human Rights in Yugoslavia*, 595-98. For updates concerning human rights and dissent, see the authoritative *CADDY Bulletin*.

48. Helsinki Watch, "Update on Yugoslavia, May 15, 1989," p. 3. For partial lists of political arrests, trials, and sentences, 1956-84, and banned publications, films, and plays, 1959-84, see *Human Rights in Yugoslavia*, 495-560; for updates, consult *CADDY Bulletin*.

49. *CADDY Bulletin*, no. 51 (January 1989): 2.

50. Ognjanović's interview with Nebojša Popov, 78.

51. Ljubomir Tadić, *Da li je nacionalizam naša sudbina?* [Is Nationalism Our Destiny?] (Belgrade: samizdat, 1986), 4.

52. See Toma Ognjanović's interview with Professor Zagorka Golubović in *South Slav Journal*, no. 40-41 (Summer-Autumn 1988): 45.

53. Ognjanović's interview with Nebojša Popov, 78.

54. *CADDY Bulletin*, no. 53-54 (July 1989): 9.

55. *CADDY Bulletin*, no. 57 (January 1990): 7.

56. *CADDY Bulletin*, no. 60 (July 1990): 9.

57. Zagorka Golubović, "The Impact of Nationalist Antagonisms Upon the Perception of Present-Day Yugoslavia," *East European Reporter* 4, no. 2 (Spring-Summer 1990): 84.

58. *CADDY Bulletin*, no. 60 (July 1990): 9.

59. *CADDY Bulletin*, no. 61-62 (December 1990): 23.

60. *CADDY Bulletin*, no. 63 (February 1991): 11.

61. Tadić, *Da li je nacionalizam naša sudbina?* p. 212. Emphasis added.

62. "Program of the Democratic Party," *CADDY Bulletin*, no. 58 (March 1990): 21-23.

63. Mihailo Marković, *Democratic Socialism: Theory and Practice* (New York: St. Martin's Press, 1982), 143.

64. See the special issue of *Demokratija*, 19 June 1990, pp. 1-8, for the June 1990 demonstrations dispersed by the police and misrepresented in the media; for the Democratic Party's appeal to the Serbian public to support the united opposition in the second round of the 1990 elections, see *Demokratija*, 19 December 1990, p. 1.

65. *CADDY Bulletin*, no. 63 (February 1991): 6.

66. Ibid., 6-7.

67. Mihajlov thought that "'Milošević's fall could pave the way for the election of a new, noncommunist Serbian government. There would then be a serious chance for new federal elections and for negotiation of a new federal constitution." See Mihajlov, "Can Yugoslavia Survive?" 91.

68. Slobodan Milošević, July 1989 Interview with *Le Monde* (Paris), excerpted in *Naša reč*, no. 408 (September-October 1989): 23-24.

69. Gruenwald, *The Yugoslav Search for Man*, 194.

70. Elie Abel, *The Shattered Bloc: Behind the Upheaval in Eastern Europe* (Boston: Houghton Mifflin, 1990), 161-86; Milan Nikolić, "Yugoslavia's Failed *Perestroika*," *Telos*, no. 79 (Spring 1989): 119-28.

71. Dobrica Ćosić, quoted by Abel, *The Shattered Bloc*, 161.

72. Janez Jerovšek, Veljko Rus, and Josip Županov, eds., *Kriza, blokade i perspektive* [Crisis, Blockades, and Perspectives] (Zagreb: Globus, 1986), 337. Note the curious contradiction in this study: While its analysis is Hayekian—in the classical liberal tradition—its conclusion is *Praxist*—socialist democracy! Idem, *Kriza, blokade i perspektive*, 357.

73. O. Gruenwald, "Novi horizonti Treće Jugoslavije" [New Horizons for a Third Yugoslavia], *Kronika* (Concord, CA), no. 22 (Winter 1988): 43, 46; Mihajlo Mihajlov, "Demokratija kao Sudbina" [Democracy as Destiny], *NIN* (Belgrade), 9 November 1990, p. 54.

Name Index

Subject Index